Sacrificed

Memoirs of SSG Jamie & Melissa Jarboe

Melissa Jarboe

Melissa Jarboe

Sacrificed - Memoirs of SSG Jamie & Melissa Jarboe

Cover design by Tori Munsell

ISBN-13: 978-1499791266
ISBN-10: 1499791267

This book is dedicated to the memory of men and women like my husband, SSG Jamie Jarboe, who gave his life for the love of his country. To the men and women who selflessly serve our nation.

CONTENTS

ACKNOWLEDGMENTS

First and foremost I would like to thank each and every veteran who has ever served to give me the freedom and the opportunity to share my journey. You represent a debt of service that can never be repaid.

Please allow me to give thanks to God for the ability to hurt and to heal.

My husband SSG Jamie Jarboe, who showed me the true meaning of selfless sacrifice, unconditional love, and unwavering dedication to the beautiful United States of America.

My two beautiful daughters, Celesteal and Alexa, who have sacrificed so much in their young lives and never once asked, "Why?"

To my dearest Daddy Jarboe for always being there for Jamie and me when we needed you!

To each and every one of you around the world who let Jamie and me into your lives as part of your families. Your prayers and strength and love helped us every day remember that there's a world outside the hospital who did not forget us.

To Jeff Canfield (my consulting editor) for helping us share our story with the world by turning our journal into a book. For one last time, thank you.

To Tori Munsell for designing an amazing cover!

Last, but certainly not least, to each and every one of the Military Veteran Project volunteers who each day help me carry on Jamie's dying wish to care for his fellow service members. There's a special place for you in my heart.

i

Foreword

When a young man or woman in uniform is critically wounded in service to our country, a circle of caregivers surrounds that individual almost immediately. Doctors, nurses, parents, siblings, friends, clergy. The list is long. After I was wounded during World War II, the role of caregiver was shared by many since I was single. But for countless wounded service members who are married, this role of primary caregiver falls on one person alone—the spouse.

After Melissa Jarboe's husband, Sgt. Jamie Jarboe, was gravely wounded by enemy fire on April 10, 2011, while on patrol in the Zhari District of Afghanistan, Melissa's life changed in an instant. She was no longer the concerned wife, nervously but eagerly awaiting her husband's return—Melissa was now an ever-present caregiver, advocate and rock of support for her beloved husband, who would remain hospitalized for 11 months thereafter.

The remarkable aspect of Melissa's story is not only her perseverance in being a pillar of strength for Jamie during the many months following his injury, but also her remarkable ability to thrive through it all. Melissa tells the important story of so many military spouses who find themselves coping in the midst of a sudden—and often traumatic—combat-related injury of their loved one.

Sacrificed is the story of Melissa's unlimited outpouring of support amidst her husband's limited future. Her unconditional and selfless commitment to Jamie throughout it all is a testament to the strength of the human spirit.

-1-

Love Defined

*M*arch 31, 2012 was a moment in life that will never be forgotten. It was the day I laid next to my husband's gravesite as dirt covered his casket. With each shovel of dirt, I felt reality close in on me. Jamie wasn't coming back. This wasn't a dream. So many thoughts filled my mind after I buried my husband. Why him? How did this happen? What am I going to do without Jamie?

※

It was 2008. After years of working my way to the top of the corporate ladder, I had finally reached my goal. I was overseeing daily operations, employee relations, worker's compensation, and relationships with hundreds of thousands of businesses across the nation and around the world. I had everything a woman could've wanted. I had a nice home, new cars, a huge wardrobe, and two daughters I was leading by example.

I laid my head on my pillow each night and thought about the man of my dreams. Above all, he would have to be a role model for my daughters. I envisioned a knight in shining armor riding up on a white horse and whisking me away. My career was demanding, and I chose to keep my social life at home with the girls. We went to the park, Chuck E. Cheese, or the movie theaters to see the newest Pixar cartoon. But, I never took time for myself—time to meet my knight in shining armor.

After talking with a few friends, I made the decision to join a dating website. If anything, it was cheap amusement for those nights I traveled out of town and was stuck in a hotel. I would flip through profiles, look at photos, and learn about people I'd never met. One night at a hotel in Kansas City, the fire alarm went off. Instead of grabbing my suitcase or personal items, I grabbed my laptop. That way I could check e-mails in the parking lot until we were cleared to go back in.

My phone buzzed as I sat outside in my car reading through e-mails. I'd received an alert from the dating website. Eagerly, I grabbed my phone to read the e-mail.

> From Boe78: "Where I come from if someone looks at your profile twice without saying anything, they are considered rude."

Wait a minute! Did this really just happen? Instead of getting an e-mail about how I sound interesting, or a short message about my dog; I just got called-out by some random guy! I thought, "Are you kidding me? Well fine! Two can play this game!" I responded by saying, "Where I come from, if someone looks at your profile twice without saying anything, they are obviously not interested."

"There! I showed this guy," I thought as I smiled about my sarcastic comeback. Then, I went back to checking e-mails. Just then, my phone buzzed again. Much to my surprise, it was Boe78. His email said:

> "Now that I have your attention, my name is Jamie.
> I'm a soldier in the Army, and I would like to get to
> know you."

Around the middle of 2009 my phone rang, and once again I was surprised that it was Boe78. He asked me how I was doing and said he wanted to catch up. We spoke briefly, and then decided we would meet for dinner in Kansas City. We would finally meet after nearly a year of talking, texting, and e-mailing. It was during that conversation that he asked to see a photo of me. I'd never posted a photo on the dating website or sent him one. So I agreed and sent him a photo. Within minutes he called me back. With excitement in his voice, he asked me if I knew I was beautiful. I laughed and told him, "It's your story, so tell it how you want to."

As I'm sure you've figured out, Boe78 was Jamie Jarboe. We began dating exclusively, and life was good. I can remember looking into his eyes as he talked about his day, and his career plan to retire from the Army at twenty years. We dated until one day when I was using Jamie's phone and he received a message from a person I didn't know, and I didn't want to know. Sadly, I walked away from Jamie at the beginning of 2010. I didn't answer his calls, text messages, or e-mails.

I had been hurt throughout my life. Instead of forgiving someone who hurt me, I would simply block them out of my life.

This pattern left no room for error, and no reconciliation with friends or family. I'm sure it stemmed from my childhood. In childhood I innocently sat back and watch the world with hopeful eyes. I would dream about what my future may hold, but time-and-again that hope withered away. After walking away from Jamie, I focused my energy back on my career. I worked twelve to fourteen hours a day, not because it was necessary, but because I was passionate about my company and my employees. I always wanted to succeed.

In April of 2010, my career took me to Fort Riley once more. As I walked with a group of contractors through a planned construction site where soldier's barracks would be built, I noticed a group of soldiers doing PT (Physical Training). As they ran along the road, we all joked that none of us could exercise like that, or would even have the discipline it took to get up at 5:30 AM each morning to run seven miles. As I walked back to my car, a few of the soldiers crossed my path. And, wouldn't you know it, Sgt. Jarboe was one of them!

"You sure look beautiful," Jamie said as I stood looking at him.

While trying to present the appearance of an uninterested businesswomen, I replied, "Thank you, however, I'm running late for my next appointment."

As I began to walk away, I felt Jamie's hand against mine as he said, "Make me your next appointment please."

My heart skipped a beat. I looked into Jamie's eyes and told him, "I already did that for the last two years, and look where it got me. I'm sorry, I just cannot do this."

As I drove away, I remember looking in my rearview mirror and seeing Jamie standing there watching me drive off. I struggled with thoughts and curiosity of where my life would go if I had given him one more moment of my time. I decided to call Jamie a few days later. Once more he asked me to go on a date in Kansas City. Since he was stationed at Fort Riley now, he said he would like to pick me up so we could ride together. My heart was pumping a hundred miles a minute when he pulled up in his big white truck and opened my door for me.

As we drove to Kansas City, Jamie talked about his life, the mistakes he'd made, and how he refused to allow me to be one of those mistakes. I quietly listened to Jamie as we pulled up to the Kansas City Royals stadium. I laughed a little as I asked him if that was his idea of a romantic date. He got out of the truck, opened my door, caressed me as I stepped down, and he said, "It's the only place I could find that will make a funnel cake for the woman I love."

A few months later, Jamie received orders for the National Training Center for an upcoming deployment to Iraq in the next year. The girls and I helped him pack. Then, we kissed him goodbye and told him we would see him when he comes home. Within days of leaving Jamie called and said he was getting sent home early. Immediately I asked if he had gotten in trouble. After all, he's Jamie Jarboe, and had a history of being a little troublemaker. His reply was, "No, it's serious honey. I'll be home in two days."

My heart was fearful of what Jamie was going to tell me. For the next few days I tried keeping my fears to myself. It seemed to work until Jamie walked in the door, put his arms around me and said, "We're being rerouted from deployment to Iraq and we're being sent to southern Afghanistan." Jamie and I both stood in our kitchen holding on to one another. We sat down to talk about the difference between Iraq and Afghanistan. This would be Jamie's third deployment. He was deployed to Iraq twice—once for nine months and then again for fifteen months. However, Afghanistan was a whole new world to him. That night, I looked up at him and asked him to tell me what he was thinking about. He pulled my hand towards him and said, "In all my life I have never felt as loved as I do with you, and I know I cannot live without you. Melissa, will you please marry me?"

I was in complete shock. I took a deep breath and told Jamie, "I would love to marry you, but I want to make sure we do it right. We need to include my children, my father, and our families in that decision." I could see him smile after he kissed my forehead. He said, "You are so damn stubborn woman." I smiled as I told him I wanted to do everything right this time to set a good example for my children. Jamie nodded his head yes, and said, "I completely agree, my love."

The next day I called Mike (the CEO of our company) and asked him about the upcoming plans for my partnership. I wanted to know if it would complicate things if I were to get married prior to becoming a partner. He suggested that I get a prenuptial agreement in order to protect my assets and all that would be attached to my upcoming partnership with the company. He felt it would protect all the parties involved. My next phone call was to my attorney. I asked him to start drawing up the paperwork with my assets and earnings to have it presented to Jamie. If he was serious about marrying me, he would understand. I knew in my heart that Jamie would never hurt me or take anything he didn't earn. But, this was just a safety measure. For goodness sakes, Jamie never even knew how much money I made, nor did he even ask. I just had to protect the district I had built from the ground up.

When I spoke to Jamie about the prenuptial, he said he understood. That weekend we went to Kansas City for a get away with the girls. We stopped by to visit my father, and Jamie didn't waste any time. He asked my dad if he could speak with him privately. A few moments later they both came back smiling and talking. What I wouldn't have given to be a fly on the wall for that conversation. On the drive home from Kansas City to Topeka, Jamie asked if I could take a few days off to travel to Indiana to meet his father and family before he deployed. It had been nearly three years, and I'd only spoken to Jamie's father a few times. I told him I would pack my bags and be ready when he was.

We left from Topeka for Indiana on February 11, 2011. We drove straight through for an entire day. We enjoyed one another's company and planned the future for our family. That night we finally made it to Jamie's father's (Andy's) house. Jamie introduced me as I walked in to meet Andy. I extended my hand for a handshake and caught Andy by surprise as he wrapped his arms around me and said, "In this family we hug." That night we sat up with Jamie's father and his girlfriend. We talked about life and our future plans. It was one of those nights you look back on think, "That was one of the best nights in my life."

The next day Jamie drove me around town, showed me his high school, and the skate park where he spent most of his childhood. He also introduced me to his childhood friends. After we met with everyone, and he showed me everything in his life that made him the man who stood before me, he asked if I was ready to go Indianapolis. As we drove toward the capital city of Indiana, we began to talk about our future family.

"I don't care if we have a boy or a girl as long as our child is healthy and we're happy," Jamie said. "But, I would really like to have a boy to carry on my family name—a son that could follow in my footsteps just like I did with my old man."

7

Then, much to my surprise, Jamie parked the car in front of the Indianapolis Speedway Museum. Both of us had been car fans since we were young, and this was a dream come true for us both! It took us nearly thirty minutes to walk into the museum because we kept stopping to look at the cars, the track…we just enjoyed every moment.

Once we got inside, I went to the classic cars and Jamie wandered over to the muscle cars. Each car was in mint condition and parked in a precise manner. After we took our time looking at our favorite cars, we eventually met in the middle and began to tell one another what we'd seen. Jamie was standing there with his hands in his pockets, and when he went to remove his hands I heard a "ting" on the ground. Then, Jamie began chasing and fumbling around on the ground for what he'd dropped. He smacked his hand to the ground and caught it. Then, he looked up at me on one knee and said, "Your father has given me his blessing, and I couldn't imagine one more day not being married to the woman of my dreams. Will you please spend the rest of your life loving me and do the honor of becoming Mrs. Jamie Jarboe and marry me?" Without hesitation, and with tears in my eyes, I said, "Yes." Then, I sealed my answer with a kiss! Jamie and I stood in the middle of the museum holding one another, kissing, smiling, and living in our moment.

On the drive back to Jamie's dad's house we talked about planning the wedding, dates, and how thankful we were to have one another. There was a brief moment of silence in the car as some distressing news came over the radio. A Corporal had been killed in action in the Kandahar province of Afghanistan. He died of wounds sustained when insurgents attacked his unit using an Improvised Explosive Device. Jamie shut the radio off and pulled the car over. His hands were shaking, and his face lost color as he looked at me and said, "That's near the area I'm being sent to, Melissa."

I could feel tears welling up in my eyes. I was at a loss for words. All I could do was reach over and hold my fiancé while his emotions took over his body. Jamie looked up at me and said, "Out of anything in the world, I want to give you the fairy tale wedding you deserve. But, I also want to know if something happens to me that my wife and family will be taken care of. Let's just go to the courthouse tomorrow and sign our marriage certificate. We don't have to tell anyone, *but I'll know* I'm taking care of my family."

My mind went blank. I told Jamie, "I don't need you to take care of me financially. I have always done that."

Without hesitation he said, "For once in my life, I want to know I'm doing what's right and marrying the woman of my dreams. The one who has captured my heart, made me a better man, and who knows in return I'll give her all I am."

ಬ

On February 14, 2011, at 11:00 AM, I became Mrs. Jamie Jarboe. No one knew but Jamie, Jamie's dad Andy, and me. Jamie and I returned home to Kansas. Before we unpacked our bags, he gave me three DVDs and said, "Sit down. We need to watch these, and you need to understand."

He told me to put in the first DVD. It was documentary called *Restrepo*. I cried through most of the movie while Jamie held me. The next movie was *The Hurt Locker*. Again, I cried as I got anxious with each minute that passed. I knew that soon this would be my husband going to war. The third movie was *P.S. I Love You*. I had no words for Jamie. Each movie left me speechless. All I knew was that I didn't wait my entire life for the man of my dreams to leave me anytime soon.

Before we knew it, there was cold brisk air pressing against my face, and Jamie's warm hand holding mine. I remember the night of Jamie's third deployment like it was yesterday. The snow calmly falling as we drove to Fort Riley, Kansas. That night he would be leaving for Afghanistan. Jamie was excited to introduce me to his platoon sergeant and captain. I felt a sense of warmth from both the men who were to lead Jamie in combat over the next year. Jamie was eager and excited at the opportunity to once again fight for his country. He loved everything about being a soldier; and for once in his life part of something great.

As the soldiers began grabbing their gear and getting ready to go, Jamie walked me to my car. He wrapped his arms around me and told me he would see me soon. He told me he loved me, and no matter what…to remember what matters. As I looked into his eyes I said, "God first, spouse second, children third." He smiled, then replied, "I'm going to miss kissing those beautiful lips, gazing into your beautiful eyes, and I'll miss our beautiful life." We said our final goodbyes. I looked in the rearview mirror as he watched me drive away.

Within the next few days Jamie would make time to call. He asked about our lives, made sure we were all right, and most of all he would tell us how much he loved and missed us. I made the decision before Jamie left to never worry him. I kept our phone calls focused around everything good in our lives. I never mentioned the bad or negative.

Jamie wasn't able to tell me his location or where he was going. But he would tell me it was only a matter of days before they would get to their base in Afghanistan…and he was ready! Like many people, I wasn't familiar with Afghanistan. I knew very little about the location of the country, the climate, or any of their customs. So I did what most nosy wives do—I searched the Internet.

As I read through articles about Afghanistan, all I saw was despair and a world torn apart by disloyalty. It was a country divided, and Jamie was in the middle of it all. Sleep didn't come easy that night. The next morning I decided I would isolate myself from any media, the Internet, and I would only listen to what Jamie told me. Besides, he was the only one that mattered. He knew how he was and it wasn't worth worrying myself over. After all, he promised to come home to me.

Two weeks has passed since Jamie left. He was able to use the Internet a few times to message me on Facebook. He told me he was all right, and he had made it to his destination. I waited patiently for a phone call. I needed to hear his voice and know he was all right.

The evening of March 20th my phone rang. It was my birthday phone call from Jamie! I was smiling from ear to ear as the girls and I tried telling him how much we loved and missed him. I could tell from his voice he was happy to feel the love through the phone. I could also tell he was distant and shaken. After the girls spoke with him, I took the phone upstairs to my room and sat in the back of my closet for privacy. He kept talking in code about the "zoo" and the "animals" and how the "rain" fell hard.

I tried to keep up with the conversation, but I wasn't able to understand everything he was saying. I just listened as Jamie rambled, for what seemed to be, forever. Then he asked, "Do you know how much I love you, Melissa?" I replied, "Yes, enough that you don't have to tell me every day because you've never left my heart. You're always with me."

The phone went silent for a moment. Then Jamie said, "Babe, I'm sorry I have to get off the phone. I'll call soon. Take care of the girls and keep sending the care packages. We love them!" I told him, "It's all right. Just as long as I can hear your voice for a few seconds, and you can hear mine, life is good. I love you Jamie Jarboe! And remember, you were created with purpose—now rock it!" He replied, "I love you Melissa, and I can't wait to hold you once more. Goodbye."

As I went downstairs to get the girls ready for bed, my mind was on Jamie and his shaken voice. Then, as I laid in bed that night I thought about our life and the fairytale wedding ceremony we dreamed of; the little boy we wanted to carry on the Jarboe name; the family vacations; and I thought about Jamie.

Each day the girls and I woke up, got ready for school, packed a care package, wrote a few letters, then started our day. Each day I waited for a phone call from Jamie. Some days he would call, and someday he wouldn't. I understood. I just longed to hear his voice.

-2-

Scripted Words

April was finally here. Jamie had been gone for a little over a month. We marked each day off the calendar to keep track of when Jamie would be coming home to us. One day I came home to find the basement flooded with water. One of the pipes had broken. The girls and I got ready to pull up the carpet and clean the basement when my phone rang. Finally! It was Jamie. I answered the phone full of excitement, and Jamie said, "Guess you miss me a little bit, huh?"

He began telling me how great the care packages were and how his guys were doing. Of course he wanted to hear about the girls and me. We talked on the phone for nearly an hour when I asked him what time was it there? He said, "3 AM." I said, "Pulling an all-nighter?" He went on to say that it had been crazy the last few days, and he just needed to hear my voice. He was barely sleeping. He was going "outside the wire" everyday; and sometimes twice each day (depending upon circumstances).

I told him I was proud of him for everything he'd chosen to do. Then, I asked if he'd spoken to his father? He said no. I told him how much it would mean to his father to hear his voice. He laughed and said, "Babe, I wish you were selfish and greedy." Then he laughed again and said, "What did I do so right in my life to have a woman who loves me so much?" I replied, "Everything my love. You've done everything so right."

I lowered my head as I hung up the phone. Each time I was done talking to Jamie, my heart hurt and my body grew weak with an overwhelming sadness that would take over. For many months, Jamie and I had discussed his career in the military, and my career in the business world. In January of 2012, I was going to become a partner in the employment agency I'd built in the Midwest. Currently, I oversaw operations for nine offices. I loved every minute on the job. I thoroughly enjoyed helping people, networking with customers, and managing the operations. Jamie hesitated on taking partnership with me. He never went to college and didn't have a degree. However, I told him we wouldn't fail as a team!

After talking with Jamie, I went back down to the basement and began moving wet carpet again. Then my phone rang. It was Jamie. I answered the phone full of excitement saying, "You just can't get enough can you my amazing husband!" He laughed and replied, "No, I can't!" Then his voice changed. He asked me sit down because he wanted to talk. I sat and listened as he chose his words carefully. "If I told you I'm all right with dying right now, I'm lying. I'm fearful of it. I just got the life I always dreamed of, and I refuse to let it go."

As I listened to him, I could hear the fear in his voice. I said, "Jamie, the life we have together, and the moments we've shared in love are powerful. I have to disagree with you. For me, if I were to die tomorrow, I would die with faith, hope and love—the greatest being love. For I've been completed by having you in my life, and through knowing that God has a purpose for me, and I'm living the life I was created for."

Jamie was silent. Then a few moments later he said, "I want so much for us; so much for the girls; and I want so much to have a son. I'm not ready to die, Melissa, and I can't let go of you either."

Not knowing what to say at this point, I just told Jamie how much I loved him and that I was thankful. I explained how I give thanks to God each day for blessing me with such a man, and with such wonderful children and a great life. After forty-five minutes of us reassuring one another concerning our life together, our faith, and remembering our love, Jamie had to hang up. However, this time when he said I love you, I could hear tears in his voice.

&

The next morning I woke up and decided to focus on our wedding ceremony, which we had planned for April 7, 2012. After years of courting, Jamie made one last proposal on February 13, 2011. Instead of waiting until he got home, we went and signed our marriage certificate at the courthouse in Frankfort, Indiana, on Valentine's Day 2011. We eloped and didn't tell a soul back home in Kansas. Instead, we began planning an elaborate wedding ceremony. Today was April 10th. With less than a year to plan our wedding, I began to focus on our future.

As I drove to my office my phone rang. It was an unfamiliar number. Thinking it was Jamie, I answered the call full of excitement. The voice on the other end didn't sound anything like my husband. The person talking to me was cold and direct.

They asked to speak with Melissa Jarboe. I could feel my body growing weak. The person on the other end of the call introduced himself as a soldier from the 1st Infantry Division, Fort Riley, Kansas.

"Ma'am, I'm going to read this script verbatim. I do not have any answers to your questions. On the 10th day of April 2011, 4th Cavalry, 4th Regiment, Able Troop, was on patrol in the Zhari District of Afghanistan when their troop took enemy fire. As a result, Sgt. Jamie Darrell Jarboe was a casualty of."

The person on the other end of the phone gave me his name, and then asked me to write down a number for further information.

My mind went blank. All I could do was listen and write down the number. I tried to keep my composure. I thanked the soldier for contacting me, and for his service. Immediately after hanging up, I called the 800 number I was given. The lady that answered asked me a series of questions regarding my physical location.

"How is my husband? Where is he? What happened?" I asked her repeatedly, ignoring her questions.

"Ma'am, you need to calm down and answer my questions," she replied.

"Have you spoken to Jamie's father yet?"

"No," she said, "we don't have his contact information."

I got Jamie's father, Andy, on a conference call as I screamed, cried, and refused to give the lady my physical address. I thought to myself, "If I don't give her my location, she wouldn't be able to send anyone to tell me Jamie had died."

Jamie's father held back his emotions, and he did his best to calm me down. The lady asked once more for my contact information, and she told us she didn't have any further information on our soldier at that time. She knew he'd been in a series of surgeries. However, she was waiting for more accurate information, and when she had it she would contact us. She told us to stay at the physical locations we were at, and confirmed that we had the 800 number. She said we could call once in the morning and once at night. As I hung up the phone, I looked around my office. I was alone. I sat quietly as my mind went blank. Then I fell to the ground as I cried and screamed, "Why!"

As I laid on the floor staring at the ceiling, I tried to gather my thoughts so I could call someone to be with me. I picked up the phone and I called my cousin Jason. He was in the military and had been deployed. He would understand. I got his voicemail.

The next number I dialed was my cousin's best friend—my ex-husband Earl. He answered my call, and immediately I began crying as emotions took over my body. I told him Jamie was shot, and I couldn't leave my office. He said, "Stay there, and I'll be there as soon as I can."

I tried to stand, but my body went limp. I tried once more, and I fell to floor. I curled up in the corner and focused on Jamie. I prayed to God to stay with us. I prayed for him to give Jamie my strength to come home to me as he promised. With tears streaming down my face, I prayed for everything in life to be all right. Just then Earl came into the office and picked me up off the floor. I began hitting him and asking him why wasn't it him? Why was it Jamie? Jamie didn't deserve this! All he ever wanted was to have a family! Why?

Earl sat me in the chair and put his arms around me. He told me he didn't know why this happened, but he knew Jamie would pull through. I contacted the 800 number to request to move physical locations, from my office to my residence. They approved and updated my location. However, they couldn't give me any new information.

As Earl drove me home, what seemed like minutes was actually hours. I asked Earl to pick up Celesteal (my oldest daughter) from his house and bring her home to me. I needed my oldest daughter next to me. I wanted to sit down with her and tell her the little bit of information I knew. I sat at the kitchen table thinking about what would become of our family. How were we going to live? What were we going to do?

As I stood up and starting pacing, Celesteal walked in the door. I looked at her with tears in my eyes as I told her Jamie was injured, and was in surgery overseas. She was speechless. She held on to me, holding back her tears to stay strong for me. Moments later Alexa walked in—our precious little baby of the family at five years old.

Celesteal and I sat down with Alexa in the kitchen to tell her that Jamie got hurt while he was at work.

"Is he coming home Mommy?" Alexa asked.

"Yes honey, he's coming home to us just as he promised he would."

The next question was harder to answer.

"Mommy, who would hurt Jamie?"

I hesitated for a moment. Then I told her the truth.

"Jamie was out patrolling the area to make sure it was safe, and a man shot him."

And then she asked, "Why would a man shoot Jamie? Mommy, he's not a bad guy."

"The man didn't know Jamie," I told her.

"Is the man that shot Jamie all right?" she replied.

I thought for a moment. Then I answered, "I hope so my love. I hope the bad guy is home safe with his family. We should say a prayer for him, his family, and all those who are over there where Jamie is."

The three of us bowed our heads, and I prayed, "Dear God, please give Jamie our strength. Please watch over the man and his family wherever they may be. Take the strength from our body, the love from our hearts, and give it to those who are empty. Let Jamie feel our love and our presence. We give thanks for allowing us to hurt and to heal. Amen."

ॐ

As nighttime came I laid on our bed with Jamie's uniform and a teddy bear, and I played the voicemails he'd left me over and over. Finally, around 10 PM, my phone rang. The man on the other end told me Jamie had been shot in the neck, and the bullet shattered his spine. He also had a collapsed lung was pending transfer to Landstuhl, Germany. He asked if I had a passport. I told him I didn't, but I would do my best to get one. He asked if I was able to travel to Germany to be bedside to Jamie. I answered yes! I told him that whatever they needed me to do, I will do it! Just tell me, and I'll make it happen! The call ended with him telling me they would know more in the morning.

I laid my head on the pillow on his side of the bed and cried myself to sleep. In my dreams I saw Jamie. I could feel his hand holding mine. I was awakened by my phone ringing. It was a confirmation call that Jamie had made it to Landstuhl, and that a doctor from the hospital would be calling me in the next few hours. I was able to leave my physical address and start packing. They were doing their best to get Jamie stateside due to the severity of his injuries. I went in and woke up my girls with a kiss, and I told them Jamie would be home soon. I promised them that everything would be all right.

-3-

Walter Reed

As I packed, I tried to think what Jamie might want when he woke up. I packed his favorite items: his DC hat, his shoes, his comfy sweatshirt, and the teddy bear he gave me on our second date. My phone rang again around noon. This time it was the doctor from Germany. He asked if I was alone, and I told him no. I was with family. He went on to tell me, my husband will never walk again.

The doctor explained that the 762 bullet from the AK 47 entered the left side of Jamie's neck, and exited below his right shoulder shattering his 2nd, 3rd, and 4th thoracic vertebrae, and then severing his spinal cord. He went on to say that Jamie was unable to speak due to the damage. However, he was being brought out of sedation and asked if I would like to let him hear my voice. I said, "Yes, of course!

The doctor transferred the phone into Jamie's room in the Intensive Care Unit. Jamie's nurse answered the phone and held it up to Jamie's ear.

"Hey honey, you're coming home where you belong, and I'll be here waiting for you," I told him. "We all love you, and I'll see you soon. Get your rest."

Just as I finished, I could hear the monitors starting to beep, and the nurse telling Jamie to relax and calm down. Then the phone was abruptly hung up.

Not knowing what had just happened, my mind went blank. I tried to put myself in Jamie's position. What was he thinking? How scared was he not understanding, remembering or knowing exactly what happened? I called the number back, and the nurse told me they sedated him for the time being so his vital signs would stay down. The nurse told me that Jamie was trying to talk, but he had had a tracheostomy and that's why he couldn't speak. I thanked the nurse for his time and his service. I asked him to take good care of my husband. *I needed him in my life.*

My phone didn't ring that evening with updates on Jamie's status. So, I called the 800 number. I found out Jamie had endured seven surgeries the day he was shot. I was told the military's travel department would call me in the morning to make arrangements for me to be at Jamie's bedside once he arrived in the States. I asked where he would be sent. He said he wasn't sure, however, the travel department would assist me in the morning. After our conversation, I put the phone aside and curled up with Jamie's uniform on his side of the bed and fell asleep.

I went to my office at 5 AM the next morning. I made the best effort I could to tie-up any loose ends. It was necessary so that my staff could move forward while I focused on Jamie. My career had involved climbing the corporate ladder for the last five years, and now I was in charge of overseeing the operations of an employment agency. I loved my job. I was also preparing to move forward with the acquisition of forty-seven percent of a multimillion dollar business (located in the Midwest) that I had spent years creating.

That morning I wanted to keep myself busy, and I didn't want to alarm my staff. I acted as though my life wasn't going to change. Jamie was wounded in combat, but he was alive and he would be home in a few weeks. Then, we would continue to live the life we both dreamed of. At 8 AM I received a call from the military travel department. They had confirmation Jamie would be flown that evening to Walter Reed Army Medical Center in Washington D.C. They wanted me to be there with him. I made sure they had contact information for Jamie's mother and father. For Jamie's sake, I requested they also be allowed at his bedside.

"Ma'am, the Army's travel department will only be able to fly two people to Walter Reed Military Hospital. Do you want any of *your* family there?" asked the military liaison.

"No. *Jamie's* family needs to be there. They're my support." I responded. "I would be eternally grateful if you could get me on your earliest available flight."

They scheduled me for a 1 PM flight, which would put me in Washington D.C. at 5 PM. I contacted my CEO (a former West Point graduate) to request time off, and informed him of my travel arrangements. My brother Jason drove me to the airport.

"My heart hurts for you," said Jason. "I can't imagine what you're about to go through. I'm so proud of you for caring for your husband, and not running away like most people would."

"Why would people run away?" I asked.

"Most people wouldn't be willing to put their lives on hold, leave their jobs, or their children to care for someone they'd only been married to for a few months."

"Jamie isn't just *someone*. He's my husband! He spent three years courting me, putting up with my long hours of work, an obsessive amount of travel, and he never gave up on me *or us*. I take our wedding vows seriously. They're sacred. I know if it were me, Jamie would do the same."

As he dropped me off, I assured him I would keep in touch when I got to the hospital. He gave me a hug as he said, "You're in my prayers."

&

As the plane took off, I looked around and saw people smiling, laughing, and resting. They seemed to have no worries or concerns. Yet, I had a thousand different thoughts running through my mind. My thoughts involved various plans of how I would deal with each level of Jamie's care in order to ensure his mental well-being. I would make sure he knew he is loved.

When I got off the plane, I received an e-mail stating I needed to meet military representatives at baggage claim. I was greeted there by a young woman who had "Jarboe" written on a piece of paper. She would be my companion on the way to the hospital. Another military representative picked up my baggage and we were on our way.

"How long have you been doing this particular job?" I asked.

"The past few months. I'm what's called a third-party administrator for the Department of Defense."

"Do you have any updates regarding my husband's medical status?" I asked rather anxiously.

"No. I'm sorry, but we're not privy to that information."

24

"No worries," I told her. "I know God has a plan for all of us. If we relinquish our worries to Him, our lives will be blessed however He sees fit."

She smiled at me as she replied, "In all the months I've been doing this job, you're one of the most courageous women I've met."

Armed guards surrounded our car as we drove up in front of Walter Reed. After presenting our identification cards they instructed us to pull forward to the main entrance. As we got out of the car, the Army representative received a call with a confirmation of Jamie's room number. My heart started beating faster and faster with each step I took as we walked up to the SICU (Surgical Intensive Care Unit). I took a deep breath and reminded myself that God is in control. I had to cast my cares and worries onto Him.

As I entered Jamie's SICU room I was greeted by a nurse who was taking his vitals.

"Your husband is still sedated. He had a rough trip from Germany," she informed me.

"How long before he wakes up?" I asked.

"I can wake him up by lowering his sedation medication for a moment—long enough so he can see you and know you're here."

"Thank you."

Within a few moments Jamie opened his eyes. For the first time in months I was able to touch my husband; to kiss his forehead; and tell him I loved him. For a few moments he tried to speak, but couldn't hear his own voice. So, he began shaking his head from side to side and trying to scream with no sound. I placed my hand on his head and said, "Jamie, honey, I'm here.

You're alive. I'm here, and I love you. There's nothing that will separate us."

Just then he stopped and looked at me. As tears fell from his eyes, I leaned down and kissed his forehead, then his cheek, then his lips, and I told him everything will be all right.

"Do you trust me?" I asked him.

He nodded his head yes.

"I'm not leaving your side," I told him as he closed his eyes.

As I examined all of the medical devices on Jamie's body I saw he had a tracheostomy in his airway, a C collar around his neck, four drains coming out of his chest, a feeding tube in his nose, an IV, and several other cords all over his body. He was also hooked up to a breathing machine to help him breathe because he couldn't do it on his own. As I looked at Jamie's face, I'm sure he could see the pain and tears in my eyes. Once more he began shaking his head and getting anxious.

"His vitals are getting too high. We need to sedate him," said the nurse.

"I understand."

I kissed Jamie on the cheek and told him I loved him. I stood next to his bed while the monitors were beeping. Instantly I felt pain in my body as it grew numb. I tried to find somewhere to sit and gather my thoughts.

"Are you okay?" asked the nurse.

"I'm seeing black dots, and there's a surging pain going through my body."

She paused for a moment, and then said, "Honey, you need to get it together. Are you laying in this bed? Did you get wounded in battle? If your answer is no, then you need to realize that you don't matter. This is your husband...*he matters*."

As she left the room, I looked around and realized she was right. I'm standing on my two feet, and I'm breathing, speaking, and feeling. Yet, before me is my husband who cannot breathe on his own, stand on his own two feet, speak with his own voice, and is paralyzed from the chest down.

The nurse and doctor came in and said they needed to take him into surgery to do a wash out of his wounds. They were concerned the entrance wound might be infected. A few moments later, Jamie's mother and father arrived. The doctor took us to the waiting room where he explained they would be taking him back to the operating room, and it may be late when he comes out.

The mood in the waiting area was one of unease. As we waited for Jamie to return from surgery, we paced, we mulled over all that was happening, and we prayed. A few hours later, the doctor returned and told us that everything went well. He suggested we go to the hotel, get some sleep, and then return tomorrow morning. The military supplied free hotel rooms for each of us. We had no worries about expenses. Our only worry was Jamie.

When the doctor finished, I asked about visiting hours. He said visitors were allowed after 8 AM. We all went to the hotel, and we decided to meet at 7:30 AM the next morning to go back to the hospital.

-4-

Moving in a Different Direction

When we arrived in the morning Jamie was still sedated, and his bed was elevated up high.

"We'll be waking him up from sedation soon," the nurse explained. "However, we need to keep him at a low stimulation because his body needs the rest."

She went on to say how most families wait in the waiting room where they can watch television, use the Internet, and eat.

"Are you saying we need to leave?" I asked.

"All I'm saying is, he needs his rest."

"I understand, and I agree," I told her. "But, if my husband wakes up, I don't want him to feel abandoned. I'll stay by his side, and when he wakes up I'll be the first person he sees."

A few moments later, Jamie opened his eyes. He tried to speak again, but I ask him to speak slowly and I would do my best to read his lips. I showed him his mother and father were there with me. He started trying to tell me what happened. He began to cry once more, and then the nurse came in and told us he may have to be sedated.

"I understand," I said. "Jamie, be strong and gain control of your emotions. Let us focus on today and look forward to tomorrow. I'm not going anywhere, and we'll get through this together…no matter what."

As the day went on, Jamie would slowly drift off to sleep and then wake up a few moments later. Each time he opened his eyes, we reminded him where he was, and he would try tell us about how he was shot just three days earlier. We never went into detail about the extent of his injuries until he asked if he still had his legs. We reassured him he still had his legs. For his own comfort we even took a picture of his legs and showed it to him. Due to the amount of pain medication he was receiving at that point, there was no need to go into great detail about anything. We didn't want to do or say anything to create worry or fear. He was safe on American soil, and he was alive! For this, we were all thankful.

Jamie asked what all the cords attached to him were. We asked the nurse to educate us about each one. We wanted to have answers for him when he woke up. He woke up shortly after we received an education about the cords. So, one by one, we took pictures of the cords and his father and I showed him what he looked like and explained how most of the cords were temporary.

"I don't want anyone seeing me like this," Jamie whispered. "It's embarrassing to know I was shot, and I cannot even breathe on my own. People will laugh at me. Now, promise me no one else will see me like this."

I shook my head in acknowledgment, and kissed Jamie's hand. His father and mother also shook their heads in agreement, and promised no one would see him. I sat in a chair next to Jamie's bed rubbing his head to ease the tension.

Jamie mouthed the words, "I love you," as he looked at me and smiled.

Each time he would do this, I would smile and say, "Not as much as I love you baby."

His mother came to his bedside and asked, "What about Mimi? Can she come and visit?"

"No," Jamie said, "Especially not her. I don't want to break her heart. She's getting older, and I don't want to scare her. In a few months I'll be better, and then people can see me."

We all agreed. We sat around his bed and watched him slowly drift back to sleep.

℘

As the sun set, Jamie's mother and father got ready to go back to the hotel.

"May I stay in the room with Jamie at night?" I asked the nurse.

"Yes you may," the nurse replied very kindly. "I'll get you a chair."

She brought me a metal folding chair. I sat next to his bed in the cold metal chair for hours as I rubbed his head and massaged his hands. I did this until I fell asleep.

"Would you like something more comfortable?" I heard a voice ask.

"I don't want to inconvenience anyone. But, anything would be better than a cold metal chair."

The nurse on duty arranged for a recliner to brought in. Before I moved from Jamie's bedside, he opened his eyes and made a noise with his tongue to get my attention.

"Where are you going?" he whispered.

"I'm going to the left side of your bed to a recliner to get some sleep," I answered. "Is that all right?"

He nodded his head yes.

"If you need me, just make that noise again and I'll wake up."

As I stood up and stretched, Jamie made a "chipmunk" noise with his tongue, and nodded his head no.

"Babe, I'm tired. I need to take a quick nap so I can take care of you tomorrow."

He moved his lips and said, "I can't see you when you're on the other side."

I moved the recliner to the foot of his bed. Then, he could see me if he woke up.

"Is this better?" I asked him.

He nodded his head yes, and puckered up for a kiss.

೩

Several hours passed, and I woke up as I heard Jamie making his noise. I got up quickly not realizing the sheet was wrapped around my feet. I tripped and fell flat on my face on the concrete floor. As I pulled myself up to check on Jamie, his eyes were big as he mouthed the words, "Are you all right?" I smiled big and said, "Yes honey."

I grabbed the suction to clean up the bile he'd spit up in his C collar. I saw him smirking.

"Did you think that was funny?" I asked.

"Not that you got hurt," he whispered, "but watching it happen in slow motion…yes, it was funny."

As we giggled about the hardness of the concrete floor, I told him, "I don't matter as long as you're comfortable. I'll be all right. But, the left side of my face *does* hurt."

He smiled and whispered, "Go back to sleep babe. I love you."

During the next several days we were bombarded with social workers—Army *this*, and Army *that*. Doctors, residents, nurses, therapists…everything. The physical and occupational therapists all came in together. I asked their advice concerning anything I could do to assist with his exercises. I hoped they could show me what would help Jamie improve. Since Jamie was only allowed to receive fifteen minutes of physical or occupational therapy three times a week, I was more than willing to help in any way possible.

Jamie was paralyzed, and he was listed as a "paraplegic." We were told that eighty-three percent of the casualties of war are from IED (Improvised Explosive Device) blasts, and that amputees are typically what Walter Reed Hospital treated. The physical and occupational therapists were not familiar with Jamie's condition. They said I needed to continuously move his legs and arms to prevent blood clots from forming and to keep his joints and muscles contracting and moving.

I made a schedule for Jamie's physical and occupational therapy [PT and OT]. Our schedule started at 5 AM with a bed bath. At 7 AM we started PT, and at noon we began OT and then again at 5 PM. I spoke with the nurses, doctors, and therapists to ensure the schedule was approved. I also asked if there were any other measures I should take to ensure his forward progress. The doctor said he should lay flat at all times and remain "NPO" (meaning nothing by mouth). After that, we started Jamie's first physical therapy schedule. It was a wonderful feeling moving his legs and being able to touch and help him!

Jamie would rest in between therapy sessions. I sat next to his bed reading about his injury, his paralysis, and what I could do to better assist him. When I was able to bathe him, it was our only time together when I could move around him or touch him and his skin didn't hurt. I would usually put on music of Jamie's choice, and in the mornings I used aromatherapy when bathing him to help wake him up. When it was time to do PT and OT we used different music and aromatherapy. That way Jamie would associate the smell of the room with the type of physical therapy or workout.

The doctor informed us Jamie needed to have surgery on his spine. Because of the bullet wound, he was missing his T2, T3, and T4 vertebrae (located at the base of his neck). The plan was to put rods on each side of his spine in order to stabilize it. The problem was, he wasn't stable enough for this type of surgery. His white blood cell count was high and so they were concerned about an infection.

After the doctors left, Jamie whispered that he was thirsty. I pushed the nurses button since he couldn't move his arms or legs. She gave us a little green sponge and grape juice. She said he could have half a glass in the morning. His eyes lit up when we started giving him the juice. We asked if it was the best grape juice he'd ever had. He smiled big, nodded his head yes, and said, " Oh yeah!" That night I laid in my recliner next to Jamie's bed and told him stories about the girls, about our life, and how much he was missed. I continued until we both fell asleep.

ଔ

At 2 AM I was awakened by Jamie's monitor alarms going off. His blood pressure was stable, but his respiratory rate was high (38-44). He also had a 103 temperature. Four nurses responded and tried to get him stable. They continued to try to calm him down, and finally I went over to his bed and ask him to try taking deep breaths since he was on the respirator which helped him breathe. The nurses were in and out for most of the night. I asked what I could do to assist. They told me to keep the cold packs on his body to help bring down his temperature.

Early the next morning a doctor came in and told us they decided to take Jamie back into surgery to do a minor procedure called a bronchostomy. On their way to surgery they stopped to take an X-ray of his lungs. A few hours later it was determined Jamie had fluid in his lungs and pneumonia. The doctor told us he was no longer able to have fluids by mouth. Additionally, they were going to take him to surgery again in the morning to insert a feeding tube into his stomach and remove the one from his nose.

"Why can't he have fluids, and why does he need a feeding tube?" I asked.

"At this point it's precautionary measures," the doctor explained.

Later we found out that due to Jamie's injury he wasn't able to swallow normally. Everything went from his mouth or nose directly into his lungs. The main reason they turned off his feeding machine three days after his injury was because it was filling his lungs with fluid.

After the doctors left, Jamie and I decided to start reading a great book—a book of understanding. I began reading at the beginning.

> In the beginning God created the heavens and the
> earth. The earth was without form, and void; and
> darkness was on the face of the deep. And the Spirit of
> God was hovering over the face of the waters. Then
> God said, "Let there be light"; and there was light.
> And God saw the light, that it was good; and God
> divided the light from the darkness. God called the
> light Day, and the darkness He called Night. So the
> evening and the morning were the first day. Then God
> said, "Let there be a firmament in the midst of the
> waters, and let it divide the waters from the waters."
> Thus God made the firmament, and divided the waters
> which were under the firmament from the waters
> which were above the firmament; and it was so. And
> God called the firmament Heaven. So the evening and
> the morning were the second day. Then God said,
> "Let the waters under the heavens be gathered
> together into one place, and let the dry land appear";
> and it was so. (Gen. 1:1-9)

It had been over a week since Jamie was wounded. We were
told he was scheduled to have his "hardware" placed in his back
on the 18th. However, due to the infected area, they had to
postpone. Then, he developed pneumonia and the doctors wanted
to hold it off further. Now, April 25, 2011, was the new goal for
surgery when Jamie would get his hardware in place and begin
moving forward. We were excited and hopeful as we look toward
this new date. We didn't allow any fear of the unknown to
consume us.

During the next week, as we waited on his surgery date, when
Jamie slept I was able to do some work. I sent e-mails and
conducted conference calls from his room. I made contacts

concerning Jamie's injuries, and tried to determine what we needed to do to our house in preparation for him to return home. Would we be able to even live in the same house? I wanted to know how long it would be before we would able to go home, and when would we be a family again? Most of these questions went unanswered because events would change from day-to-day. Before we knew it life was moving in a different direction.

-5-

Path is Chosen

"I'm afraid to die," Jamie said.

"Jamie Jarboe, you didn't come all this way to die in Washington D.C.," I told him. "God is good, and the path is chosen. It will be an amazing one. We just have to relinquish our concerns to God."

Jamie smiled and whispered, "I love you."

Once again I replied, "Not as much as I love you Jamie Jarboe."

Jamie's surgery went relatively well. The doctor explained how Jamie's back had bone fragments all over it from the blast of the 762 bullet. They tried to remove as much as they could.

However, in the end they left most of the fragments so they could use them to place the "hardware." After the surgery, Jamie rested most of the day. The doctors said they would check on him each day for the next few weeks.

We'd been at Walter Reed for two weeks. We were now eligible for assistance from the Soldier's Family Assistance Center [SFAC]. Myself, as well as Jamie's mother and father, were put on orders from the military. We would receive $71.00 a day, and now our lodging was also covered by the military. This was unexpected. The SFAC was a great relief to many families who had left their lives behind to care for their service member.

Jamie's father and I coordinated it so that between the two of us Jamie was never left alone. During the day I would stay in his room for twelve hours, and then Daddy Jarboe would be there for twelve hours at night. This way we were there for him at all time. It gave Daddy time with his little boy, and it gave me time with my amazing husband! These plans helped us know that life was moving forward.

One morning I snuck in early by taking a cab from our hotel, which was just a few miles away. I wished I would've taken a picture when I entered Jamie's room. When I walked in I saw Daddy Jarboe sleeping next to Jamie's bed. I thought to myself, "That's the cutest thing!" As I stood by his bed, Jamie opened his eyes. He smiled as I kissed his cheek.

"How did you sleep?" I asked him.

"I can barely sleep at night with all the noise," Jamie replied. "Boy, you smell good today."

I laughed and said, "Yes, I showered today."

"You don't shower every day?"

"No, Jamie. The first few days here I never left your side. I stayed here four days straight, and I was a mess…I was stinky."

"Well, I'm ready for my bed bath Mrs. Jarboe," he said laughing.

I turned on his music and began washing his face with one wash cloth, and then after throwing that one in the dirty clothes I grabbed the next one.

"Why do you keep getting a new washcloth each time?"

"To ensure I don't spread infection or anything. I want to play it safe babe. You're too important to me."

He nodded his head, smiled once more, and then he whispered, "I'm so glad I married your OCD butt."

Moments later Daddy woke up and told us he was going to head down to the hotel to get some sleep. As he left, the nurse came in and told us the ENT (Ear Nose and Throat) doctor would be coming to evaluate Jamie's tracheostomy. I looked at Jamie and said, "See babe, we're almost there. By the fourth of July we'll be sitting on the beach sipping a mao-tai."

As the ENT doctor came in, he said they wanted to replace his tracheostomy since the German one Jamie had was broken. Due to his spinal precautions, they laid Jamie flat on his back. Then they slowly removed the old tracheostomy and inserted a new American one. Then they covered Jamie's air-pipe and asked him to speak. For the first time in nearly two weeks Jamie heard his own voice.

"I love you," Jamie said in a strong, healthy, Jamie Jarboe voice.

Oh, how we all had missed his voice!

∞

Only two days after Jamie's surgery we were told they

needed the room for the SICU. So now they were in the process of transferring him to Ward 58 (neurology). We gathered all his belongings on a cart, and two nurses assisted in transferring him. As we walked up to his new room, the two SICU nurses told me to keep an eye on Jamie. They said the wards can be busy at times, and with his extensive injuries it would be important to keep a constant eye on him.

The first thing we noticed about his new room was how bare it was. We also noticed there were no monitors. He had no equipment to regulate or document his blood pressure, oxygen levels, or his respiratory rate. I asked his new nurse if it was common practice for a soldier to have surgery, and then be moved up to a ward with such limited monitoring systems. Here response was that April and May are the busiest times of the year, and many of the beds for ICU are for new patients coming in from the battlefield. She said they would come in every eight hours to check his blood pressure, respiratory rate, and temperature.

After a few moments the speech pathologist entered the room. He said it was time to take Jamie down for a "contrast swallowing study." This would help them determine whether they could clear him to eat clear liquids and softened food. The unit was understaffed and overbooked. They even had patients in the hallway! They had to call for volunteers to assist with the transfer of Jamie since he was unable to move his arms, his chest, or his legs.

It took four people to move him from his bed to a wheelchair. Once he was transferred and comfortable, we went down to the X-ray area. After two hours of transferring him to an X-ray chair from a wheelchair; having him swallow thick fluid; having him swallow thin fluid; and then having him eat a cookie, he was cleared to eat softened puréed foods. We were finally moving in the right direction!

Jamie's dad showed up as we were about to head back up to his room. As the volunteers began transferring Jamie from the X-ray chair to his wheelchair, one of them lost their grip and dropped Jamie. Completely out of instinct, I rushed to aid Jamie. I put my hands around him and held him. I kissed his face to calm him down. When I looked into his eyes, I could see he was hurt. We felt like it was our fault. We should've protected him. I asked the speech pathologist if we needed the volunteers to assist, or if his father and I could transfer him. She said it would be fine if we wanted to help and comfort him.

We situated the sheets under Jamie and counted to three. On three we lifted him slowly and steadily back into his chair, and then we waited to situate him according to his comfort level. Then we let the nurse take over and push Jamie to his room. Daddy and I walked behind the wheelchair and discussed what had just happened. When we arrived at his room we requested an incident form and asked how to file a complaint.

"I can take your complaint," the nurse said. "What is it?"

We told the nurse what had happened, and he said, "I'll take care of it."

When we got back to the room Jamie was sound asleep. I kissed him goodnight, and as I left I asked his dad to please keep up-to-date notes for the evening. My patience was wearing thin with the medical care Jamie was receiving. We had done our best to give the military's medical personnel enough space to do their jobs. However, day-after-day we were seeing inconsistencies. These inconsistencies were hindering Jamie's improvement. We didn't know who to speak with or who to voice our concerns to. We made sure to keep daily logs and photos. Then if necessary we would be able to pinpoint issues and concerns.

The social worker working on Jamie's case came to see us

later that week. She told us we needed to pick a Veteran's Administration spinal cord injury facility for him. We asked her if we had to go to a VA facility, or if we could go to a private care facility. She said she wasn't aware there *were* any private care facilities. We asked her what our options were, and she gave us a list of VA facilities including ones in California, Minnesota, and Florida. I asked her to wait as I woke Jamie up from his nap to get his opinion. Without hesitation, he wanted to go to Tampa, Florida. That was where his aunt and uncle lived. We figured it would be nice to be near family. The social worker was able to set up a phone conference for April 29th with the James A. Haley VA in Tampa.

"Is Jamie coherent," the social worker asked on her way out.

"The nurses say he's just tired due to his injuries," I explained. "The doctor was supposed to meet with us today at some point. Jamie hasn't been seen by any since his surgery."

"All right. I'm sure you're on top of it," she said as she left.

The following day we had *the meeting*. This was an important conference with a female physician, a social worker, an AW2 representative (Army Wounded Warrior Program), and several other individuals I'd never met. In this meeting we discussed Jamie's medical condition and the prolonged care he would need. (Unfortunately, Jamie wasn't allowed to attend the meeting since they were short-staffed. Plus, Jamie was sleeping once again.)

During the conference I was told that the availability of beds at the Tampa VA was minimal. I told them of my concerns, one of which was the fact that Walter Reed was predominantly for amputees. But, my husband was considered a paraplegic or a quadriplegic who wasn't receiving the necessary physical and occupational therapy. I felt he needed to begin rehabilitating after his *fifteen* surgeries. He had only been out of his bed three times since he was injured. We'd been told he wasn't able to go to the workout room because they were short-staffed.

He needed spinal cord rehabilitation to get better. So often, I was filling in for the therapists, and I didn't have any medical training. I was simply doing what I was told in order to help maintain my husband's condition. The representatives took fifteen minutes to discuss my concerns, and then told us they would be happy to save a bed in Tampa for Sgt. Jarboe when he was medically able to transfer. They set a tentative transfer date of May 9, 2011. I went back to the room to tell Jamie the wonderful news. When I got there, he was still sleeping, and, once again, he was nonresponsive.

For the next four hours I sat by his bed waiting for him to wake up. Finally, I leaned over and began kissing his arm, his shoulders, his neck, and his cheek to wake him up. Jamie was still nonresponsive. I pressed the nurses call light to report his condition.

"We're going to have to start straight cathing him," his nurse explained. "Have you ever done that before?"

"No I haven't. Can you show me?"

As she walked me through the steps of straight cathing Jamie to drain his bladder, we talked about his condition. She was of the opinion he was going to have a very complicated life once he got home and into the real world. A wounded warrior with such complex injuries can often become depressed or even addicted to their medications. Many wounded vets would rather take medications and sleep so they don't have to live with the fact that they're injured.

"It's similar to how he reacts now," the nurse explained.

45

"While you were out he asked for more pain medication but couldn't specify where his pain was. And, as medical attendants, we have to listen to him and ensure he's comfortable."

"So what's the standard protocol for patients who abuse their medications?" I asked.

"Well, we can monitor and note it in the system, but once a wounded warrior is addicted, their entire demeanor can change," the nurse said. "Very often they end up pushing loved ones away."

"I'll always be here for my husband," I replied very adamantly. "I'll do whatever I can to protect him from himself."

Just as our conversation ended, Jamie opened his eyes. I leaned down and kissed his lips and asked, "Did you sleep okay?" He nodded his head yes. The nurse asked him if he was in any pain. He said no.

"Melissa, what I like about you being here is that when you're next to him, he doesn't need as much pain medicine."

As the nurse walked out of the room I asked, "Is that true Jamie?"

He whispered softly, "Yes it is. When you leave I want you to hurry and come back. I can't sleep, so when I take the pain medicine it passes the time until you return.

I was on the verge of tears, but I tried not losing my composure as I asked Jamie to be careful with the narcotics and pain medicines. He'd finally come home to me, and I refused to lose him to drug addiction. I sat next to Jamie's bed and laid my head on his chest knowing he wanted so much to be able to move his arms and comfort me. But, he wasn't able to.

I tried to process the conversation I had with the nurse about Jamie's medical condition and the pain medicines. Even when he didn't need them for pain, they were giving him pain meds simply to help him sleep. I wondered if I could do anything about it. I asked myself, "How can I fix this?" I wanted to learn as much as I could. I began contacting friends from all over the U.S. who understood Jamie's condition, his medical care, prescription drugs, and other aspects of his long term care.

The next morning, as we started his bathing and therapy, I informed Jamie he was accepted to the Tampa VA Hospital. We were so happy! We would be near his aunt and uncle. I asked him if it was all right for me to make arrangements to fly home to Topeka to see the girls for the first time since he was wounded. I would also be able to pack our belongings. He smiled, nodded his head yes, and then fell back to sleep.

-6-

The Unthinkable Happened

As noon approached, I put down my computer. I'd been reading articles about spinal cord injuries. During his therapy, I began moving Jamie's left leg and stretching his muscles. I did the same with his right leg, then afterward I massaged his feet and legs to keep the blood circulating properly after an hour-and-a-half of therapy.

I said Jamie's name, but he didn't respond. I waited a few moments and said his name again. There was no response. I immediately pressed the nurse's button, and moments later a nurse entered the room. I asked if she was Jamie's nurse for the day since no one had been in that morning. I knew because I had been there since 5 AM.

"I'm not his nurse, but I'll find her for you."

An hour passed, so I pressed the button again.

"I've been trying to get a hold of Jamie's nurse, but I haven't been successful," the *same nurse* told me.

"Can you assist us," I asked.

"Sure. What do you need?"

"My husband was awake this morning, but I haven't been able to wake him up since. It's 2:30 in the afternoon, and I'm concerned. I tried to wake him up several times, but he's not responsive. I was told he sleeps a lot due to the medications, but he hasn't had any medication today."

"Let me find his nurse," she said as she left the room.

As I sat next to Jamie's bed, I tried moving his arm to startle him. There was no response. I turned on the TV. There was no response. Finally, I said in a loud voice, "Jamie wake up please!" He didn't respond.

Around 4:00 PM his nurse came in and asked what we needed. I told her I was concerned because my husband was non-responsive and had been sleeping all day.

"Ma'am, have you really been here all day?" she asked.

"Yes, I haven't left his room."

"All right. I'll notify the doctor on call."

Jamie's dad arrived and I filled him in on how Jamie had been non-responsive. I asked him to call me when the doctor arrived. I had to get some rest at the hotel.

Around 11:00 PM Jamie's father called and told me the doctor came in and tried to speak to Jamie, but he was still non-responsive. The doctor said they would change his medication. I told Jamie's dad that Jamie didn't have medications that day until

3:00 PM. I didn't believe it was his medications causing him to be unresponsive.

"Honey, I'm not sure. I only know what the doctor told me," his dad said.

"All right, I'll see you in a few hours."

&

When I arrived the next morning, I asked the nurse what changes were made to Jamie's medications. She said nothing she was aware of. Jamie's dad said he slept all evening. I leaned down to kiss him good morning, he opened his eyes a little, but then went back to sleep. I started his bed bath and finished up his therapy as I did previous mornings.

"I need help," I told the social worker when she arrived. "Something is obviously wrong with Jamie. He's still non-responsive."

"That often happens to military men who've been traumatized," she responded. "Don't worry about it. Soon we'll be in sunny Tampa, Florida, and everything will be all right."

"I'm hesitant about flying home because of Jamie's condition."

"Melissa, don't worry. Go home, see your children, and when you get back we'll be on our way to Florida."

It was now the beginning of May. It had been three days since Jamie became non-responsive. He wouldn't eat his puréed foods and he would barely sip on his strawberry shakes. Each day he grew more distant. I finally asked the nurse if the doctor would be available to see him since he hadn't been visited consistently since we left the ICU more than a week earlier.

"The doctors make the orders, and we follow the orders,"

the nurse informed me. "Since we're following the orders the doctor is giving, there's no need for him to come in since he's pending transfer."

"Would you call the social worker please," I asked the nurse after expressing my concerns a second time.

When the social worker arrived, I asked her once again if it was common for a soldier to be lethargic to the point he doesn't respond and sleeps all day. She asked if Jamie was taking any anti-depressants.

"No, he's not. Should he be?"

"It might be something we should discuss when we get to Florida."

I spent the night with Jamie before I left to fly home. Before leaving, I voiced my concerns to the new nurse. She assured me she would tell the doctor. When his dad arrived I asked him to keep me updated on Jamie's condition, and when he wakes up to remind him I loved and missed him.

✄

The flight home was nerve-racking. All I think about was the fact that I didn't have any good news about Jamie to share with the girls. Then, I started thinking about all the wonderful family fun we had before Jamie deployed (going to the T-Rex Café, playing at Dave & Buster's and Chuck E. Cheese's, and going swimming at the park). What a blessed life! We did everything we wanted a few months before Jamie deployed. Finally! My heart fluttered with excitement as I pulled into the driveway and saw the girls. At the same time, I felt sorrow because our family was still not reunited.

The girls ran and jumped into my arms. I'd already told them the good news about Jamie being transferred to Tampa,

Florida, and that we were making arrangements to take them to Disney World. I reminded the girls that before they knew it we would be on the beach as a family, building sandcastles and enjoying life! After dinner that evening I called Jamie's dad to check on Jamie.

"Jamie's been acting even more strange since you left," his dad told me. "He started having nightmares and has been waking up whispering things out of the ordinary."

"Can you ask for the psychologist, neurosurgeon, or general physician to come back in and examine him? I'll be back there tomorrow night," I told him.

As the girls and I packed our swim suits and Jamie's clothing for Florida, Jamie's dad called and said the psychologist stopped in to observe Jamie.

"He's concerned about Jamie's lethargy and how he's nonresponsive at times throughout the day," his dad told me. "But, that's all he said."

As I flew back to Washington D.C. I felt ashamed for having been home, snuggling with the girls, and having fun without Jamie. I said to myself, "I left my husband to be greedy and go home. How terrible am I? My husband was laying in a hospital bed and I flew home to pack clothing!"

When I arrived at the hospital to see Jamie, he was still nonresponsive. I called for the nurse. She finally came in after I waited twenty-five minutes!

"Have you spoken to the doctor regarding my husband's condition?"

"Don't worry. He's on a lot of different medications right now. Being non-responsive and lethargic are common side effects."

"Can I get a blanket and pillow so I can spend the night next to his bed?"

"Of course," the nurse answered.

My alarm went off the next morning at 5:00 AM. I turned on Jamie's music, sprayed aromatherapy near the door, and then got the warm water ready for his bed bath. As I was washing Jamie from head-to-toe, I noticed a very distinct smell. It smelled like rotten fruit. As I began moving Jamie's left arm, I noticed the sheet was wrinkled. As I pulled the sheet out from underneath him, the unthinkable happened.

Not Medically Stable for Transfer

I'd gone home to get my girls in anticipation of transferring Jamie to Tampa, Florida. The girls were not only excited about seeing Jamie, but also about making the trip with us. Although, it had been tough to leave Walter Reed Hospital knowing the difficulties we were encountering with Jamie's lethargy, and the apparent uninterest of the doctors. But, what I found as I bathed Jamie was beyond words.

As I stretched out the sheet under his back, I saw a little black bug fly out from underneath his body! I tried moving Jamie's left shoulder and arm to see where the bug had come from. When

I placed my right hand underneath his left shoulder I could feel moisture. As I removed my hand, I could see it was saturated with blood and tissue. I pressed the call light.

"Has my husband been turned every two hours?" I asked the nurse, showing her his blood on my hand and the towel.

"That's not on the orders," she said.

"Can you check the bandage on his back where he had his spinal fusion?"

She called for another nurse to assist as they turned him to remove the bandage from his surgical site. As they rolled Jamie on his side he moaned in pain. I stepped over by the nurse who was trying to remove the bandage. The blood had soaked through the bandage and had saturated the sheets as well as Jamie's entire body. The smell was overwhelming as she removed the bandage.

"When was the bandage put on," they asked.

"On April 25th when he had his spinal fusion."

"Have the neurosurgeons been in to check him since the surgery?" asked the nurse.

"No. They came in the day of the surgery, and I haven't seen them since."

One of the nurses began to lift him up by putting her hands on his left and right shoulders, then lifting him straight up. When she did, blood and fluid began seeping out of his back. Immediately, she was told to lower him slowly. After checking they discovered Jamie's bandage hadn't been changed in nearly two weeks! The nurses left and requested to have the doctor come in to evaluate him.

The doctor on-call arrived an hour later.

"After examining Jamie," the doctor said, "we're going to

have to take him down for a complete surgical wash-out of the infected area. Who's his main doctor?"

"We're not aware of who his main doctor is. We haven't seen a doctor in two weeks. We've only seen a psychologist," I explained.

After Jamie's surgical washout, they placed him back in the SICU pending surgery the following day. They needed to get the opinions of other doctors, and since it was Sunday they were limited on staff availability.

"Doctor, tell me what happened to my husband."

"Your husband has an infection," he told me. "We're doing everything at this time to ensure it hasn't reached his spine or the bones in that area. Unfortunately, his transfer to Tampa will be canceled. He's not medically stable for transfer right now."

৪৩

Monday morning (May 9, 2011), Jamie was taken into surgery *again*. I sat in the waiting room for hours. Finally, the neurosurgeon met me there.

"Does your husband have a history of Post Traumatic Stress Disorder," he asked. "Does he usually have an aggressive behavior?"

"We haven't seen any signs of that in past few weeks," I told him. "Why do you ask?"

"When we were bringing your husband out of the anesthesia, he must've regressed back to the day he was on the battlefield. We'd like for you to come into the recovery room and see if you can wake him up."

I followed the surgeon as he walked briskly toward the recovery room.

"How did Jamie's surgery go?" I asked.

"It went well. We removed most of the infection. However, when a resident was removing some infected tissue and bone fragment, I believe he may have nicked the back of Jamie's esophagus."

"Are you sure?"

"I can't confirm it. But, first thing tomorrow we're going take him down to do a swallow study and find out," the surgeon said.

I went into Jamie's room and sat by his bed. I put eucalyptus lotion on my hands, and then waved my hands slowly above his face. Jamie opened his eyes and began moving his mouth, but he couldn't make a sound. I placed my hand on his head.

"Everything is all right," I told him. "We're on American soil. You just got out of surgery, and I'm right beside you."

The nurse placed a purple speaking valve over Jamie's tracheostomy in order to listen to him speak. We'd used it a few different times. However, he complained saying it was hard for him to breathe.

"The last time we put that on him, he said he felt like he was suffocating," I told the nurse.

"I need to get solid answers from him, not from you translating," she responded. "He needs to learn to answer his medical questions."

After she placed the speaking valve on him, his oxygen level decreased along with his respiratory rate. He decreased to ten percent oxygen. The doctor came back in the room and stood beside Jamie as I stayed at the corner of his bed.

"Can you remove the speaking valve doctor?" I asked. "For some reason it's been suffocating him lately."

"Sure," the doctor replied as he removed the valve.

As soon as he removed the speaking valve, Jamie was able to take a deep breath.

The doctor asked, "Are you going to stay all night?"

"Jamie's father is going to stay tonight, and I'll be back in the morning."

"As I told you, I'm concerned that during surgery, while they were doing the washout (removing bone fragments from theT2 and T3 level), and as a piece of bone fragment was being removed from the T2 level, that they may have nicked your husband's esophagus.

"Mrs. Jarboe," the doctor asked, "are you familiar with esophageal perforations?"

"No," I said. "What am I looking for?"

"If your husband's heart rate increases, or he developed a fever, you need to have the nurse's page me immediately. We're also going to set up another swallow study for tomorrow."

"Despite the fact this has happened, we still have confidence in your ability doctor. Just please take care of my husband as you would yourself."

Jamie's father walked in just as the doctor was leaving. We saw the doctor go to the nurse's station and speak to the nurse attending Jamie. After a heated discussion and altercation, the doctor left the IMCU area. Several hours passed by, and the nurse didn't come to his room to evaluate him. It was nearly 9:00 PM— almost six hours after his surgery! Jamie developed a rash over part of his upper body and said he felt hot. His heart rate and blood pressure also increased. I rang the nurse's bell, and a male nurse came in.

"Is it normal for my husband's vitals to increase and for him to have a rash developing?"

"Yes," he responded. "Now I have paperwork to do. Do you need anything of great importance?"

"No. I'm sorry. Thank you for coming in."

Another three hours passed by and Jamie's rash got darker. His blood pressure was also up, so I rang the bell again.

"Are you going to insert a catheter for my husband since he's paralyzed and isn't able to control his bodily functions?"

The nurse said, "I'll need to look in the notes and see if it's ordered."

"It was verbally ordered by the doctor over eight hours ago. He's paralyzed and can't control his body! Please help us!"

The nurse went to the supply cabinet, got a catheter, and inserted it. Within moments the bag was full. Jamie had expelled over 900 cc's of fluid in just minutes. Moments later his rash went away.

ⅎ

It was now May 10, 2011. All day we'd been waiting for Jamie to be taken down to X-ray, but no one had come to pick him up. That afternoon the neurosurgeon showed up. Jamie's dad and his aunt were also there, and we were allowed to stay inside the X-ray room. Jamie refused to complete the swallow study if I wasn't present. The technicians allowed me to hold the contrast in the cup and place a straw in Jamie's mouth for him to take a sip. I gave my camera to Jamie's father to take pictures of the results as they showed up on the screen.

As Jamie took a sip of the contrast and held it in his mouth, the technician told him to swallow if he could. When he swallowed we could see the contrast leaking outside of his esophagus. A hole was confirmed in the back of his esophagus from surgery the day before.

As we were finishing, Jamie asked how the swallow study went. I told him he did a great job swallowing, and we would wait to see what the doctor says. I asked Jamie's dad to stay by Jamie as he laid on the X-ray table. As the X-ray techs opened the door, we saw the first doctor we met the night Jamie arrived at Walter Reed. There were two others with him. The doctor was informed that there was an esophageal perforation.

As they transported Jamie back to his room, the doctors conferred with nurses about the perforation, and that they should be very cautious with his care.

As the doctor was about to leave, I asked, "Do you have a plan of care for my husband?"

"We're working on one, Mrs. Jarboe."

"You know doctor, Jamie has endured nearly thirty surgeries in the last month, and we have the utmost faith and confidence in your ability. But, out of concern for his well-being, would you let me know if this is out of your scope of practice?"

"Thank you," the doctor replied. "This is the first time I've dealt with this type of injury. I'm going to consult with experts across the country to ensure the corrective procedure we take is the right one for him."

As I sat in Jamie's room, I looked over his body once again. He had cords wrapped around his body, and a "wound vac" covering his spine to remove extra tissue or fluid from the numerous washouts and surgeries. As I started his afternoon exercises, I greeted the infectious disease doctors, G.I. doctors, ear, nose, and throat doctors, and another team that came to place a PICC line in Jamie's right arm. I was told that they have seven different services of doctors following Jamie case—of course for precautionary measures.

I made inquires about esophageal perforations. I found treating physicians in this area, and I discovered that this type of injury is rare. An esophageal perforation is typically found in cancer patients. It could be fatal depending on the perforation and fluid leakage. I wondered what our chances were that we would be transferred to another hospital to meet with one of these doctors, or have the doctor come to Walter Reed to perform the surgery. The doctors proceeded to tell me how they were consulting with specialist from across the nation. They believed they had found a corrective surgery, and told me they would discuss it with me more in the days to come.

-8-

Emotionally Overwhelmed

Jamie slept the next few days, not even opening his eyes. The doctors came in and out of his room. They promised me they had found the corrective procedure to get Jamie back on track. I was feeling overwhelmed emotionally. It was all getting to me, but I tried not to show it around Jamie. Yet, I could feel it building up inside of me.

I found myself walking up the stairs to the balcony overlooking the lobby at Walter Reed. As I stepped closer to the edge, I leaned over and looked down. I thought how easy it would it be for me just let go. I thought of Jamie's fragile state and the lack of compassion I was experiencing from the staff. Each moment it seemed like our life together went from bad to worse. I felt like it would be easier if we could just to be together in the next life.

Tears ran down my face as I sat next to the ledge. My mind was clouded and my body ached. What was I going to do? As I looked at the people walking below me, I heard my phone ring. It was Celesteal calling to tell me she missed us. When I heard her voice, I remembered *why* my life was so valuable. As I stood up, I looked over the ledge again. In that moment, I chose to put God first, my spouse second, my children third, and nothing else mattered.

I went back down to Jamie's room and I asked his dad to give me a moment alone. It had been a month since Jamie was shot. Here he was laying in an SICU bed *again*. I kissed his hand, then I kissed his arm, and then I kissed his shoulder. When I leaned up to kiss his cheek, he opened his eyes and smiled at me.

"I love you beautiful," Jamie whispered.

"I love you too, and I want what's best for you," I told him. "Is it all right if Celesteal comes to visit?"

"Yes," Jamie replied softly.

His dad and I began working on bringing Celeste to Washington D.C. The next day we arranged for her flight.

ॐ

The doctors had found a surgical correction for Jamie's esophageal perforation! They were going to insert an esophageal stent (similar to a Chinese finger cuff) into his esophagus to block the hole.

"Do you have any other options right now," I asked. "Do we need to transfer him to another hospital for a surgical procedure with someone who's experienced in this type of problem?"

"That won't be necessary. We have seven teams of doctors right here who've been working with your husband. They're confident in their ability to help him."

"Just out of curiosity," I asked, "how many times have you performed this surgery, doctor?"

"This will be the first time."

"Has anyone in the hospital performed this surgery before?" I asked.

"No," he replied. "However, before IED and amputees, no one had cornered that market either. But, now we're saving more lives and leading the way for our amputees."

I smiled as I said to the doctor, "I commend your efforts, and I appreciate your what you've done. However, there are spinal cord injury doctors available here in the states that have cared for a paralyzed patient before. You haven't. There are surgeons who specialize in esophageal injuries. You don't. Why can't he be transferred to another facility?"

Obviously agitated, the doctor replied, "There isn't much time to transfer him. He needs surgery immediately."

The next morning we were met by another doctor who told us that somehow a blood clot had passed through Jamie's heart and was now in his lung. During one of his recent surgeries they had inserted an IVT (inferior vena cava) filter to prevent this from happening. To further help prevent it, the doctor now wanted to increase his blood thinner.

As Jamie was resting I noticed he was developing a rash around his neck and his ears again. I felt his head and his hands. I discovered that his entire body was warm. Immediately I called for the nurse so she could check his vitals. His blood pressure was two hundred over one hundred, so something was obviously wrong. They checked his gastric outtake, his feeding tube, and his catheter. The catheter was kinked! Once the kink was fixed, Jamie's urine bag filled with over 500 ml. of fluid.

The hematologist left, and SICU doctor came in. He informed us that the X-ray that morning showed fluid outside Jamie's lungs. They wanted to remove the fluid by inserting a needle in his lower right back. They asked if I could assist them with the procedure. I told them I would be more than happy to.

We lifted his upper body and placed his legs on the side of the bed. The doctor asked me if Jamie could put his arms around my neck. We would be chest to chest. I was thankful for the opportunity. It was the first time in over a month that I was able to hug my husband. The fluid that was removed from the outside of his lung and in between the wall cavity was a greenish-yellow color. It filled a bag with over 400 ml. of fluid!

"Doctor, what caused such a fluid build-up," I asked, after the situation was under control."

"It's undetermined," he answered. "Your husband is lucky we were able to remove the fluid and prevent anything further from occurring."

"Thank you, doctor."

After the doctor left, Jamie and I spoke for a short time before he fell asleep. I told him I understood that he was in pain and discomfort, and how never in a million years could I imagine how he feels. Even so, I knew one thing—we had to listen to the doctors and nurses. They were there to help us, and to bring him home to the girls and me. Jamie agreed.

Then, he told me of his fears and concerns; the fact that he was a twenty seven-year-old sergeant in the military and he couldn't even move his own legs; he couldn't breathe on his own;

he couldn't eat on his own and he couldn't walk or use the restroom. I rubbed my hand on his head until he fell asleep. Then, I laid my head on the side of his bed, and I imagined a life outside the hospital. I felt certain we would make it there soon.

ဆ

The next morning a nurse came in to do an assessment.

"Jamie has the start of a stage two bed ulcer. Do you have any idea how it would have gotten this bad?" asked the nurse.

"It's from incontinence and fecal matter being left on his skin for too long. He can't control his bowels. If he has a bowel movement and the nurses are too busy to deal with it, he has to wait," I explained. "If the nurses need assistance, his father and I are very good at helping change the bed sheets or clean him."

We knew this was degrading to Jamie. We continually reassured him that he would learn independence, but for now he should do his best to be patient.

Each day I looked at my husband, I remembered the man who watched me drive away the night he was deployed. I remembered the visions we had of a homecoming. He was so looking forward to having me jump into his arms and swing me around, and then to have the girls run up to him and give him a hug. He dreamed of being able to tuck them in at night knowing they were safe, and then wake up the next morning and have breakfast with his family. *That was the life we dreamed of.*

Jamie fell asleep after his bed bath and physical therapy. I sat next to his bed and ran my hands over his feet and his legs. As I did, I prayed that God would always stay with us, and that we would always remember to put him first. I promised Him we would follow his path diligently. I acknowledged that trials were going to come, but we would welcome them with open arms and give thanks to Him for allowing us to hurt so that we could learn how to heal.

As I contemplated the surgery to insert an esophageal stent (to cover the hole accidentally created on May 9, 2011), I wondered what the options for Jamie were since they had never performed that surgery at Walter Reed. I asked the doctor in charge of the SICU about his options, and whether he could be transferred out to have an experienced physician perform the surgery.

"There's no need to transfer your husband, Mrs. Jarboe. We've spoken to specialists across the country, and we're willing to do the surgery in order to help get Jamie stabilized. It's really not in his best interest right now to transfer him. He's still in a very fragile state."

"We're looking forward to having the surgery done," I told the doctor. "I just don't want my husband put through any more discomfort."

Understandably, on the morning of his surgery, Jamie was scared. We couldn't remember if this was surgery number thirty-six, thirty-seven…we'd lost count.

"All I want is to go home and be a husband and father," Jamie told me.

"Soon, my love," I responded. "I promise you, it doesn't matter where we're you will always be a husband and a father."

He smiled and asked, "Do you ever see the bad, or only the good?"

"All I see is the good," I told him. "As for the bad, we relinquish it to our Lord our Savior."

As they prepared Jamie for surgery, all I could do is watch and smile at him while a they took him down the hallway. I asked the orderlies to stop so Celeste and I could give him a hug and kiss. We reminded him that we would be right there waiting when he returned.

Many hours later, the doctors came out and told us they believed the surgery was a success. The only concern they had was the plastic stent. Where it was placed had a small fold at the top towards Jamie's trachea. I asked if it was something they wanted to redo or correct at a later time. The doctors said no. They explained how complex the surgery had been. They had to place the JP (Jackson-Pratt) drain in the back of Jamie's neck at the T2 level. This was due to the fact that they were concerned about fluid leaking out into the spinal region. They placed the JP drain in place to suction out any extra fluid that may build up.

The surgeon was emphatic that the JP drain not to be replaced. He wanted to keep it place for up to three months. A few moments later, as the GI surgeon was preparing to leave, I asked them to explain to me what procedures had been done in surgery. I suggested it would be good for us to have pictures and documentation to carry with us so we could communicate with all the medical providers who would be assisting with Jamie's care. Within the next hour, the doctors brought me pictures and extensive findings from the surgery they had performed.

೮

Jamie was pretty tired after his surgery. His aunt was there and said she'd like to take Celesteal for a tour of Washington D.C.. I told her that would be a great idea. She asked me to come with them, however, I didn't want to leave Jamie's bedside. I knew if he woke up and didn't see me, he would be worried. Jamie slept for the next four days. He was heavily sedated, and he had good vital signs. This was a much needed rest for his body considering everything he'd endured during the past month. It was now mid-

May and I felt confident we were finally moving forward.

The doctors did their rounds early the morning after his surgery. They discussed transferring Jamie from the SICU to the IMCU (Intermediate Care Unit). This would be a step toward getting him back to the ward and his PT and OT. Meanwhile, as he was in the SICU, and even in the IMCU, I was still handling his bathing, physical therapy, occupational therapy, and speech pathology. We were told by the speech pathologist that Jamie needed to exercise the muscles to ensure that when it was time, he would be able to swallow without aspirating.

Each day at 5:00 AM I started his bathing, and then I brushed his teeth. After that, I helped him do his physical therapy. I helped him move and stretch his legs as well as his occupational therapy structure, which included his fingers, his hands, and his arms. This helped to ensure that his muscles wouldn't contract while also preventing fluid from building up in his joints. We repeated all of this at 7:00 AM, noon, and again at 5:00 PM. I managed all of Jamie's physical and occupational therapy and care.

Once Jamie was transferred to the IMCU, the doctors ordered an MRI and a CAT scan for Jamie. They sent a private, fresh out of his schooling, to transport Jamie's bed down to the basement. Getting him ready for a transfer was very hard work. They had to transfer monitors, oxygen tanks, disconnect his feeding tube, his IV, and ensure that monitors were hooked up accurately. They would usually hook up the oxygen tank in the back, and then put a mask over his tracheostomy. We waited patiently as they got him ready.

As we were walking toward the elevator, Celesteal and I decided to have a little fun. We told Jamie and the nurse that we would race them downstairs. We took the stairs while they took the elevator. Needless to say, we beat them. Once got to the CT area, the tech told us we weren't allowed to go in the room with Jamie. This was the first time we hadn't been allowed.

We went across the hallway and waited. Within fifteen minutes the nurse came out and told us he was done. We checked on Jamie because transfers were always hard on him. I noticed Jamie's oxygen level was at sixty-eight percent and dropping.

"Didn't you notice his oxygen level during his test?" I asked the nurse.

The nurse said, "No ma'am. I wasn't allowed to be in the room either."

"How can his oxygen level be at

I checked to see if there was airflow through the mask leading to the tracheostomy, and there wasn't. The nurse checked and couldn't feel any airflow. He began knocking on doors in the basement to ask for assistance as Jamie's oxygen level continued to drop. After a few minutes an X-ray tech brought a new oxygen tank for him. Within seconds after connecting the new tank, Jamie's oxygen level increased.

"Jamie, are you all right?" I asked him.

He nodded his head and said, "I'm scared, but I'm all right."

"Just a few more bumps in the road, and everything will be okay," I assured him.

So many thoughts went through my mind as we were waiting for the elevator. Jamie could tell I was scared. He began to make his chipmunk noise. When I looked at him, he smiled, shrugged his shoulders, and then used humor to overcome the obstacle we'd just endured. He mouthed the words "boom boom firepower." I couldn't help but laugh at my husband.

When we got back to his IMCU room, I called Jamie's LNO (Liaison Officer). His LNO was soldier from Fort Riley, Kansas, and was assigned to care for the needs of First Infantry Division soldiers at Walter Reed. I filled him in on how many setbacks we'd had in the past month due to incompetency, lack of knowledge, lack of documentation, and lack of teamwork. I said, "My husband is paying the ultimate price." Jamie's LNO said he would make the CSM (Command Sergeant Major) at Walter Reed aware of our concerns. I expressed my thanks, and within a few minutes Celestial and I were walking along with the LNO to the CSM's office.

After being greeted, I conveyed my concerns. I showed him the pictures of Jamie's stage two bed sore; the infection of Jamie's spinal hardware; and video of how the nurses move Jamie as well the three times they've dropped him within the last month. The Command Sergeant Major thanked me for my due diligence, my loyalty to my husband, my dedication to a wooded warrior, and he assured me that he would get to the bottom of what was going on. He said we should have no further concerns.

The LNO escorted us back to Jamie's room. Jamie's father had been with Jamie while I was gone. I spoke to his dad and asked him what he thought we should do. Each day Jamie is scared about what could happen at any moment. As I was speaking to his father, Jamie's doctors came in as part of their rounds. I told them our concerns, I showed them the pictures and documentation, and filled them in on the meeting I just had with Walter Reed's CSM.

As a result, I requested a transfer to a civilian hospital that could adequately care for my husband and his fragile state.

"What hospital would you like your husband to be transferred to," A Navy doctor asked me.

"What are our choices?" I asked. "Do we have specific options of where we can go? He needs to be seen by a doctor that's familiar with para and quadriplegics."

The doctor's response was short.

"If you don't have a specific hospital in mind, then we cannot assist you."

He left the room.

The next morning his occupational therapist came for a visit. She said she heard he would be transferring to the ward soon. She wanted an idea of how his arms and muscles were functioning, so she did a couple movements of his arms to gauge how his body was doing. She asked what kind of pain or discomfort he had when he moved his arms. Jamie told her it felt like one thousand needles were poking his arms at the same time. But he said that was okay. At least he could move them.

A few moments later the ENT doctor came in again. He said they wanted to downsize his tracheostomy from a size eight to a size six. Jamie wasn't to enthused. However, Celeste and I jumped into our "cheerleading" mode—meaning we show a lot of excitement and enthusiasm in order to get Jamie to trust and feel encouraged. We told him this was one step closer to eating, and a step closer to drinking a Mountain Dew. We reminded him that the doctor was there to help, and we encouraged him to relax and let the doctor do the same job he's done for many years.

I asked the doctor if it was okay if we stayed to watch. He said that would be fine. Within seconds the doctor had cut the sutures holding the tracheostomy in place, removed Jamie's tracheostomy collar, and then removed the plastic pipe from Jamie's neck. Without hesitation, and with an open airway, he began to insert a small black tube with a camera at the end. He said he wanted to look at the tracheal airway to ensure there wasn't any inclusions, and he wanted to see if there were any other issues that may arise. Within seconds of the doctor inserting the black camera tubing into the hole in Jamie's throat, Jamie's eyes got big as he mouthed the words, "I can't breathe!"

"My husband's having complications breathing, can you please stop the procedure and reassure him?"

"Calm your husband for me," said the doctor. "There's a muscle inside the airway that makes it feel like the air is being restricted. But, as long as his vitals are accurate, and they look good on the monitor, then everything should be all right."

A was behind Jamie's chair showing a new recruit how to fill the feeding tube bag, and how to reset the monitor for tube feed.

"Do you have a clear view of the monitor," I asked her.

"Yes, Mrs. Jarboe. And if his vitals get to an unusually low rate, the monitor itself will beep to alert us of the danger."

Within the next few seconds Jamie's skin began turning light blue. I could see his eyes were full of fear. Out of concern of being escorted out of the room, I comforted Jamie and told him everything was going to be all right.

"Stay calm, soon we'll be out of this place," I told him.

I asked the nurse if she could see Jamie.

"No," she said. "I'll try to come around the chair to get a visual of the patient."

"Would you please remove the scope from his throat," I asked the doctor. "He needs some time to catch his breath and to relax."

"I'm almost finished," the doctor replied. "You need to keep yourself calm, and calm your husband. There's no need to be anxious."

Just then I noticed Jamie's head drop to the side and his body grow weak. I asked Celesteal to leave the room and stand by the door until I call her back in. Jamie's arms that were moving around went limp, and his whole body was suddenly lifeless. I looked at the monitors. His heart and respiratory rate, as well as his oxygen level, were at a zero. The monitor wasn't making a sound. I only straight lines and zeros on his vitals.

The nurse asked the doctor to discontinue what he was doing. She felt for Jamie's pulse. The doctor removed the scope from Jamie's throat and looked at the monitors.

"Are the monitors accurate," the doctor asked the nurse.

"I'm not getting a pulse," the nurse replied.

"I guess the monitors are accurate," the doctor said as he also didn't feel a pulse. Nurse, call a 'code blue'."

I heard the nurse yell "code blue" to the nurse's station.

In reply I heard a nurse at the desk ask, "Are you sure it's a code blue."

The nurse in Jamie's room yelled, "Yes! Code blue!"

The nurse manager announced code blue over the intercom. In minutes, fifteen to twenty people were surrounding Jamie. They had to remove him from the recliner he was in and lay him flat on his hospital bed. They began chest compressions and placed a bag over his mouth to clear his airway. I stood outside with my daughter. We prayed that Jamie would have strength, and that I would have understanding why my husband has to endure so much. Within seconds Jamie opened his eyes. For Celesteal and me, the minutes he didn't breathe felt like hours.

Due to the fact Jamie couldn't speak, the nurses and

doctors requested that I stay by his bed so I could tell them what Jamie was saying. The first thing Jamie said was, "Am I alive?" I told him, "Yes!" The next thing he said was, "Please get me the hell out of this hospital before they kill me!"

Because of the code blue, the doctors felt it necessary to remove Jamie from the IMCU and transfer him back to SICU. They tried inserting a wire from Jamie's groin up to his heart, but they were unsuccessful. Then they put him back on the respirator he'd been weaned off of weeks earlier.

Jamie was adamant that he wanted to transfer out of Walter Reed Hospital. I told him that we needed to ensure the next hospital would be able to adequately care for him, and I didn't know where to begin. Jamie said he would request to transfer, and he would ask the doctor for options. I explained how I'd requested that very thing a few days ago, but it didn't accomplish anything. No one tried to help us. He said this time everyone who walks into the room will verbally hear his request for a transfer. We agreed that everyone who comes in and asks how we're doing, we will all give them the same answer: "We are fine, thank you. We formally request a transfer out of Walter Reed Hospital immediately." As Jamie and I discussed our options, we concluded we could not trust anyone inside the hospital. One nurse said she was sorry the hospital didn't meet our expectations. We told her our expectation was simple—adequate medical care.

Various examples of what we considered adequate care were: 1) Jamie shouldn't be dropped from a bed during transfer; 2) oxygen tanks should function properly; 3) doctors shouldn't "accidentally" cut open the back of Jamie's esophagus; 4) nurses should be expected to turn him every two hours; 5) if he has a bowel movement, it should be cleaned in a timely fashion. So, we didn't have *high* expectations. We felt these were reasonable and *normal* expectations. I simply wanted the hospital staff to care for my husband as they would care for themselves.

As we discussed the last month's events Jamie's arms began moving uncontrollably. His chest muscles contracted and retracted enough to cause him serious discomfort. We were told there could be many reasons for the spasms—medications, lack of movement or lack of oxygen due to being unconscious for long periods of time. Later that evening, Jamie was sent down for an MRI and a CT scan of his brain. The findings didn't surprise us. He had frontal lobe damage to his brain from lack of oxygen! So now, a month after being shot in Afghanistan, and after coming home and being cleared of any traumatic brain injury, he's diagnosed with an injury that could've been prevented!

The following morning, the colonel of general surgery came in.

"May I be of any assistance to you?" the colonel asked.

Jamie mouthed the words, "Yes, you could assist me by transferring me the hell out of this hospital."

The doctor looked to me for a translation of what Jamie whispered. I asked Jamie if it was okay for me to tell the doctor what he said. He nodded his head yes.

I told the doctor, "My husband is formally requesting a transfer out of Walter Reed Hospital, and he would like to know what his options are."

"Why do you want a transfer?" the doctor asked him.

Jamie looked to me to answer the question.

"Doctor, Jamie has been dropped three times; he has a stage two to three bedsore; he has been put in compromised situations; and due to the lack of knowledge, communication, and overall inexperience of some of the staff in dealing with a quadriplegic, we do not believe that Walter Reed Hospital is able

77

to care for him properly.

"If he were an amputee, a burn victim, or had a severe traumatic brain injury, perhaps then he would receive proper care. However, you've told us that eighty-three percent of war casualties are amputees from IED blasts, while quadriplegics make up less than eight percent of war casualties. So please tell us doctor, what are the options for my husband to receive the adequate medical care for his quadriplegia and esophageal perforation?"

The doctor explained that due to the severity and complexity of Jamie's medical condition, it would be hard for him to receive adequate medical care at a facility anywhere in the nation. He then asked *us* how we planned to be transferred. We didn't have the answer to his question, or other questions like how we would pay for medical bills, or how we would know the right doctors or facilities. It was after questions like these that we felt lost and hopeless. We all wanted the same thing—for him to live. Furthermore, we didn't want to fight with the country or the military hospital. These were places where we should feel the safest. These were places where shouldn't have to fight all.

The doctor returned a few hours later. He told us Jamie could be transferred to Bethesda Naval Hospital in Bethesda, Maryland. It was just twenty minutes away, and they would also provide an ambulance service for the transfer. Later that same evening, a nurse came into Jamie's room and asked if it was all right to speak with us. We welcomed her in the room.

"Mrs. Jarboe, do you have a piece of paper?" the nurse asked me.

As I reached for my scheduler, she said, "What I'm about to tell you will help you get to where you need to go. It will help you as a wife fight for your husband. Please use discretion, and once I leave this room, don't tell anyone I came in."

Jamie and I looked at one another. We were somewhat shocked and confused.

I said, "Please continue."

"This isn't the first time I've seen a patient hurt or tortured the way Jamie has been," she began. "It's not done on purpose by the medical staff, it's merely lack of education, lack of compassion, and the fact the *Feres Doctrine* protects them all—even me as a nurse."

"What's the *Feres Doctrine*?" I asked.

"It's a court decision that protects the military, and gives them the freedom to practice on our wounded like guinea pigs," the nurse explained. "It protects them from prosecution."*

The nurse stood slowly and put her hand on Jamie's foot.

"Never lose that fight inside of you, Sgt. Jarboe," the nurse encouraged him. Then she looked at me and said, "Never let him lose the fight inside him, and also fight for him. You're doing the right thing by never leaving his bedside."

We both had tears in our eyes. We were amazed, but we also ask ourselves what this meant. How *do we* continue fighting? It had been a month of nonstop issues! How can we continue to move forward?

ত

A few days later, Celesteal and I carried our bags to the hospital and waited for the ambulance to transport Jamie to

---

*The practical effect is that the *Feres doctrine* effectively bars service members from collecting damages from the United States Government for personal injuries experienced in the performance of their duties. It also bars families of service members from filing wrongful death or loss of consortium actions when a service member is killed or injured.

Bethesda. We were hopeful our lives would smooth out and that we would get to go home soon. We were also thankful for the lives we were given, the struggles we had, and the fact we'd hit rock bottom so many times. Knowing you're at the bottom means there's only thing you can do—look up. We were going to do our best to make it!

When we arrived at Bethesda, Jamie was admitted to the ICU. We were greeted by the nurse whose job it was to review Jamie's medical history and do a body check. They ask me to leave the room. Jamie and I held our ground and say no. I always stayed. The nurse confirmed Jamie's stage three sacrum wound, the JP drain in his back, the oxygen amounts needed, his low blood pressure, and the ongoing tingling in Jamie's body. Celesteal and I sat in the room while they gave Jamie pain medicine for the tingling in his hand. They asked him if he wanted more pain medicine. Jamie nodded his head yes. I asked Jamie if he was is in pain, or if he was agitated.

Jamie was already taking methadone, percosec, oxy gabapentin, lyrica, valium, and now they were adding dilaudid. I knew that medications can be addictive for anyone, not just those with a family history of abuse.

I suggested to the nurse, "I don't think it's a good idea to give him narcotics unless he's in severe pain, especially if the other five pain medicines aren't helping.

Jamie mouthed the words, "I agree. I just want to sleep this day away and forget everything."

As he fell asleep, his body started having spasms (the same as it had a few days earlier). The uncontrollable spasms were in his chest muscles, shoulders, and arms. This was even worse than before. We asked the nurse what was causing it, and she told us it was typical when patients receive pain medicine over a long period of time.

The next day we were greeted by the new list of doctors we had acquired at Bethesda Naval Hospital. Jamie's general medicine doctor came in and went over the case notes he'd received from Walter Reed. He confirmed that Jamie's T2, T3, and T4 vertebrae were shattered and his spinal cord severed. He went on to say that Jamie will never walk again. That was the news we never wanted to hear. We'd hoped to get him walking once again. I remembered the day I spoke to the doctor in Germany, and the same words came out of his mouth the day after Jamie was shot. Now the hope we were holding on to was gone.

After he left, Jamie I both stared at the wall for what seemed like forever. Then I laid my head on the side of his bed near his arm. I raised my hand to caress his hand, and told him for our wedding ceremony we'd be able to dance as one. I didn't want him to worry about not walking. I just wanted him to be concerned with getting better. We needed to listen to the doctors so we could get him home. I would worry about the rest. I promised him that even if I had to sell everything we had, he would walk again.

Jamie didn't say anything for a while, and then he looked at me and whispered, "All I need is you and my girls. That's all."

I leaned in and gave Jamie a kiss, and then rested my head on his bed.

-9-

Moving Forward

I would either get up very early each morning, or spend the night with Jamie at the hospital. And so, Celesteal, being as strong as she is, would walk alone to and from the room where we were staying just a few blocks away (within the Bethesda Naval area). She never complained. She was about to graduate from the eighth grade. Her school had excused her for the last several weeks so she could spend time with us in Washington. Her last day of school was spent inside a hospital.

We wanted to get something special for our little girl to celebrate her graduation.

"What should we get her, Jamie?" I asked.

"Everything," he answered with a big smile. Then he said,

"Give her a couple hundred dollars."

"Don't you think that's too much for a thirteen-year-old?"

"No." He said. "Not for Celesteal."

As I walked down to the gift shop, I thought about how blessed our family was to have so much love between the four of us. I thought about the commitment we had to one another. It was amazing, and I was so thankful for our life.

As Celesteal got to the room that day, Jamie excitedly passed her a card. Then with all his strength he tried to speak.

"Your mother and I are proud of you, and love you kid," Jamie told her.

As Celesteal opened and read the card, her eyes got big.

"Thank you!" she said to both of us. "But, I don't need money to know how much you love me."

We knew she was sincere. We could also see she was happy with the gift we gave her.

Just then Jamie started coughing and we pressed the call light. The nurse came in to suction Jamie's tracheostomy. His cough wasn't strong enough due to the fact he was paralyzed and couldn't engage his stomach muscles. Celesteal and I watched the nurse use the suction kit. She used the sterile gloves in the packet and didn't go over twelve, which was Jamie's threshold for his suctioning (or so we were told by his ENT and general surgery doctor). I imagined a plastic hose going down my air pipe. Sucking the air and mucous out was more than I could handle. This part of what he endured four to five times a day just to be able to breathe on his own.

☙

A few days passed and we were told Jamie was no longer in

need of ICU, and they would be transferring him to the ward within Bethesda. Moments later we were packing our stuff and going down to the "5E" area of the hospital. We were greeted there by a nurse and corpsman. They asked Jamie questions. His response was, "I don't know. Ask my wife." They began asking me questions concerning the date of his injury, the location of his injury, the type of injury, how many surgeries, paralysis rate, and so on. I told them everything I knew and more.

I told them Jamie had incontinence due to the nature of his injury, and how it was important to turn him every two hours because he has a stage three bedsore from fecal matter being left on his skin. Therefore, people needed to blot his skin instead of rubbing it. I told them about the level twelve of his trach suctioning, and his involuntary spasms he developed due to lack of oxygen after his code blue. I explained the fact he's NPO and cannot have any fluids. I filled them in on the specific cream to be used on his bed sore, the mouthwash he's suppose to rinse with three times daily (due to a virus in his throat), the hypersensitivity in his arms, and the ringing in his ears. I told them of the cuffed trach he still had, and asked them not inflate the balloon because it would suffocate him. I told them how they needed to float his feet to eliminate bed sores from his heels, and to place a pillow in between his knees for comfort. They also needed to keep his spine straight, and I asked them to please change his bandages twice a day.

"Everything I've told you is in his medical file. If you can't find it," I explained, "I've printed it off so we can reference it."

The nurse looked at me and asked, "Are you in the medical field?"

"No ma'am," I told her, "That would be easier. I'm just a wife that wants her husband to come home to his family where he belongs."

"I understand, Mrs. Jarboe. I follow your Facebook page daily. Please tell what I can do to help you achieve your goals."

Jamie and I looked at each other and smiled.

❧

We all snuggled into Jamie's room and began to watch a movie. Celesteal laid on the other hospital bed, and I sat on a chair next to Jamie's bed. Jamie rested comfortably. We made each hospital room our home. We were together, and that's all that mattered.

We were told Jamie had one more surgery where they would remove scar tissue from his throat. When I asked why it had taken two months to show up, they said there wasn't a reason, it just does that from time to time. In the waiting room, a social worker told me Jamie needs to get to rehabilitation for spinal cord therapy immediately. I told her how the doctor said Jamie wouldn't be able to go to Tampa due to the distance. She said we could go to Richmond, VA. She said they had a spinal cord injury rehab area there. I told her I would mention it to the doctor.

It was mid-June, and it had been nearly two months since Jamie's injury. When it came to bathing and therapy, I'd been doing it all. While I never wanted to complain about caring for my husband, my body was growing tired of the ongoing fourteen hour days.

The doctor agreed that Jamie needed rehabilitation. The paperwork was initiated for his transfer to Richmond. I asked if my daughters would be allowed to be there with us so we could all be together as a family. It had been nearly five months since Alexa had seen Jamie. He missed her. A few days later, Alexa was flown in. After bringing her to the hospital, I told her how happy we were to have her with us. We needed our Alexa.

"Mommy, I want to see my Jamie," Alexa said smiling.

Just then, we walked into Jamie's room. She looked scared…until Jamie smiled at her. I told her Jamie couldn't talk or walk, but he'd started moving his arms a little, so he could give her a hug.

"Jamie, what are all these things on your body?" she asked him.

"They're there to protect me," Jamie whispered.

"What did you say? I can't hear you," Alexa replied.

Jamie looked up at me. I told Alexa what Jamie had said. Then she gave him a big hug. Finally we were all together again, just as we belonged.

As the girls left with their guardian, Jamie and I began to talk about his frustrations. He said he felt as if no one would take the time to listen to him. That made him feel as though he didn't exist. He wanted to have control.

"What can I do better?" I asked.

"I don't know," he replied.

I smiled and said, "You have all the control in the world. You tell me what to do, and I'll do it without hesitation."

He laughed and whispered, "You're pretty obedient."

Then he looked at me and asked, "Do you think I'm a mean person? Is that why all this happens?"

"No way," I said without hesitating. "Everything in our life is happening because this is our path. The only thing we can control is our reactions to what happens. And I do my best to remember we will catch more flies with honey than vinegar."

He smiled and laughed as he said, "Are you saying I'm an asshole?"

I giggled a little bit and replied, "No, my love, you just have an interesting way of speaking to people."

I gave him a kiss, and then laid in my hospital bed next to his as we fell asleep.

ॐ

The next morning we were greeted by Jimmy, the squad leader from the WTB (Wounded Transition Battalion). He helped us with our bags, and with the girls. The children were not allowed to ride in the ambulance with us. They rode in the van with their guardian and military liaison all the way to Richmond, VA. (about three hours away).

When we arrived we were greeted by a few people that went over Jamie's medical history. I shared with them the information I knew. They told us they would do their best to care for Jamie, and to get him up and going for physical therapy. However, they wanted to be cautious since he hadn't been out of bed for two months. They told us it may take a while.

During the first week we spent time with the children reading books, watching TV, and playing games. The nurse came in one day and asked if the children could leave for a moment. They were taken to the day room with their guardian. We spoke to the nurse regarding Jamie's bowel care. By this time, his sacrum wound was at a stage four and they were contemplating surgery. I asked what we could do to get rid of the wound. We turned him every two hours, but he keeps having involuntary bowel movements.

"He's not on a bowel program?" the nurse asked.

"No. What is a 'bowel program'?" I asked.

"Quadriplegics need to have their colon stimulated in order to train it when to have a bowel movement," she explained.

With excitement in my voice I replied, "So he can be independent! That's great!"

Jamie and I both thought this was a great idea. The nurse walked me through a few pamphlets full of information.

"Tomorrow we'll start the program, and we'll also train you," the nurse said.

To know that we'll finally understand Jamie's paralysis was a gift all its own. Moments later we were greeted by a man in a wheelchair.

"Jamie, I'll be your doctor," he announced.

Amazingly, his doctor was a T2 quadriplegic. Once again, we felt reassured that we were moving in the right direction.

-10-

Exploring the Options

June 17, 2011. Waking up to your husband next to you in a hospital bed always feels like you're still dreaming. Then five nurses walk in and you realize this is still my life. This morning we woke up early and started some physical therapy. I spent the night at the hospital, because the night before Jamie didn't sleep well. His bed wasn't comfortable. In fact, he sunk down into it. When the physician's assistant came in, Jamie tried communicating his concerns to her, but she said she couldn't understand him. I translated what Jamie was trying to say, and she said they would put in an order for a new mattress. That morning they also weighed him. He weighed 105 pounds! That was exciting because he weighed 98 pounds two weeks earlier.

The nurse informed us they would be putting a PICC line

in Jamie's arm. When he heard this, he nodded his head no.

"Don't put anything in my arm," Jamie said. "I told you I had it before and it hurt. I don't want it."

Again, she couldn't understand him. I had to repeat what he said to her.

She told Jamie that his veins could collapse, or spasms could occur with the IV needles having to be replaced every three days. The PICC line would be so much easier. Jamie nodded his head no.

"We've gone for two months without the PICC line," I explained. "I would like to proceed in the same manner simply because we've come so far, and we don't want to take steps back. Especially with a PICC line that goes right to his heart and has the potential to cause severe problems and infections."

"All right," the nurse replied, "no PICC line."

I asked her about Jamie's antibiotic. We were told by the infectious disease doctors in Bethesda that they wanted Jamie off of IV antibiotics after the 15th and he was to start on oral medications such as Isoniazid and Rifampin. However, they said they would be doing the oral medications through his feeding tube because they couldn't be crushed.

"Then what antibiotics will be on?" I asked.

"Zosyn," the nurse told me.

"We were told he needed to be taken off Zosyn after the 15th to start the next level of treatment."

I gave her the business card the doctors gave in case there were questions like this.

Jamie's primary doctor (who had been in a wheelchair for twenty-seven years) began to explain how they were going to put

92

Jamie on a yeast pill to help with his bowel movements. They also planned to start him on some steroids to build his muscles so he could get up and going. This was very exciting news! Jamie and I smiled at each other as we welcomed the good news.

The therapist came in and started doing rotations with Jamie's left arm. They did the left arm for about five minutes, then the right arm about two minutes, and then the right leg two minutes. As they got called out, they said they would be back to do left leg later.

Next, the occupational therapist came in. They wanted to get Jamie sitting up, and possibly put him in his new chair. Unfortunately, the day before it didn't go as well. His blood pressure dropped to forty-six so they immediately laid him down and discontinued therapy.

I asked if a cardiac chair would be all right to start with. That's what we had done at Bethesda and Walter Reed. Slowly we worked to get him up since he'd been lying in a bed for almost a week. The female therapist said the cardiac chair wasn't good for bed sores.

"Would two days really make that much difference?" I asked.

"Yes," she replied while increasing Jamie's bed to thirty degrees.

Jamie's blood pressure dropped to sixty-three. I asked Jamie to move his arms and squeeze on his sponges to get his blood circulating. Then, they moved his bed up to a forty-five degree angle and took his blood pressure. It went up to seventy-six! Finally, Jamie had had enough. But, not until we got him up to sixty degrees, and he was able to hold that position for three minutes!

ॐ

It was June 18, 2011. Each morning I got up around 5 AM and made my way a few blocks away to the VA Hospital, room 124. As I walked I enjoyed the beautiful sky and the air that was so fresh. It had been weeks since Jamie had been able to feel the wind on his face. I couldn't help feeling guilty for enjoying the beauty of the outdoors.

Early this particular morning we were met by the chief doctor. He reiterated how they wanted to take care of Jamie and get him up to physical therapy so his healing could begin. We all agreed how wonderful that would be. He told us that with this type of paraplegic, there were many options for us to consider. We knew it was important to get Jamie on a strict routine. A strict routine of therapy would help his internal organs. Since Jamie had a feeding type bypassing his stomach and going to his lower intestines (to protect his esophagus which had been repaired with a stint on May 23, 2011), his stomach hadn't been used. His throat muscles, which help him swallow, had also been inactive. Due to all of this, the doctor told us we had a long road ahead of us. We told him we've been following this path for over two months. We understood that it's a marathon and not a sprint.

Two nurses changed out Jamie's bedding. As they did, they lowered his bed, and then afterward they raised it to twenty degrees. I told Jamie he was at twenty degrees. (I would tell him things he couldn't see so he could try to control something simple like the angle of his bed.)

"He needs to be at twenty degrees for his tube feed," the nurse told me.

"I'm fully aware of that," I told her, "however, we were told by occupational therapy that he needs to be at thirty-five to forty degrees from time to time."

"The higher position is what gives him pressure ulcers," she replied.

I paused for a moment, and then told her, "This is the reason I'm not in politics. I'm simply relaying a message of what I was told, and I'm trying to give my husband an option to decide where his bed is going to be. You'll see this if you read his chart."

The nurse then covered Jamie's trach collar in an attempt to get him to speak. After a few seconds of him moving his arms while suffocating, I informed her that his vocal cords are damaged.

"He has granulation in his throat, and he can't speak or breathe out of his mouth or nose," I told her. "Also, in the future would you please use gloves when you're in Jamie's room to prevent germs or further infection."

Jamie and I were able to do leg and arm exercises. Most days his arms were easy exercise, but now they were hurting him more than ever. I went slow when I did his range of motions with his shoulders and his neck rolls. But now his hands were losing their form. His motion had decreased from what he was able to do previously. I needed to ask the doctor about it so I could understand why his hands were sunk in and his muscles were losing mass.

On a positive note, we discovered a wonderful pool of information—*YouTube*. I had perceived it to be only a music video outlet. We typed in "wheelchair cars" and "paraplegics." The informational videos that appeared were unbelievable! We watched people with the same injuries Jamie had doing step-by-step routines involving everything from putting on shoes to getting in and out of wheelchairs.

ळ

On Monday June 20, 2011, we were scheduled to meet

with the entire team at the VA to discuss their goals for Jamie's care. The meeting was scheduled for 2:00 PM. That same day, Jamie was only turned once in nine hours by the nursing staff! I had to turn him every two hours due to the fact we hadn't seen our nurse. It was for this reason that I had been forced to learn so much about Jamie's medical care in just a few short months. I contacted the nurse case manager to discuss a few of these concerns prior the meeting with the entire team. I got her voicemail and left a message. I never received a call back.

The team arrived around 2:45 PM. I set up my voice recorder so Jamie could hear it later. He was exhausted. They apologized for us being caught in the middle of a variety of requests from doctors, nurses, and therapists. In short their goals for Jamie to complete were as follows: 1. They wanted him at a thirty degree angle for up to two hours and no less than twenty degrees; 2. They wanted to be consistent with his bowel care; 3. The nursing team must do their best to read orders prior to completing tasks; 4. The nurses will work on rolling him effectively and doing their best to service him as a patient.

The meeting lasted about thirty minutes. The speech pathologist was amazing; the social worker was a breath of fresh air; the nurse was a very nice woman; and the recreational therapist was pretty impressive. It's easy to tell if someone takes value in themselves because they see everything they do as having value. They take their time to care for others and listen to their concerns while not interrupting (simply because they don't like what is being said).

I wanted to step back and see how things transpired in my absence. So, I took the girls to a children's museum, and then out to lunch. I'd been in Jamie's room since 5 AM that morning. I bathed him, helped him with physical therapy, massaged him, and brushed his teeth. He was a little concerned about me leaving for the day, but he knew the girls and I needed a break. I told him I would be back no later than 4 PM. This was the first time in over two months that I had left Jamie's bedside. I also felt he needed to build some trust with his nursing staff. He couldn't rely on me for everything. I hoped it would be a successful day!

∞

The girls and I had the best time! We watched *Sea Rex* at an Imax theater. Cici, Lexi, and I were in shock at all the information and the wonderful pictures! They had lots of fun running around playing. We found the human anatomy display that explained certain parts of the body. We got to see the esophagus, vocal cords, and spine, all of which helped me explain to them why Jamie was hurt so bad. Lexi was adorable as she asked me, "Mommy, doesn't the hospital have Band-Aids for Jamie to get better?"

When I got back to the hospital, Jamie said he felt like the nurses wouldn't listen to him. He told me how they made him wait for an hour for a necessary change. He said he tried to communicate with them, but they just walked away.

I called for the nurse. Without making any accusations, I simply asked her how her day was going. She walked me through her day. She told me she had two additional patients put on her roster because another nurse had left early. I asked her if she was aware that Jamie had been in need of a change earlier in the day. She said yes, and then told me she had done her best. I believed she wasn't trying to hurt Jamie's feelings, or ignore him. The fact is she had too many patients. My heart went out to all the medical staff. It had to be a difficult job to attempt to please everyone while forgetting about yourself.

I assured Jamie that the nurse was not trying to be mean or rude. I explained how she was overloaded with patients. I told him

I was sorry he had had such a terrible day. Then I tried to tell him about my day out with the girls and how it was so nice to see the girls smile.

"It must be nice to see the things you got to see today," Jamie said rolling his eyes.

"Are you having a pity party Sgt. Jarboe?" I replied.

He smiled and said, "Yes, what's it to you Mrs. Jarboe?"

"It's *everything* for my husband to be happy. I just happen to have video of the day we had. Would you like to watch?"

His face lit up. He smiled as I pressed play button on my phone. Now he could see how wonderful of a day we had and hear the excitement and laughter.

ജ

Jamie and I had been discussing new options. After five out of six incidents reported to Walter Reed Hospital were determined to have a solid basis, they transferred us to Bethesda Naval Hospital. We asked what options we had. The general surgeon reiterated to us that with the severity of Jamie's injury they would prefer he stay local. And, since Bethesda had the same doctors, we shouldn't have any issues.

Then we were told we he had four options for spinal cord rehab. Our options were in Minnesota, California, Virginia, and Florida. We were never given any other options. We spoke to a couple that had the same injury and issues Jamie and I were dealing with. We found out we did have a choice. We had a choice to make a decision on Jamie's healthcare for the rest of his life. We requested meetings with the doctors and social workers at Virginia VA.

-11-

Frustration Mounts

We discovered that we didn't have to receive medical treatment at the VA, Walter Reed, or at Bethesda. Jamie could be treated anywhere as long as a referral from Tricare was approved.

I began communicating with Tricare, Craig Hospital, and the military chain-of-command. We continued to meet with doctors and social worker at the VA in Richmond. While we appreciated their efforts, it was obvious to us that the hospital was understaffed and over budget. We had also heard enough to know that their staff was overworked and underpaid. That may also be the case in the next hospital, but of course we hoped it wouldn't be. In our present position, we were constantly being put in between the staff and the "politics" of the nurses, doctors, therapists, and social workers. This being the case, we knew the military wasn't who, or what we needed to be dealing with.

We had made our decision, and we were going to stand by it. I was being told by numerous individuals that we might be denied by Tricare. However, we'd already spoke to three Tricare representatives and requested approval. They asked us if we wanted to go against the doctors recommendations and risk Jamie's medical stability by transferring him out of the military hospital system. I explained how we'd been told by numerous doctors that Jamie was stable enough to fly, and that we would be provided with adequate staff. I also pointed out that even though we were told Jamie would not be able to fly, his medical notes (page 1926) clearly stated that flying was okay.

Even so, the team in Bethesda preferred for him stay close. After numerous phone calls from individuals regarding a declination, my reply to them was the same. If we receive a favorable reply, I will formally request that the name, telephone number, email address, and physical address of the individual be sent to me within twenty-four hours. If the cost becomes a factor, then I will start paying for my husband's medical care myself!

It had been a long day. But, finally we are able to take control of Jamie's future. It was good to know that he had the ability to make decisions, and that I was his voice.

ಝ

Jamie grew stronger each day. After two months of resting, fighting, and praying, I saw a little bit of my husband that I'd missed so much.

"What kind of man was he before he was shot?" a nurse asked me.

"He was the same man you see today," I responded

passionately. "He's the kind of man who would do anything to come home to his family alive. He was saved to be on this earth. His time is unknown. Each minute to me is heaven having him by my side."

That morning at the hospital was great. Jamie was sound asleep when I got there. As I sat in the chair next to his bed, I examined emails, looked at houses online, and I thought of everything in our lives we would be able to do once we got home. I found myself thinking back to when I fell in love with him. As I stared out the window, I could hear him playing his guitar for me outside my bedroom window the night he asked me for a second date.

When Jamie woke up, he looked at me, stretched his neck, and he said, "Good morning."

"What would you like to do first today?" I asked him.

"A massage."

I started with his feet. I went from his toes up to his ankles. I remembered reading an article online about muscle stimulation. I tried to mimic the article by patting Jamie's feet and legs. He looked at me as if to say, "What the heck are you doing?" I told him it was an old Chinese technique to help circulation. He laughed and nodded his head.

The nurse came in to give him his meds, after which we started watching funny YouTube videos to pass the time. Then, the wound nurse came in and started doing a body assessment of Jamie just as the PA had done earlier. They determined that Jamie not only had a substantial amount of bruising, but that his pressure ulcer had also increased in size. Now it had a yellow appearance.

While the wound nurse was moving Jamie, and while she was examining the wound, she told him he needed to quit sitting up so much. Jamie typically stayed at twenty-two to twenty-six degrees on his bed. He'd only been sitting up getting ready to be in his wheelchair for about two hours. The nurse reprimanded Jamie saying that his antibiotic was giving him loose bowel movements, and that that was the cause of his pressure ulcers and bruising. She insisted that it wasn't from not being consistently turned night or day. However, we knew there had been days that a nurse hadn't attempted to turn him for up to nine hours. In those times, I had to complete the process with assistance from our thirteen year old daughter.

After the nurses left came the moment we'd been waiting. PT and OT came in for Jamie to finally get up in his wheelchair and go outside! The transfer went smooth, and he was able to be outside for almost an hour. Afterward, he was tired and took a nap all afternoon. So, the girls and I went to see Cars 2. When we got back, we started packing up Jamie's room for our transfer.

As we were packing, I received a call from the nurse case manager. Her message went something like this: "We are working on the transfer. These things don't happen overnight. Please be patient as we are working on getting this handled."

I told Jamie the news. Our goal was to be in Colorado by the 4th of July—*for our own "Independence."*

Ⅎ

A "good morning" would be great. However, last night I went back to the hotel to see the girls, and to get some sleep. I woke up to a phone call from Jamie. He was able to text me through his IPad. He stated that it had been four hours since they checked on him, and he doesn't have his call button. He asked me to call the hospital. After two minutes of ringing, someone at the hospital finally answered the phone. I asked the nurse on the other end to please check on my husband. Then, I texted Jamie and he didn't respond.

I sat next to his bed that morning until he woke up. He typed on his IPad that he didn't have his call light within reach at two different times during the night. He said the nurses were hurting him when they moved him. I pressed the call light, and they answered.

"May I have a list of the nurses who were in my husband's room last night," I asked.

A nurse came to the room and asked, "Is there a problem?"

"Yes. I need the names of the individuals who cared for my husband last night."

"Is there a problem," she asked me again.

"Yes, and I'm waiting for a list of names."

Belligerently, the nurse blurted out the names of those who were in Jamie's room, and then she walked out of the room. I thought to myself, "Why does my husband have to endure such horrific treatment when I'm not here. Why is he being hurt time and time again. I would be sleeping in Jamie's room until we're transferred out of the hospital.

ᏏᏯ

Our goal today was to get airline tickets for the guardian and the girls to go home. We also needed to talk to doctors about medications, bandages, and about having Jamie turned. We also needed to find out when we would leave for Colorado!

During PT the doctor gave Jamie a message to call a certain doctor at Craig Hospital. He explained that Craig Hospital had some reservations about taking Jamie due to the stent in his neck. I called for Jamie, and I was referred to an administrative coordinator. I left a message for her since the doctors were unavailable. It was 2:30 PM. Jamie was getting in his wheelchair for recreational therapy for the second time.

What we'd found at the VA was that they don't try to speed anything along—*healing or rehabilitation.* They always seemed hampered by insufficient funding (due to budget cuts) and being understaffed. Jamie had PT for an hour in the morning, and then from 11:00 AM to noon. Then, he had recreation from 3-4 PM. We were used to Walter Reed and Bethesda where Jamie would be active and up in his chair for four to six hours a day playing Checkers, Connect Four, and whatever else he could get his hands on. The first week in Richmond, Jamie was confined to his bed. His pressure ulcer had gradually become bigger and more complex. His sore wasn't from sitting up. According to the doctor, it was from laying in bed too long on the same area.

During recreational therapy we went outside to enjoy the shade and the hot sun. The speech pathologist came out and told us we can go ahead and try the speaking valve as approved by ENT. I asked her if she could please chart and make an order for it. She said she would. Then, she asked why. I told her the recreational therapist said Jamie was confined to his bed all weekend because the proper order wasn't submitted for him to do any type of PT, RT, or *any* activity for that matter. KT (Kinetics Therapy) came in for twenty minutes on Saturday to do some range of motion, but otherwise it was up to Celesteal and I to keep moving forward and help him with his activities. The recreational therapist said she could talk to someone regarding the orders, and that we should mention this to our doctor. We thanked her for the insight.

My phone rang. It was a wounded warrior wife checking in on me. I informed her of the delay. I told her I wasn't sure of the full story, but at this point the VA was telling us Craig Hospital would not accept us. She told us to keep moving forward. She encouraged us that we would be free soon.

Jamie, Celesteal, and I went to the store (along with the RT). Jamie wanted to buy some DVDs and speakers. While we were shopping we received the phone call from Craig Hospital. It was comforting to hear them welcoming us with open arms. The woman who called told us about their concerns with the surgery Jamie was suppose to have in a week or two for his stint. They desired to wait until after his surgery. But, I let her know that his surgery wasn't for another month, and that we didn't want to be in the Richmond VA Hospital for one more second. This was due to the inconsistencies we encountered, the staffing issues, and the facility not being able to provide the quality care my husband deserved. He had already fought for his life the day he was shot, so why do we now have to fight once more?

The woman at Craig Hospital was told that Jamie was in such a fragile state that he wasn't able to much. That wasn't true! I let her know the extent of Jamie's ability and how he's more than capable to do what is needed and when it's needed. Yes, he did have problems getting up after a week in bed. He did have issues sleeping after they changed his medications, took him off his methadone, muscle relaxers, and his sleeping medicine. I told her how Jamie had to contact me late one night because he'd called for a nurse who didn't show up for four hours! I assured her that this was a decision Jamie and I were both determined to make. We wanted the quality care he deserved and we wanted to use our secondary medical (namely our Tricare). I told her how grateful we would be if she would assist us.

She assured me she would look into our situation again and get back with me. Meanwhile, I had the doctor paged so that we could get some clarification on Jamie's "fragile nature." Clarification as to why he's only able to get up three hours a day.

Clarification on why he wasn't receiving the yeast pills the doctor wanted him to start on a week ago. Clarification on why there's *still* no sign in his room stating he cannot speak. Clarification on why his tube feed was changed, and clarification on the values concerning patient care at the VA Hospital.

As we walked back to the room, we were met by another soldier's wife.

"I've actually heard about you," she told us. "I've heard how Jamie presses his call bell all the time; how he *must* have twenty-four hour care; and how we don't like any of the nurses."

"I'm so sorry for any distress your family due to the nurses speaking out of turn," I responded.

"No worries," she assured me. "I'm sure they talk about us too. There's next to *no professionalism* here with the nurses yelling down the hallway at 2:00 AM. Or, the nurses coming in to our room talking on their cell phones to friends or family."

My heart goes out to our veterans! I'm thankful for all the soldiers of the past who paved the way for Jamie and future soldiers. Presently our soldiers have a choice; they can go to a private facility and see their family physician while they live their lives. A choice that was provided for them by soldiers of the past. If I've learned anything from the past few months, it's how much compassion and love I have for our veterans.

℣

This evening we spoke with the PA (Physician's Assistant). We needed to clarify the inconsistencies in the reasoning behind Jamie not being transferred to Craig Hospital.

"Is Jamie medically stable enough to transfer," I asked.

"Yes," she answered. "But, we don't want to cause stress to his body by unhooking him from his tube feed (his nourishment and water). He was dehydrated when he got here, and for four days he was too weak to move."

"Are you referring to the first four days we were here—when they misappropriated his medications and took him off of his pain medication?"

"Of course you know Tricare will only pay part of the rehabilitation fees as a private provider," she said, changing the subject.

"That isn't true. We've spoken to Tricare, and they're waiting for the referral. And, due to the fact that Jamie is still on active duty, Tricare will be his *secondary* insurance. So, hypothetically, DOD will pay seventy percent, and Tricare will cover the other thirty percent."

We told her once again that we wanted to be transferred immediately out the VA Hospital in Richmond and transferred to Craig Hospital in Denver, Colorado. This was our fourth request. We also expressed how we wanted them to stop trying to change our minds, and stop ignoring our requests while bringing idle excuses as to why he can't be transferred. It had almost been one week since our request was made.

The only thing they were doing was telling Craig that Jamie was too weak to participate in PT, and that he could only be up and awake three hours a day. That was false. They told Craig he was too fragile to transport. That was false. They told Craig he was hooked up to too much equipment. That was false! The truth was, he had a feeding tube in his small intestine, which was bypassing his stomach. He had a jejunal and a gastric intake and outtake. He had an IV for Zosyn and fluids. He was on room air and had a mask over his trache for humidity reasons (only it's at twenty-one percent). He can't walk or talk, but he could make choices, and he'd made his choice.

A few minutes after the doctor left, the military liaison came in.

"I came in to see how Jamie's doing, and wondered if I could speak to you privately Mrs. Jarboe," she said.

"You can speak to me in front of my husband," I told her. "We speak freely with no secrets. And, he makes decisions just as I do—we do it together."

"Jamie, are you happy with your care?" she asked him.

"No," he answered. "I'm not happy. I had a nurse last night, and when she was moving me from side to side she thought it was all right for poop to be on my leg even after I asked her to remove it. Her reply was, 'Don't worry, you're getting a bath in the morning.' I asked her again to remove the poop from leg. She left the room.

"There's been nights my call bell is nowhere near my bed, and I've sat here for four hours waiting for someone to help me. I was manhandled by a nurse and had to call my wife from my iPad at 1:00 AM for help. The nurse was brutally violent with me to the point I had tears in my eyes. She wouldn't stop pushing me over. While she was moving my bedding, I couldn't breathe. But, she refused to stop and let me rest. She just wanted to get her job done and leave because she'd worked a double shift due to being understaffed.

"Nurses left scissors in my bed. They've left breathing treatments on my oxygen tube for two hours; or they never gave me the breathing treatments just leaving the clear tube in my bed. They've dropped the suction 'Yonkers' on the floor, and then picked it up and placed it in my bed for me to use without replacing it. They complain about their government cheese being in slices, and the government equipment never working. My bed was broken and wouldn't go down for four days. Finally, they switched it out and got me a new mattress and maintenance came and fixed the bed.

"Nurses have made comments about how the beds typically don't work. We've been told they're short-staffed, underpaid, and they're facing more cutbacks. At this point the nurses know we're unhappy, and we feel their resentment and retaliation. They come in and ask condescendingly if we need help. The fact that this is all reactive and not proactive makes our choice even easier. We want to transfer."

"We have a meeting next week, and we're going to get everything fixed," the military liaison said.

"That's fine," Jamie said, "fix it after we leave. We want to transfer, and we want to transfer now!"

"I'm not in charge of transfers," she said. "That's out of my hands. But, call if someone is hurting or manhandling you."

As I thought about our conversation, I concluded that whether or not the military was taking care of their hospital personnel was not *Jamie's* problem. I'm sure they have a lot to complain about. However, Jamie was the one shot in battle! At this point he's been told that his spine is severed and he'll never walk again. He may also lose movement in his arms. Fine. We can accept and work with that. But, dealing with the emotions and fears that we're dealing with now—that's *not* all right. We cannot accept it because our well-being and spiritual beliefs are what keep us alive. It gives us hope.

The bottom line is, we don't feel safe and we want to transfer. Why can't they just let us go? They're portraying him as a fragile and incapable quadriplegic. Yet, that fragile and incapable quadriplegic did two hours of PT, forty-five minutes of KT, and one hour of RT. Plus, he spent time with his family shopping today. I believe in him! He believes in himself! We're what matters!

Medically he's a miracle, and we know that we can move mountains. They will see it soon enough.

-12-

PTSD, TB, and a Downtrodden Marine

Each day we tried to start new while giving the hospital the benefit of the doubt. However, each day there was an issue with care—whether it was leaving Jamie without his call light, or no response to the call light for four hours. Or, "stimulating" him for bowel care, and then leaving him in it for an hour to "make sure he's done." He had bruising on this thighs from where a nurse grabbed him; feces left on his legs, stomach, and all over his bedding; and no use of his orthotic boots to keep his feet straight or protected. He was still not being turned properly (often for nine hours). These issues were obviously not going away. If anything,

111

we were now getting nurses who were so defensive when they came in the room they were counterproductive.

Jamie and I wrote a letter and e-mailed it to one hundred thirty-six people. (We wanted out of the VA now!)

To whom it may concern:

Please accept this as our written request to be transferred immediately from Veteran Rehabilitation Hospital in Richmond, Virginia, to Craig Hospital in Denver, Colorado. We have verbally requested this transfer four times in the last week. We have been told by the PA that Jamie may be transported; however, they are concerned about stress of transport.

Furthermore, the PA told us Tricare won't pay for all of our rehabilitation at a private hospital. That comment is of no relevance. That seems to be the level of professionalism that is conducted here—scare tactics, very similar to the two nurses on night shift aggressively turning my husband last night, and then ripping the sheet out from under him. He is dealing with retaliation and personal attacks each hour you leave him in this hospital.

We have spoken to Craig Hospital. They were told Jamie is in a fragile state and unable to do physical or recreational therapy longer than 3 hours. This is not accurate. This is only due to minimal time slots available by staff here at Richmond. Please correct this miscommunication to reflect accurate information.

There has been a message left for Jamie's doctor in Bethesda informing him of our request, as well as letting him know that we will return to Bethesda to complete any necessary surgeries at his discretion from Craig Hospital.

We have no interest in waiting for corrections or meetings to be made. We want to be transferred by Friday July 1, 2011. (Especially taking into consideration the four day weekend.)

Thank you for your time and consideration.

Respectfully,

Jamie and Melissa Jarboe

ಚಿ

After the letter was sent today, Jamie and I decided to move forward with our day. We were determined not to let anything derail our last day with the kiddos before they left the next day with my mother to go home to Kansas.

We started doing some of his physical therapy. Jamie and I worked doing reps with his bands. He did fifteen reps with his arms—three sets on both arms! Then the man from KT came in and did Jamie's range of motion. As he worked on Jamie's arms he told him that his muscles were getting stronger.

"Keep up whatever you're doing," the therapist said. "It's hard to build with only thirty minutes a day, three days a week."

As the therapist was doing his working with Jamie, he noticed something he felt I needed to see.

"Come here and look at this, Mrs. Jarboe," the therapist said, motioning for me to come over to the bed. "That looks like dry fecal matter under his left leg. It looks like it's been there for quite some time."

Now I'd have to remind myself to lift his legs and look under them. Each morning I would typically come in and wash Jamie down with soap and water. This was to make sure I removed all the dry skin and any germs or bacteria. I was a little upset with myself for missing this. On the other hand, the nurses had missed it too. It took all the restraint I could muster not to press the call button and have her come back down to show her the oversight. Instead, I put gloves on and started washing him down. There was no sense making him wait any longer.

While cleaning him up, and after using seven wipes, I started examining the rest of him. I noticed fecal matter on the catheter for his bladder. I started wiping it with rubbing alcohol. It took four alcohol pads to get him clean!

"I'm sorry you have to do this," Jamie mouthed to me.

"Why? I'm not. This is what we're supposed to do," I said. "We're supposed to take care of one another. What would you do if it were me?"

Jamie opened his eyes wide and said, "Yes!"

"Well then, it's not a big deal."

After I finished, Celesteal showed up. We were planning an outing to the infamous Walmart. Jamie had PT at 11:00 AM, and I was trying to help him build trust in others. I knew exactly what he wanted, but it was better if I gave him some distance to help him rely upon and build a bond with his therapist.

I was only gone for an hour and a half when my phone rang. It was the physical therapist asking if I could come to the PT room. Jamie wanted to show me his progress! I told her we would be there as quickly as we could! Jamie was proud of himself—he was able to sit up a little longer with the assistance of two people! His therapists (both physical and occupational) were ecstatic! We got back to the room around 12:30 PM, and Jamie said he was a little tired from being in his chair. He rang the nurses bell to have them come and put him in bed.

While we were getting him into bed, another nurse came in and said, "What are you doing? He has an appointment at 1:00 PM!"

"He's tired," the nurse helping us replied.

Frustrated, the nurse looked at me and asked, "Why is he in bed? He has appointments, and if he isn't at his appointments I'll get in trouble."

I stopped getting Jamie undressed.

"He made the decision to get into the bed," I explained. "He knows his body, and he's tired."

Still pushing the issue, she said, "Well he told me at 10:00AM that he wasn't going to get into bed until 2:30 PM. Therapy said he can be up in his chair until tolerated."

Then she walked out. The other nurse and I got him situated. When she came back in to adjust Jamie, 1 had a few words for her.

"You know, I understand and appreciate your concern. However, Jamie makes the decisions. It's his body and his care. He tells me what he wants, and as his wife I follow through. When he can't speak, I speak for him," I told her. "I didn't care for the way you talked to us or the other nurse. And, when we rang the call bell you didn't come for over thirty minutes. If *we* had to wait on you, that means *Jamie* had to wait on you. That's not going to happen."

She looked at me and didn't say a word. She began speaking directly to Jamie. She asked him if he was comfortable, then she then left the room.

The rest of the day was calm! The doctor came in with the PA and asked if we had any questions about transfer. We didn't have any at that time. We were patiently waiting. We thanked them for stopping in.

The guardian, Alexa, and Celesteal came to the hospital to spend some time with us since they would be going home the next day. Tomorrow was going to be a sad day. We would miss our "Cici" and "Lexi Lous." But, we knew when it was time, we would be together again. That day would be very special!

Though today was difficult, I was thankful Jamie was still here to go through these obstacles. No matter what challenges we faced together, we did our best to overcome them. We tried to do it with grace and a smile, especially when I considered the alternative—I could've been at home mourning the loss of my husband along with so many other military widows.

The night before Jamie was shot we discussed our beliefs about life and death. The day that we're called to serve the Lord is the greatest day of our lives. Death is a privilege if we live our lives as intended. We don't have to be perfect, not making any mistakes. Instead, be imperfect, make tons of mistakes, but just never make the same mistake twice. Learn, listen, love, and live. That's what we did today. We learned, listened, loved, and we lived. We *will* move forward.

⁋⁋

I woke up with Jamie in the morning. He called me from his iPad last night. I communicate with him via the iPad by asking yes or no questions. Then he simply presses a button in response. I asked if he wanted me to stay the night. He pressed one button, I kissed the girls goodnight, and walked up to the hospital.

Everything went well through the night. We both slept well. I left at 7:00 AM to go to the hotel. I planned to go to the airport to see the guardian and girls get on plane. After a few minutes, I decided to go back to the hospital to be with Jamie. I told my beautiful daughters we would all be together soon, and that we loved them more than life. We all stood strong, making the departure a happy one. We were happy that we had been able to see one another, and we stayed that way as we separated.

After arriving at the hospital I gave Jamie a kiss. A few minutes later the doctor came in and said some of Jamie's levels were elevated. They wanted to send him for Cat Scan. I told Jamie, "Remember God first. He matters, so let's keep our faith and He will provide." The doctors and nurses wanted to take extra precautions. A few minutes later the transport for the CT scan showed up, and the X-ray tech came to take more blood from Jamie.

They were hoping the stent in Jamie's neck wasn't leaking, and that the trach in his esophagus hadn't become infected. As we headed down for the CT scan, we were thinking of ideas to celebrate the fourth of July in his room.

"I'm thinking Luau!" I said.

A meeting was scheduled with the doctors for the following morning. Hopefully we'll see what options Jamie has, and then go from there. Altogether, it's been a fairly relaxing day. I needed to run to Bath-n-Body Works to get some eucalyptus spearmint lotion and oil. Since Jamie was able to smell again, it was one of our favorite ways to relax. I was also going to find a sound machine with reiki music and ocean sounds. We would get this all taken care of in due time.

As for the nurses and military liaisons telling me I was stressed, tired, and worn out—anyone who knew me, and had seen me in action running operations for the past five years, understood this was nothing compared to my career. My reply to those concerned souls was: "If you're concerned for my well-being (which *I do* appreciate), step-up and follow through with your own job (meaning chart accurately, pay attention to details, and keep your personal opinions to yourself). If there's something medical you'd like to discuss, please feel free."

Typically, being in the hospital wasn't hard. I had a recliner. We also had movies and Internet games. And, most importantly we had each other. Again just because our home was in the middle of a hospital didn't mean it wasn't our home. It may not have looked like everyone else's homes, but it was our home.

There were several different doctors reading Jamie's CT Scan. We were just relaxing today as we focused on our love for God, for one another, and for our children who had left Virginia a day earlier to go home to Kansas.

It was a calm, easy night. Jamie was going to get up in his wheelchair, and we were going to go outside under a tree to read the *Love Dare* book. We'd already read it once together. It was amazing how it related directly to us—to what we were going through at that moment. When we finished, we were planned on giving it to our nurses. Sarah (a nurse) watched us as I read to Jamie. I felt she had a better understanding of us. As I told the doctors before, we make our home wherever we are, and just because our home is in the middle of a hospital is inconsequential to us.

Once we know exactly what's going on with Jamie's body, we will understand our future much better. The doctors were running tests and cultures trying to figure it out. His heart was enlarged and his vertebrae were possibly infected. We understood that C Diff (a bacterial infection) was a possibility. However, maybe it was just Jamie being his silly old self. Maybe he would get better in his own time. That's exactly what we had—time. We had time to love, to laugh, and to live. I stayed next to my husband that night.

ౚ

After staying during the evening, bathing Jamie, exfoliating his feet, brushing his teeth, and rolling him on his side to ensure he was comfortable, I arrived at the hotel around 10:30 PM. I was up at 6:00 AM the next morning walking back to the hospital. Jamie was pretty tired that morning. He said he had a good night. When I got to his room he was getting ready to be bathed by a nurse. I typically stayed to help and watch.

I seldom told the nurses that I bathed him because I began to notice they would expect me to do it all the time. I didn't want that to happen because they could do certain medical things while bathing that I could not. They took off bandages and cleaned out his wounds (pressure ulcer). Plus, this way he would get doubly clean.

The PA came in to speak with us.

"Was respiratory able to get a sample from the suction in Jamie's trache?"

"Yes," I told her. "They did get a sample, and it was green."

"What about a bowel sample?"

"I'm not aware of any samples being taken when they did his bowel stimulation."

"All right," the PA said.

"Why are samples being collected?"

"Well, we're going to take him off the Zosyn and put him on Rifampin and another medication."

"Take out my IV! Right now!" Jamie said.

"We will soon," she responded.

Just then the infectious disease doctor walked in. He

119

started talking with the PA and the doctor. When they were finished, I asked them to explain in English what was being discussed.

They said they were concerned with the CT scan. One reason for the concern was that Jamie appeared to have some pockets in his upper lungs as well as some other effects. They wanted to test him for Tuberculosis. The infectious disease doctor checked the incision in Jamie's back, his JP drain under his shoulder, and then he felt his neck for pain.

"Do you remember a few weeks ago when I asked you why Jamie's oral medication was switched from Zosyn to Rifampin?"

"Mrs. Jarboe," the ID doctor explained, "Rifampin can be crushed and fed orally."

Then I looked at PA Adkins.

"We felt that the Zosyn was enough *at that time*," she explained.

I knew I had nothing nice to say, so I said nothing. I started rubbing Jamie's feet and doing his stretches in order to calm myself. They ended the conversation by saying that they would look into it, and then get back with us. They also said it was all right for Jamie to get up.

At that point Jamie and I weren't real concerned about the TB. Jamie got up in his wheelchair at 10:45 AM and then had PT at 11:00 AM. He was able to on the mat and stretch out his arms with the assistance of his trainers. He actually held himself up a little bit! After that I asked him if he would like to take his lovely wife to lunch. Even though he couldn't eat, it was the first time he was able to sit up with me. We actually looked at one another and acted silly as we ate. It meant so much to both of us.

After PT we went to the store, and then to the hotel to

check out some movies for the weekend. On the way back Jamie said the sun felt great on his arms and legs! We talked about our future, and the new house we knew we are going to have to build. We discussed and tried to figure out our bills in case I wasn't able to go back to work.

"I don't want you to forfeit your partnership," Jamie told me.

I was invited to accept a partnership in my company in January 2012.

"I'm okay with putting my career on the back burner and staying home to be a wife and a mother," I told him.

"You would really do that?"

"Yes."

When we got back to the hospital, the PA found us. She looked flushed. She said they needed to get some more tests done immediately. She also told us Jamie might have to be isolated for the weekend pending further results.

We went to his room and read up on Tuberculosis. At this point we were focused on health, happiness, our love for our family, and the beautiful life we were going to have.

In the moment, I was reminded of a scripture:

> And Adam said: "This is now bone of my bones and flesh of my flesh; She shall be called Woman, because she was taken out of Man." (Genesis 2:23)

ॐ

When I woke up, I was eager to get to the hospital. The night before, Jamie had told me to sleep in until 8:00 AM. But, I hadn't done that since I was fourteen. I told him I would try, but I liked being there early in the morning. I saw a lot more that way.

For a brief moment that morning, I thought about the fact that Jamie was so exhausted. He would fall asleep at a moment's notice, and then start having dreams. His arms would jerk around, and periodically he would mouth words. I videotaped it on my phone and showed it to the doctors. They said it wasn't a nerve issue. They said he dreaming, or it was part of his PTSD. They suggested keeping an eye on it, so I installed a surveillance camera in the room.

Each day I watched the same thing over and over. He fell asleep, his arms started moving around, and sometimes he clenched his hands together. At other times he held his arms up as if he was shooting his machine gun. I could see his face filled with anger, but then at other times I'd see a smile. Either way, when he woke up he didn't have any recollection of his dreams or his actions.

I asked the doctor if it would be okay to show Jamie the videos of him sleeping. They said it was okay, so I showed him.

"I can't believe I'm doing that," he said as he watched the videos. "How long has this been happening?"

"For the past two weeks," I told him. "Each day it seems to get worse. Yesterday you were shooting your gun and throwing grenades."

Now I understood why when I asked him a few weeks ago if he was sleeping well, he said no. He told me then that he kept waking himself up with the sudden jerks, or the immediate impact of the severity of his dreams. Whenever he would wake up, I could touch his chest and feel his heart beating fast.

After having video proof of his reactions, the doctor changed Jamie's sleeping medication. The change in meds eliminated the muscle movements, but I didn't know how it affected his dreams. I found that throughout the day he would still have sudden movements produced by dreams. I'm hopeful that each day as he conditioned his body mentally, physically, and emotionally that the dreams would eventually go away.

The next day when I arrived at the hospital, the nurse was in Jamie's room, and he was up and at it. He asked me to soak his hands and clip his nails. I started filling a bowl of water while the nurse did what she needed to do medically. Once she left, I gave Jamie a kiss and told him good morning.

He said he slept well, and that he was excited to do some exercises. He really wanted to stretch out his left arm and build it up. His left hand had been tingling more lately, and he was hopeful that if he moved it around more it would go away. His ring finger and pinky on his left hand were hard to open, close, or make a fist. This was due to the fact that this part of his hand took the impact of the bullet.

We sat and talked for a bit while I cut his nails. We discussed a young marine at the hospital who was also paralyzed from the waist down. We'd met him a few days earlier as we were going to PT. We stopped to talk with him, and casually said, "Hello, how are you?" Instead of giving us a casual response, he replied, "I'm doing shitty, and I'll never walk again." We paused for a moment without responding, thinking perhaps he would correct his feelings. Instead, the young marine went on to tell us how his wife had left him, and he's scared he wouldn't get her back.

This was all too common! At Walter Reed I witnessed so many military wives absent from the bedsides of their husbands. I saw doctors, nurses, and military liaisons giving them free movie passes, free transportation, gift cards, and even sending them out to fancy dinner parties. On the one hand, it seemed like a nice gesture to the spouses and families. But, then I thought with everything Jamie had endured, I would not be so naive as to be coaxed away from his side while putting all my faith and confidence in the medical staff. If I had, where would Jamie be now?

We listened as the young marine vented his frustrations concerning his marriage, his accident, and his new life that he didn't care for. He wasn't a casualty of war. He was a casualty of youth. He was twenty-one and his wife was only twenty. They were married almost three years earlier before he left for the Marine Corps. He joined the Marine Corps to give her the life they would've never had working dead-end assignments at factories. He wanted her to be proud of what he'd accomplished.

The day of his accident he and his wife were scheduled to sign-off on separation and divorce paperwork. Looking back he thought the accident actually helped save his marriage because the papers were never signed. Now, three months later, they were still married and that made him happy. However, his wife was hardly ever there! When she was on base, she spent her time tanning every other day. He had to get up in the mornings and go to the Fisher House to see her. He said he loved her and was willing to overlook that. Apparently, she was a "high maintenance" type of girl, which meant he'd always cooked, cleaned, and cared for her.

As we listened to the young marine share his feelings about his life, we looked at each other and mouthed the words, "I love you." We could see the dramatic affect the accident and the long term medical prognosis was having on them. Now I understood much better why many people couldn't believe that I could speak so positively, or even understand my gratitude. There were people who couldn't fathom dealing with the life we had the past few months. To us it was just that—our life. We didn't think of it in terms of: "Oh my gosh, Jamie is paralyzed!" We thought of our life as: "Oh my gosh, Jamie is alive!"

After listening to the young marine for nearly an hour, Jamie put on his speaking valve.

"Dude, just live your life," Jamie told him.

Then he looked at me to take off his valve. It was hard for him to breathe through the trache when he had his valve on.

"What do you think," the Marine asked me.

"The only actions you can control are your own," I said. "When it comes to your actions, you're the most powerful person on this planet. If you believe in yourself, almost everything else should fall into place. Furthermore, trying to control or make someone into something they're not…that's a hard thing. A penguin will never fly no matter how hard you try to train it, or no matter how many feathers you glue or tape on it. They won't fly.

"Look at your wife, and listen to her concerns. I don't believe a traumatic event makes or breaks a marriage. The two people involved decide whether or not to save the marriage. You need to live for yourself awhile; find yourself; and find the higher power and the path you've chosen to go down. That path is different for everyone."

The young marine replied, "Each day I see you early in the morning and late at night near your husband. You barely leave. How do I get my wife to do that, and how do you do it?"

"I believe that before Jamie and I were created we were made for one another. Every trial and triumph in our lives has prepared us for this event, and it's all part of a bigger plan for us. Every day, I choose to do what I do for him. I also know that if the roles were reversed, and I was in the hospital bed, he would do the same for me"

Jamie nodded his head in agreement, and then asked for his speaking valve. "Much like you," he said, "I lived and loved a woman that didn't return it in the beginning. I had to grow, and I had learn who I was, and love myself, before she could love me. Melissa was hard on me from day one—even before I got the chance to take her on our first date."

I began laughing because he was right. Then I said, "I expected more from him because I knew he had the right intentions. I also knew he was limiting himself. I knew he was capable of so much more. I believed it so much that after asking him if he read any books lately, I asked him to do one thing for me (if he believed in us and loved me as he said he did). I asked him to read *The Love Dare*, a devotional book dedicated to couples."

"And I read the book," Jamie said. "You know the worst part? The book called me out and made me think about how fake the world is. It showed me how full of crap people are, and how full of crap I was. I was so worried about making myself happy with superficial things in life that I'd lost track of what was real. I wanted someone to love me for me, but I didn't even know who I was."

The young marine came closer to us, and we showed him Jamie's iPad. We had downloaded the *The Love Dare*—all three hundred and sixty-five days. We let him read the first chapter as Jamie and I smiled at one another.

"I'd love to give you our hardcover copy," I told him, "but I gave it to our nurse a few days ago."

"That's all right. Maybe someday. I just want to get over this."

"I don't know if you realize this," I told him, "but the days when Jamie couldn't get up (when he was in such terrible pain), I would gaze out his window and see you outside. With the scar on your neck, I figured you had a trache. With your legs positioned as they were, I assumed you were paralyzed. Yet, during those days,

Jamie wasn't able to give me hope by opening his eyes or talk to me. But seeing you gave me hope for our future. To me that was everything! So, I want you to know that you were my positive encouragement in a time of weakness. Thank you."

The young marine smiled and said, "I really didn't do much. I was just myself."

"*Exactly*," I responded.

We left after wishing him the best. As we were leaving, Jamie looked at me and said, "Wow, what a downer! I feel bad for that kid. He's so young, but he has so much going on."

"There's a plan for him," I said. "I don't feel *sorry* for him. But my hope is that his life will get better, and that *he* will make that decision."

Jamie looked at me and said, "How do you always do that?"

"Do what?"

"Make the worst situation sound good."

"It's simple. My husband sacrificed so much for my daughters and me (a selfless act). You may not walk anytime soon, but you gave the children and me the opportunity to have you in our lives. The day we walk through the White House, and take the girls with to see all the history and meet the President of the United States, we understand that was made possible by you—my amazing husband.

"When our daughters get ready to go to college and their tuition is paid for, we know it was you who made that happen. As we get to wake up next to one another in our bed for one more day, that was made possible by you. So I see all the great things that can come out of a series of events. I'm all right with the ups and downs, it's the unknown that concerns me."

127

"All I ever wanted to do," Jamie said, "was take care of you no matter what. Now, let's go look at houses and find out where we're going to live when we get home to Topeka!"

-13-

Please, Let Us Go!

It's Sunday, July 3, 2011, and I'm happy. I'm calling it "no tuberculosis Sunday." The results came back negative on Jamie's TB test! We've got to go out and enjoy the world. We just can't leave the sidewalk.

I've spent most of my time this morning house hunting. Finding a handicap accessible house is harder than putting a ramp at the front door. At this point it would be better to build a house from the ground up rather than buy and remodel one—especially if we're going to have more children. We would love to have a son to carry on the family name. It will be nice that the kids are far apart in age. This way we can give them each valuable parenting time and watch them grow. Life is so beautiful!

I was awakened the following morning at 1:00 AM to

Jamie calling my cell phone from his iPad. Typically this meant he was scared or concerned. I asked him if he was okay. He tapped the button twice for no. I told him I loved him, and I asked him to hang up so we could text each other. That way I could understand what's going on with him before I jump out of bed, call the nurse's station, and call the security escort to take me up to the hospital.

The area we were in wasn't the best. As a matter of fact, it was far from it. The hotel where I was staying had been broken into just a week earlier. Thank goodness we all had locks on our doors and no one could enter. But, I told Jamie how the fact that someone took the time to break in caused me not to feel comfortable walking up to the hospital between the hours of 10:00 PM and 4:00 AM.

We started texting and he said he didn't feel right. The meds were messing with him, but he wasn't sure why. His nurse came in his room, and we communicated via text message. She gave no reasons for Jamie feeling the way he did. She just told him to relax and take it easy.

The day before had been a very busy day for him. Being cleared and getting up in his wheelchair (around 10 AM), we spent an hour looking at house plans, apartments, and cars to help our transition. That's the one thing I didn't want…complications so big I couldn't correct them. I was doing my best to be proactive—to eliminate the issues before they rise. However, the hospital in Richmond was quite the opposite. They were *reactive* to issues. They saw how far they could allow issues to progress on their own, and then once the issues were at their peaks, then they got together and started addressing them. Yet, no matter how hard one tries to change the proverbial "leopard" it will always show its spots.

I left around noon for the airport to pick up daddy Jarboe.

He was quick! His plane landed and he was outside within fifteen minutes. He was so full of energy, and he'd missed us so much! It was like the family was back together. We arrived at the hospital around 2:00 PM. Jamie had just received his meds, so we went outside for a little bit to enjoy the weather.

We showed daddy all the Youtube videos we'd found of people in wheelchairs doing everything from putting their shoes on to transferring to their car. I showed him the Easy Stand 5000, which Jamie and I were both excited about! Then ran across the muscle stimulation (which I was a firm believer in). Jamie and I planned on doing our best to get one of those gadgets, or at least find a facility that had them. We weren't desiring them from a sense of false hope that he would walk someday. We wanted to build up his muscles and give his body the proper circulation. We'd talked many times about him being in a wheelchair and our outlook concerning that. If he was meant to walk one day, then we would be thankful. Until then, we were going to condition and care for his body every day to ensure he was healthy, happy, and comfortable.

Around 4:00 PM Jamie said he was tired, so we took him back to his room. I took daddy to the hotel, and then we went out to eat. We told Jamie we would be back by 6:00 PM. Unfortunately, due to the traffic and detours, we didn't get back to the hospital until 6:20 PM. I called Jamie so he wouldn't think we'd forgotten him, and to let him know we wanted to hurry back to see him.

As we were walking to Jamie' room, we saw his neighbor who had similar injuries. He'd gotten his injuries weightlifting. He literally broke is back! He told me a little about his injury as we were walking up to Jamie's room. Daddy went on in, and I stayed outside talking to the man and his wife. They were a very nice couple. As I was speaking to them, Jamie's caregiver nurse came out and said, "Ugh! He wants out of the damn bed again!"

I was caught off guard, and I assumed she didn't see me standing there as she complained about my husband!

"Is there an issue with Jamie getting up to spend time with his family?" I asked her.

"No," she said. "He wants Dilaudid too."

"Well, if that's what he wants, that's what he wants," I replied. "Is the IV coming out (as it had been ordered a day ago)?"

"We know about the order, but if he keeps getting more drugs, how are we supposed to take it out?"

At that point I walked in Jamie's room and kissed him hello.

"I want up," he told me.

"That's what I heard."

"I didn't get in bed until 5:15 PM."

"What?" I said surprised.

"We rang the bell at 4:00 PM, and they said they would be right in. I had to start my wheelchair and go up to the front desk to ask for help."

"I'm sorry for leaving. That's just unacceptable on *any* level."

The nurse who gave him meds was the one who had to put him back in his bed. As I was speaking to Jamie, his caregiver (the same one that came out of his room in disgust) entered his room again.

"Let's get you up," she said.

She began moving things around very hurriedly, and

putting in his sling to get him up.

"Is something wrong?" asked Jamie.

"No, not at all."

"Are you sure?"

"No, it's okay" the nurse assured him. "I've just been busy all day, and it's my sixth straight day working and I'm tired."

At that point she obviously realized how she sounded. Then, she started being a little more chipper. She got Jamie up in the wheelchair and off we went outside to enjoy the night. We went far away from everyone else. We had so much going on that small talk was way down on our list of desires. Jamie, daddy, and I found a nice spot and began talking. One thing his dad talked about was how thankful he was each day, and that I was one of the things he was thankful for. To me, that was the sweetest thing ever! Jamie agreed. I told him just as he tells me: I treat him the way I know he would treat me, and I do my best for him.

We joked and laughed as we enjoyed the rest of the night. We talked about little silly things and joked about how when we have another child it's probably going to be twins or triplets. Jamie said, "Oh no! I can't handle that!"

Daddy and I just laughed at him and smiled.

&

The next day started of great! Jamie and I spent a little more time on the Internet that morning, and then we went to a luncheon with all the veterans. Jamie still couldn't eat, but he wanted his dad and me to go and have some food. While we waited in line for forty-five minutes, Jamie was greeted by a lot of veterans who asked him how he was doing. Some would also ask where he was when he was injured, and what were the extent of his injuries. He would try to speak to them, but then he would have me answer their questions because his speaker valve took so much energy.

At that point, reciting information about Jamie's injury and experiences was as easy for me as breathing. He was injured April 10, 2011, at 7:30 AM. He'd been outside the wire on patrol in southern Afghanistan. He was shot once by a sniper. The bullet penetrated his neck, pierced his esophagus, trachea, vocal cords, and collapsed both lungs before exiting out his back where it tore through his spinal cord shattering the T2, T3, and T4 vertebrae. On April 25, 2011, he had spinal fusion done from C7 through T5, however, he was diagnosed with pneumonia a week prior causing the hardware in his back to be infected. He has a virus laying dormant with antibiotics, and within the next one to three years they'll remove the hardware from his back and treat the infection. Then, they'll replace the hardware several weeks after. He's not able to eat or talk on his own, but he's been breathing on his own for the past couple weeks.

Usually, the people who ask us would immediately say, "I'm so sorry," or "You're all too young to go through this." I would thank them for their concern. But, we knew we had a path set out for us before we were created. This was designed as our fate, and we both accepted it with open arms. People would literally fall over in their chairs when they heard our story. To Jamie and me, this was our life. Each day we got into our routine and we understood more and more. We just didn't know any differently.

After we were done eating, I pushed Jamie manually in his three hundred pound wheelchair. His hand was hurting from pushing the lever to go forward. Talk about team work! He was able to relax, and it was a great workout for me. We went outside and took some pictures. Then we called it a day and went back to his room.

In his room, the med nurse came in and gave him calcium water. Then the caregiver nurse came in and said she wanted to replace his Foley (catheter). After forty-five minutes of running around, she said they didn't have his size. Even though it was overdue to be replaced, she said her hands were tied because they didn't have the proper size. Then another nurse came in. She asked the caregiver what she was concerned about. The caregiver explained how she had flushed Jamie's catheter, but the water didn't come back out. She wanted to switch it out, but couldn't at this point.

I looked at daddy Jarboe and shook my head. This was all too familiar—the nurses were distraught, overworked, and they lacked ongoing training and supplies. It seemed that every time I turned around they couldn't do their jobs because they didn't have the proper equipment. As a result, they simply passed it off to the next shift. However, the one who suffered was my husband. My thoughts were interrupted by the nurses rolling Jamie back-and-forth to check his bandages.

"Concerning his JP drain, was it changed yesterday?" I asked.

"Yes," the nurse responded.

"And his bandage gets changed once a week even if it's dirty?"

"Well, typically it's not dirty," the nurse said.

I showed her a picture of his JP drain. It was dirty. In fact it had been dirty for well over twenty-four hours! Additionally, three shifts had overlooked the dry blood on his bandage.

"I wasn't aware of that," the nurse told me.

"I understand you weren't here, but please make sure it's documented for future reference. I'll be bringing it up tomorrow to the doctors and the appropriate management."

She began pulling Jamie's pants down. He'd had a bowel movement, which should happen, but hadn't happened for some time. He was having bowel stimulation done each morning at 5:00 AM. This was when they were supposed put a pill in his rectum, and then every fifteen minutes they were supposed to return and stimulate his rectum. I asked Jamie if this was being done. He said they were putting the pill in, but then they were leaving him in his bed for an hour and then changing him.

This frustrated me further, and I thought, "Now, I need to come in at 4:30 AM because apparently I wasn't asking the right questions." The doctors were the ones who ordered this procedure. They explained the stimulation process to us so we would understand it. Perhaps some of the staff missed *that* memo too! At that point I was a little upset. I didn't feel the need to yell or curse, but I did feel the need for chocolate and food. (That was my outlet. Hence, the ten pounds I'd gained. But, so be it.)

After the nurse was done doing her job, she rolled Jamie on his side.

"Do you see anything in his chart about being transferred," I asked. "If so…when?"

"I don't know anything about that," she said as she walked out of the room.

Within a few minutes of her leaving, Jamie's feeding tubes started beeping. It had been turned to "hold" and she obviously didn't remember to click it back on. We pressed the call button and waited twenty-five minutes while we listened to the beeping ten times a minute. Instead of being upset, we literally just laughed and zoned out the noise.

When the nurse came back in to do his feeding pump

(around 3:00 PM), she remembered she should've recorded his stats which hadn't been done since 7:00 AM.

"Let's hope your heart rate went down," the nurse said.

"What was his heart rate this morning?" I asked.

"113."

"Really? Then, why did you tell me at 9:00 AM this morning that his stats looked great...no issues? Yet, now almost eight hours later you're telling me his heart rate is high!"

"Well, that may be his regular heart rate."

"No," I told her, "he normally runs 60-80."

The nurse acted very nonchalant as she responded by saying, "No worries. He doesn't have a fever and his blood pressure is all right."

So, once again, I walked over to my purse and pulled out a Snickers bar and shoved it in my mouth. Chocolate therapy! The nurse left after getting Jamie's heart rate, which was 95! She forgot to take his temperature and blood pressure! I thought to myself (very sarcastically), "Heck, why would that matter?"

Another nurse came in to do his meds.

"Can you check his stats after you give him his meds?" I asked.

"No problem," the nurse replied.

After checking Jamie's bracelet, he said, "I'm in pain. I want Valium."

"All right. I'll get it ready."

I looked at the clock and realized she's bringing him his 2:00 PM meds at 3:00 PM. So I asked, "Ma'am, what meds are you giving him?"

"Methadone 7.5 and 2 Percocet," she explained.

"Wow!" I said looking at Jamie. "Babe, are you sure you need Methadone, Percocet, and Valium?"

"No," he said, "I didn't know I was getting Methadone, and Percocet. Scratch the Valium."

Great idea! Now my question was, why didn't the nurse tell him this? I asked Jamie about the previous night when at 1:00 AM he got his meds and didn't feel right.

"What did they give the other night at 1:00 AM when you said you weren't feeling well?"

"I asked for Dilaudid and Valium, and they also gave me my other meds."

"What?" I said shaking my head. "So they gave you Methadone, Percocet, Valium and Dilaudid!"

I walked over to my purse, and wouldn't you know it...*no more chocolate!* I kissed Jamie on the cheek and told him I was going to the computer room to write in my journal. He smiled and said, "You're out of chocolate?" I laughed and said, "Yes."

Some days I was a little upset and fragile. I understood why as I read my journal. I wasn't quite sure how I made it through those days. Looking back I understood better why I would isolate myself to some degree. I communicated a lot through Facebook and through text messaging. Very seldom did I speak to people on the phone. It was easier for me as I tried to stay focused on all the present challenges.

I wrote in my journal, "Tomorrow is going to be a beautiful day. We'll find out when we transfer!"

శ్రీ

"Happy Tuesday, feels like a Monday!" I wrote in my

journal.

I received a phone call that morning at 3:50 AM from Jamie. He needed me to come up the hospital. I arrived around 4:20 AM. He was supposed to have his bowel stimulation at 5:00 AM. He was concerned they weren't doing it properly. While doing his full body check at 4:30 AM, I put his speaker valve on so he could tell me what he was thinking. When I took it off, he starting talking without it. Typically people would be jumping for joy, but not us. We knew this meant his trache was plugged with mucous.

We rang the call bell and the nurse came in.

"What's the problem? I'll go get a speak valve for him," said the nurse.

Jamie replied, "I don't need it."

"Why not?" asked the nurse. "I can't hear you without it."

I couldn't believe what I was hearing. Jamie told the nurse he didn't need the speaking valve, and the nurse said she couldn't hear him without it! I almost laughed out loud as the nurse *still* walked over to the get the valve. How could she miss the fact that the only reason he could speak without it was because he was congested?

"He's plugged with mucous," I told her. "That's why he can talk without the speaker valve."

"Oh, I understand."

After Jamie got suctioned, he fell asleep until it was time for the bowel stimulation. The nurse came in at 5:00 AM, and then left at 5:05 AM saying, "I'll be back every fifteen minutes." Sure enough, she was!

"Babe, that's the first time *ever* that they've come back each fifteen minutes," Jamie said.

"I guess I'll make sure to be here at 4:30 AM from now on," I told him.

After that, we fell asleep until 7:00 AM!

That morning daddy Jarboe came in and we talked and laughed with him. Around 9:00 AM Jamie's favorite nurse came in to get him ready for OT. At that point I took daddy Jarboe to introduce him to the social worker and military liaison. When we got to the military liaison's office, we met with two of them. I asked about the status of our transfer, and she said they were working on our transfer to Craig.

"We discussed this last week, and we sent an e-mail to you and four other individuals regarding our request to Bethesda," I said rather frustrated. "By the time we get to Denver to be transferred, Jamie will need to turn around and have surgery the last week of July. That's a lot of wear and tear on his body, and so we requested to immediately be moved to Bethesda."

"Well, I'll look into that," the liaison said. "However, you know if you're sent to Craig you may only receive six weeks of physical therapy because your insurance won't cover more than six weeks."

"We have numerous outlets we can utilize," I told her, "including our two hands working with Craig to pay it out of pocket."

We wanted out of the VA at Richmond ASAP, and we wouldn't ever return regardless of what she told me.

"If you're sure," she said, "I'll talk to a few people and see what we can do."

As we were leaving, the E7 (Sergeant First Class) apologized for not picking me up to return the rental car I had to get the day he neglected to get the guardian and my daughters to the airport on time. I told him no worries. Then, he asked if I needed a ride. I told him that would be great around lunchtime, and to please call me.

After we left, daddy Jarboe said, "Darling, you were amazing the way you handled that scare tactic."

"If Jamie can go and sacrifice his life," I told him, "then the girls and I can sacrifice my 401K and savings to ensure he has the best medical care."

We got down to Jamie's room and went to the therapy area at 10:00 AM. We waited until 10:15 AM. Then I found the therapist only to discover that there was a miscommunication with the nursing staff. Jamie didn't have OT until 11:00 AM. We were up, and Jamie wanted a haircut. So off we went!

Jamie asked me about submitting the letter to Homes for Our Troops. I'd called every number with an area code that began with two, and I finally got a hold of our contact. She confirmed receiving the necessary letter. I told her how even though it would be nice to have the assistance, we were also more than happy to donate money and give to another family in need (as we'd posted on our Facebook).

Jamie and I felt very fortunate to be where we were. With his outgoing personality and my professional background, we knew that in no time we would experience some amazing things! Some of the things already being considered were joining the Chamber of Commerce as Ambassadors for my company; and going to networking functions and volunteering our time to help others. Life is a beautiful thing, so why not share it!

After Jamie's haircut we received a phone call letting us know that the previous night there was an explosion in which Celesteal (our oldest) was hit by debris. It occurred when a large firework exploded. She had a laceration and burn. We were told she was holding strong, and wanted Neosporin and me-derma for her birthday. What a silly girl! She was more concerned with Jamie and me than herself.

Jamie and I were so excited at the prospect of getting home and having our family back! We missed the girls so much. We also missed all the little things. We missed things like having breakfast together, going to the zoo, playing at Chuck E. Cheese, or swimming in our pool. We were a very active family and loved to get out and about.

Jamie went to his PT/OT appointment at 11:00 AM. Daddy and I left to get an early lunch so he could focus on himself and his therapy. We got back around 11:50 AM. We inquired concerning the correct scheduling. Each week there was a mix up where someone was zigging when we were zagging. Jamie needed consistency and he needed rehab. However, at this point I was helping him with the majority of his exercises.

KT was also inconsistent. Speech had adjusted his iPad, but the psychologist had come in only once in the past three weeks. The truth was, we could've done this at home with our kids! We'd spent a lot of time watching Youtube videos of paraplegics demonstrating how to put on their shoes, how to transfer to a car, or how to brush their teeth—just about everything! I called the KT therapist over to the PT/OT area. I requested that he update his schedule because he'd told me he didn't have Jamie in his schedule book. He said that was why he'd forgotten to come the past few days. We'd only seen the KT therapist around six times in three weeks, yet that therapy was so valuable for Jamie's stretching and moving around.

When Jamie transferred back to his wheelchair he was flushed. He had no color and he said he was dizzy.

"Can I please push your wheelchair to work off the candy bars from yesterday," I asked him.

"Sure," he said.

As we were about to leave, the OT therapist asked, "When did you get your haircut."

"This morning," Jamie told him.

Laughing, the OT therapist said, "It looks funny."

I waited for the therapist to say, "I'm just kidding," or something to let us know he wasn't serious. Instead, he kept laughing. Jamie looked at him as if to say, "Are you serious?"

"Maybe you're not used to a standard military haircut," I said to the therapist. "Jamie has been a soldier for seven years. How long have you been without manners?"

Needless to say, I didn't want to go that route, but it was such an ongoing problem. People were constantly cutting one another down, or talking negatively about other people. I felt as though I was back in high school! When we got back to Jamie's room we called for the nurse to come and put Jamie in bed. Thankfully, it was done promptly, and Jamie was comfortable.

The PA came in later, and we voiced some concerns about Jamie's bowel care. Two-thirds of the samples had not been taken that weekend as was requested for testing (due to his mucous being green and yellow and his trache being raised).

The PA said she was going to look into that issue and get back to us. Right then she wanted to look at the blister on Jamie's foot since neither the second or third shift had taken off his T.E.D. (thromboembolism deterrent) hose for his blood pressure. I noticed it that morning, and the first shift nurse took off the hose and noticed the blister as well.

We called our NCM from Walter Reed to follow up on the Bethesda transfer. She told us the doctor at Bethesda would prefer Jamie go directly to Craig instead of coming to Bethesda. I explained to her that wasn't in Jamie's best interest to do all that traveling if he was having surgery in the next couple of weeks. We needed him to be at Bethesda ASAP. She said all right. She would look into it, and then get back with us. At that point I stopped by the social worker's office to give her the NCM's number. I told her we wanted to get back to Bethesda ASAP—someone make it happen and quit making us go in circles. They were literally trying to wear us down.

"How are you holding up considering all of Jamie's injuries and medical care?" the social worker asked.

"We're strong and we're fine," I answered.

"But, transitions can be hard."

"I've been in foster homes and Jamie's a soldier. Transitions aren't an issue," I explained. "The real issues are the lack of VA funding, the understaffing, and the behavior of the hospital staff. That causes us more problems than the severity of Jamie's injuries. *We* are doing great. If you're concerned about our wellbeing, then get us out of this hospital immediately.

"Right now, I'm taking the rental car back with no return ride because the military liaison isn't answering his phone. So, I'll catch a cab back to the hospital. *My* stress level has nothing to do with Jamie and our life. We accept the difficulties. It's frustrating not to have adequate support to keep us out of harm's way. Things that shouldn't happen have happened, and they *keep* happening. But, we keep moving forward."

Photo Journal_____

Date night for Jamie and me with friends. (June 2009)

October 2010

February 12, 2011.

Engagement photo at the Indianapolis Speedway Museum.
(February 13, 2011)

February 14, 2011.

Sgt. Aguilar, SSG Feaster, and Jamie in Afghanistan.
(April 2011)

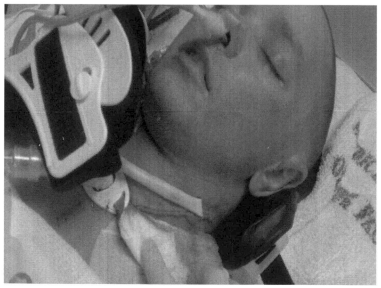

Jamie, two days after being shot through the left side of his
neck by a sniper. (April 12, 2011)

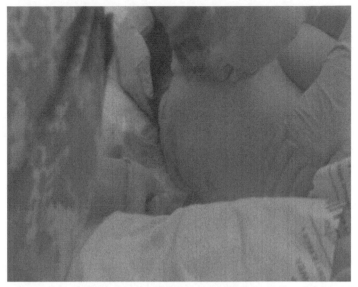

Old Walter Reed Hospital, Washington D.C., May 2011. Nurses take off eleven day old bandage from Jamie's spinal fuse surgery.

May 2011. Blood-soaked sheets from Jamie's wound.

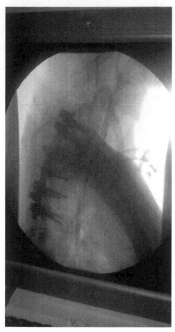

X-ray of Jamie's esophageal perforation (hole) in the back of his neck, at the T2 level. (May 2011)

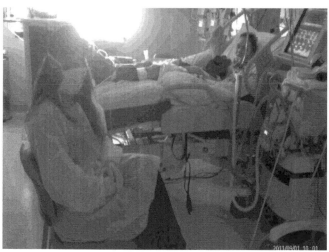

Vigil next to Jamie's bed at Walter Reed in Bethesda. The first thing he would see is me and feel my love and strength.

Our oldest daughter, Celesteal, falling asleep in a hospital chair next to Jamie. We would stay in Jamie's room from sunup to sundown.

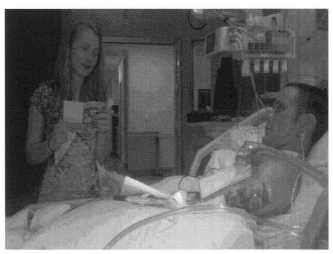

New Walter Reed, Bethesda, MD, May 2011. Celebrating Celesteal's 8th grade graduation in ICU.

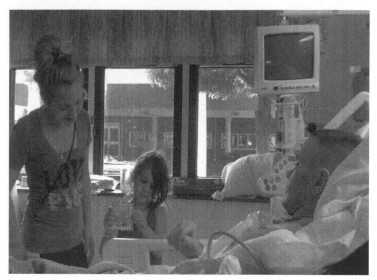

VA Hospital, Richmond, VA, June 2011. Father's Day magic
show. Celesteal and Lexi doing a magic show for the best dad
ever.

VA Hospital in Richmond, VA, June 2011. The first Lexi hug
Jamie got since he left for Afghanistan in February 2011.

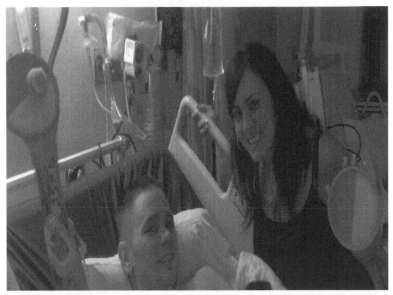

New Walter Reed Hospital, July 2011. Occupational therapy for Jamie. Once he was able to move his arms, I did everything to help build him back up—even silly games.

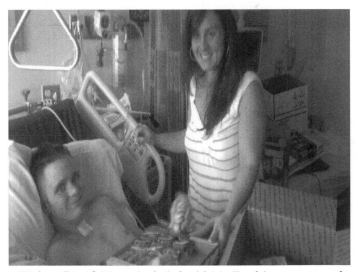

New Walter Reed Hospital, July 2011. Packing care packages. Since Jamie couldn't eat or drink, he wanted to do something for his fellow 4th Calvary soldiers.

Walter Reed, July 2011. Jamie and I would take photos to send to the girls and daddy Jarboe back in Kansas.

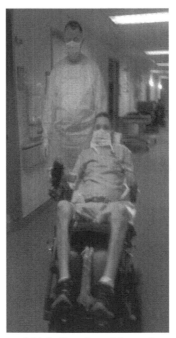

Walter Reed, August 2011. Jamie with a therapist trying to learn how to use a wheelchair.

New Walter Reed, August 2011. Photo before tracheostomy was removed.

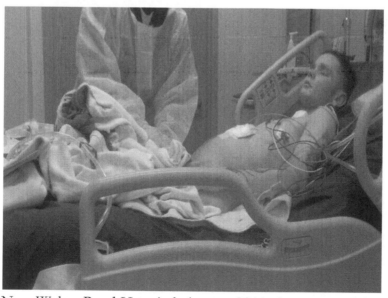

New Walter Reed Hospital, August 2011. A nurse applying pressure to stop bleeding after a catheter she inserted imploded high in his urethra.

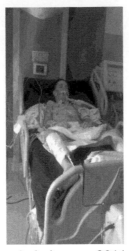

New Walter Reed Hospital, August 2011. Jamie aspirated fluid from his stomach which filled his lungs. His lungs collapsed and his body went septic. This was the fifth time he was placed on life support. I was able to kiss his lips and promise him he wouldn't die anytime soon.

Johns Hopkins Hospital, September 2011. Jamie on life support after 14 hours of surgery. I would kiss him in hopes of him opening his eyes.

Johns Hopkins, Baltimore, MD, September 2011. Jamie opening
his eyes after being on life support. He asked for a Mountain Dew.

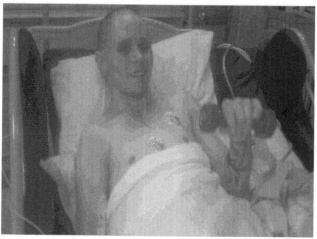

October 2011—Johns Hopkins progress! Jamie doing
occupational therapy with me, and smiling after he was able to lift
3 lbs. five times on his own.

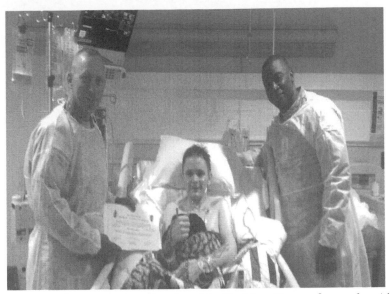

CSM Cook presenting Jamie with Golden Spurs from the 4th Calvary of Fort Riley, Kansas. (At Johns Hopkins.)

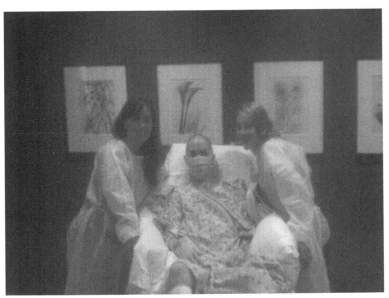

Johns Hopkins, October 2011. The first time out of his room in a month! We got to show Jamie part of the hospital floor.

October 2011. Medical transport from Baltimore, MD to Denver, Colorado.

Halloween in Craig Hospital (2011). The girls went trick-or-treating at the nurse's station and played games in Jamie's hospital room.

Craig Hospital in Denver, November 2011. Jamie being fitted for his electrical chair.

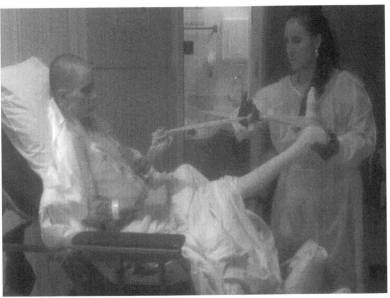

December 2011. Jamie was finally able to sit up in a chair and do therapy to build his muscles so he would be able to walk someday.

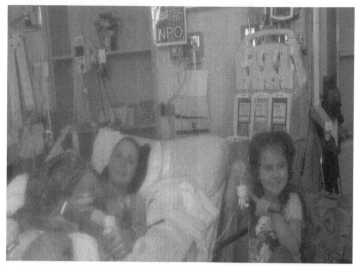

Craig Hospital, December 2011. Jamie and Lexi coloring Christmas decorations for our tree in Jamie's hospital room.

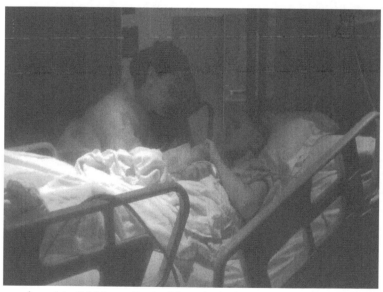

December 11, 2011 at Craig Hospital. After Jamie's surgeries the doctors said the hole in his esophagus and windpipe was bigger and they couldn't fix it.

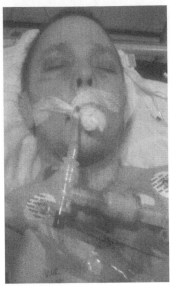

Johns Hopkins Hospital, January 2012. Jamie on life support for the 9th time due to his lungs collapsing.

January 2012, after his 123rd surgery to fix the hole (trachea esophageal fistula) in Jamie's neck (caused by a tracheostomy and esophageal stent).

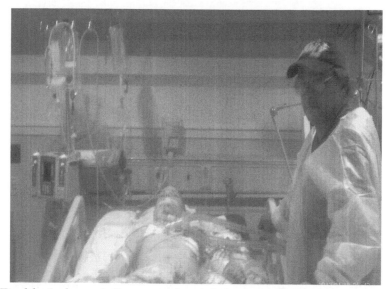

Daddy Jarboe vigil next to Jamie's bed. (January 2012, Johns Hopkins Hospital.)

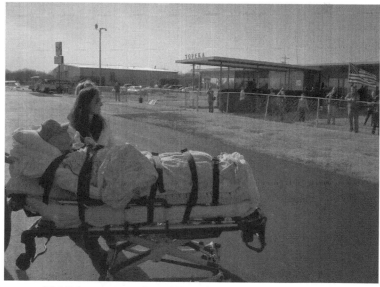

February 2012 homecoming, Topeka, Kansas. Over one hundred veterans watched for Jamie's arrival.

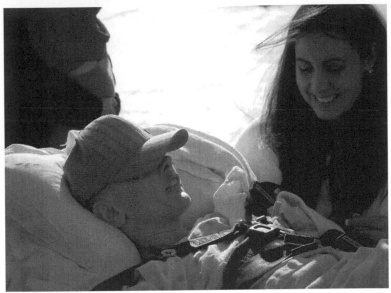

Topeka, Kansas, February 2012. Jamie's smile after he thought no one showed up to welcome him home.

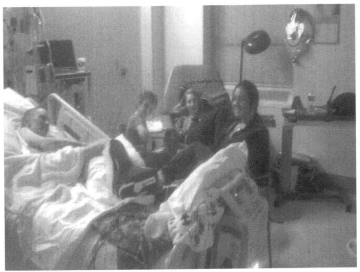

Family at St. Francis Hospital, Topeka KS, February 2012.

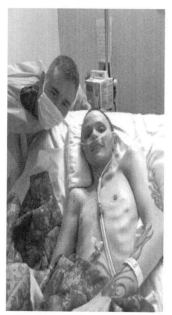

Battle buddies and best friends reunited (March 2012). Kenny Hendricks and Jamie smiling.

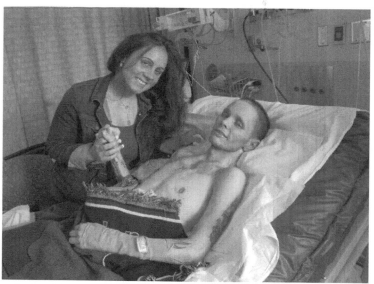

March 18, 2012. Jamie and I staying strong a week after he was rendered terminal.

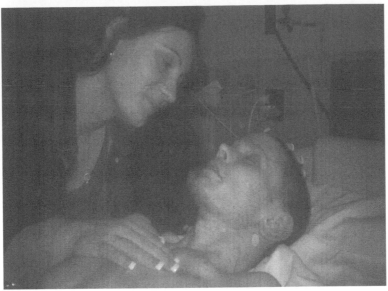

March 18, 2012, St. Francis ICU. Jamie asked me to keep rubbing his head so he could feel my touch.

March 18, 2012 (after hours of using the last moments of Jamie's life to plan the rest of my life). I laid next to him knowing it might be the last time.

Mount Hope Cemetery, Topeka, Kansas, August 2012. "Love never dies!" Jamie promised he would not die on my birthday. He took his last breath the day after.

Last family photo. Look in the mirror for our hero.
(Nathan Ham photography, Topeka, KS)

-14-

Bethesda At Last!

E-mails I sent through the chain-of-command:

> We are at a standstill at this time due to the staff telling us they're trying so hard to get us sent to Craig Hospital in Denver, CO. (even knowing the issues listed below).
>
> Now it's written, and we're hopeful they hear our concerns and grant us a transfer at their earliest convenience.
>
> Have a great afternoon!

೮೦

> Thank you for speaking with me today

regarding the requested transfer to Craig Hospital Tuesday June 28, 2011 (see email below). As per our conversation about Craig Hospital's stringent guidelines regarding bed sores, there will no rehabilitation available for Jamie as he will be on bed rest if transferred this month (July).

Therefore, our goal is still be transferred immediately from Richmond Veterans Hospital to Bethesda Naval Hospital in Bethesda, MD. We have verbally requested this along with our concerns to the following individuals attached to this email and listed below:

Nurse Case Manager

LNO (Liaison)

VA Superintendant

Jamie is concerned about retaliation from the nursing staff. He doesn't feel that he has received adequate medical care. According to our communications with the nurse case manager this morning, she stated Jamie should have surgery for his esophagus by August 9, 2011 (pending his medical stability). As soon as he's able to be transferred from Bethesda to resume rehabilitation; then our choice of rehabilitation facilities is Craig Hospital.

The change in our decision to transfer out of Richmond VA Hospital to Craig Hospital, and now from Richmond VA Hospital to Bethesda, MD, came after discussions with the PA. Our discussions were in regard to Jamie and his medical stability for transfer to Colorado. The hospital representative stated that he would be on bed rest to cure bed sores with little rehabilitation, and the nurse case manager confirmed a surgery date by August 9, 2011.

Please let us know a specific timeline regarding immediate transfer to Bethesda. Also see the e-mails below regarding concerns of an increased magnitude.

      ❧

In everyday struggles, sometimes it's hard to see the good in each person. Today we were happy when they gave Jamie a loaner wheelchair that fit him better (he weighed a little over one hundred pounds and some of the adult wheelchairs were too big). It made him smile and that brightened the entire room!

Despite issues and back-and-forth communication, overall it had been a good day. We woke up near one another, joked about his wheelchair driving, and shared kisses as much as we could. We expressed our love for one another every hour. We didn't want to seem ungrateful for the life Jamie was given. We were determined to enjoy it no matter how fragile or life-altering it may be. He had his life and we were going to live each day like we were dying.

It seemed as though every morning we had some kind of unfortunate event happen. A few weeks ago my friend Nona sent me a mustard seed from her Grandmother. Today, it made me think—I'm not acting in a godly manner. I'm allowing my environment to dictate my actions.

After reading *The Love Dare*, Jamie and I made a decision. We would treat others around us how we wanted to be treated. That meant treating others in a godly manner. This was a rule we did our best to follow. However, we found we're not like the mustard seed. We feel as if we're in the survival of the fittest. We lacked trust and confidence in the medical staff, and perhaps we needed to focus our energies on the success of our medical team.

That day we decided to move in a different direction. Instead of isolating ourselves while being fearful of our outcome, we were going to try our best to relinquish our selfish concerns.

ℜ

We've made it safe and sound to Bethesda Naval Hospital, and the environment is tranquil and calm! Today was very productive. We awakened at 4:30 AM to our nurse letting Jamie know they needed to complete labs for the orders they'd received from the doctor. Around 5:00 AM they were finished with the necessary blood work, and I asked Jamie if he would like to go back to sleep or start his KT (stretching, range-of-motion, and massage) that I did for him every morning.

We also started PT early and he accomplished his goals. He completed fifteen reps—three sets on each arm using my Pilate band. We did half-range of motion for his arms because he couldn't raise his arms over his shoulders. This was due to the hardware in his back. We then moved to his legs using the band. With him holding the bands, I assisted him in raising his legs and stretching his hamstrings. Then I completed a range of motion with his legs.

Once we finished, we started occupational therapy. This involved him washing his face, opening his toothpaste, and brushing his teeth. These small tasks were a struggle for him to complete. Jamie was reclassified as an incomplete quadriplegic, or a *tetraplegic*. Basically, with the extent of his injuries, Jamie was fortunate to be able to use his hands. We were so thankful and would do everything we could together. We completed PT, OT, and KT around 7:00 AM. Then, we both took a nap. It was so nice in Bethesda. They put an extra bed in his room for me to sleep in. Now I was with Jamie and could sleep whenever I needed to!

We woke up around 8:00 AM and completed some more simple stretches. Then we were greeted by the wound care director from Washington DC along with six of his colleagues. We welcomed them, and then we listened to the objectives and concerns. They took all the necessary pictures of Jamie's pressure ulcer (bed sores). They showed me in detail what their concerns were, and they said Jamie had a stage three, and almost a stage four pressure ulcer. They said he would need to be on strict bed rest for six to eight weeks. This would give the ulcers the proper time to heal.

They started the circulation cuffs on his legs and assisted in showing me the proper way to turn him on his side while keeping his heels floating. They were going to keep his ortho-boots on a two-hours on/two-hours off schedule. This would help with the drop foot syndrome that had begun in his right foot. Next, we met with neuro-surgery who told us the CT scan that was done the previous night looked fine, and they had no concerns at that time.

Our general surgery doctor also stopped in. I thanked him for bringing us back so quickly, and for ensuring our safety. He said he was aware of the severity of the pressure ulcer, and it's their intention to ensure it's taken care of. The JP drain from Jamie's esophagus was leaking a milky pink fluid, in which pseudonymous was largely present as well as puss. Their belief was that if they were to remove the drain, which had been in for two months, an immediate infection would begin.

There were no plans for immediate surgery. They were still on track for Jamie's stent removal surgery on August 9, 2011 pending the results of the swallow study and blood cultures. If everything came back clear, then by the following we would be good to go. In the meantime, Jamie would be on strict bed rest; no sitting up at all for six to eight weeks. We could do some OT, PT, KT, and RT, and we could transfer to the local facility near Washington D.C. VA for rehab if we desired. We immediately declined that offer. Our intentions were to stay safe and sound in Bethesda until Jamie was healed and able to transfer to Craig Hospital. The doctor respected our decision.

A few hurdles we had to overcome:

- Spit-out secretions from Jamie's mouth. He shouldn't swallow his spit. This will help dry out his throat area to give the stent optimum improvement for the next four weeks.
- Turn him every two hours to clear up the pressure ulcer.
- Antibiotics had been started aggressively to get Jamie's pseudomonilia under control so it didn't spread or flare up. They will pull creatine levels twice a week.

If everything went as planned, Jamie would be in good shape by September 1, 2011. If one issue went the opposite way, Jamie would have the hardware in his back removed. If the stent didn't seal leaks as they predicted, they would have to put his esophagus on the outside of his neck, and then move his stomach and colon up into his chest in order to be able to cut out part of his esophagus.

At that point, Jamie and I simply loved each day we had together. We were grateful and happy following the path laid out for us. We weren't worried. We were at peace because he was alive. Even during all the hardships he had, we got to wake up to one another each morning.

❧

It was another beautiful morning! Jamie had slept safe and

sound all night with no issues. He said, "It's so nice to be back with people who take time to care and listen to me!" Jamie was beginning his six to eight weeks of bed rest. Concerning his stage three bed sores (pressure ulcers), they were still running tests to determine the proper course of action. He was placed in isolation as an extra precaution due to the pseudomonas.

We'd been told he was an enigma of a rabbit's riddle. Jamie's injuries were so severe and traumatic; and then add in months of ICU and hospitalization along with the extent of nerve damage, injuries to internal organs, and skeletal and muscular damage, it wasn't as easy as just doing a few surgeries to fix everything. The bullet damaged many of his internal organs when it penetrated. Now three months later he was experiencing more damaging effects. The pressure ulcer was a major concern. The doctors at the VA had told us he could be up and moving in his wheelchair. However, when he sat in his wheelchair it created more pressure, which was evident by the visibly purple tissue. It was no coincidence that the tissue that came off was around the muscle where he sat up.

Jamie was now coded as a *tetraplegic*. This meant that he was a quadriplegic with minimal use of his arms. He was paralyzed from the chest down and couldn't sit up straight. The point being, I'd be okay sitting up in a wheelchair for four hours. Not being a tretraplegic, I'd be able to use my core muscles and back muscles to hold myself up. But, Jamie didn't have that ability. He had to rely on the chair itself to hold him in place. He was also placed back on oxygen per the respiratory and ENT doctors. He never should've been taken off! Do to his trache, he needed humidity in that area of his neck. Since turning the oxygen on, they suctioned a lot of green mucous out of his trache.

On the whole, we were thankful to be there. And while some of the test results from the VA had not been validated, we

175

felt the overall treatment of Jamie was abusive. Now we were seeing some of the results of the medical neglect and abuse. At times I blamed myself. As Jamie's medical power of attorney, I was the one who chose to go to the Richmond Veterans Hospital. When those around you are telling to you to trust that the VA is a great facility, etc., you convince yourself that everything is going to be all right. The fact is, you expect doctors and nurses to know what they're talking about.

Our trip to Richmond Hunter Holmes VA was far from all right! If anything, it was the most trying time of our lives! I felt sorry for their patients and nursing staff. Neither group seemed happy in their environment. The staff was continually subjected to pay cuts, double shifts, and unprofessional behavior exhibited by the upper management. They certainly gave the impression that they didn't feel appreciated. I wouldn't say what they did to Jamie was all right. Yet, I believe if the management had taken a different approach, including increasing the morale of their staff, that even with the cutbacks the increase in morale would've made all the difference in the world. (But, what would I know? I've only operated eight offices generating millions in revenue each year; I've had almost 3,000 employees; and I've learned that people don't leave companies—the companies leave people.)

Jamie had been sleeping on and off for two days. The doctor told us they wanted to do a swallow study to ensure there weren't any leaks in his esophagus. They would also start treating him for C. diff[1] (even though they didn't have a sample yet). They wanted to be proactive, and we agreed. The doctor wanted him to

---

[1] Clostridium difficile (klos-TRID-e-um dif-uh-SEEL), often called C. difficile or C. diff, is a bacterium that can cause symptoms ranging from diarrhea to life-threatening inflammation of the colon.

try to stay awake as much as possible. I mentioned to him that Jamie's meds were increased after we arrived at the VA. His methadone was now at 10mgs every four hours. It had been at 5mgs every six hours before going to the VA. I asked if the pain management team would be a part of Jamie's trauma team. The doctor said they would, and that hopefully at the beginning of the week they would make their rounds to discuss medication.

My phone rang after the doctor left. It was Jamie's grandmother. She'd left a message.

"Jamie, do you want to call her back?"

"Not right now."

"It would be good to at least say hello so she can hear your voice," I told him.

We called her, and Jamie said hello. His grandmother told him she missed him and wanted to see him.

"I've got a lot going on right now grandma," he said. "I'll see you when I get home."

Just then my phone died! I charged it for a few hours, and we called her back.

"I don't have Facebook," his grandma told him. "I don't get updates, and I don't know what's going on."

"I understand," I told her. "But, we seldom call people because it's hard to explain everything that's going on. It's just easier to type out all the current issues and then move forward."

She started crying. "It's just so hard not knowing."

I couldn't imagine what she was going through.

"You know God has big things in store for Jamie," I encouraged her. "That's one of the reason it's difficult for us to talk to people. We're not sad or hurt by the life we've been given. This is our life, and we're doing our best to prepare one another for our long and loving life together. It just makes it all easier."

"It would still be nice to see him," she said.

Jamie nodded his head no.

"That probably wouldn't be the best thing right now," I explained. "When Jamie's ready, he'll call for you and any others whom he desires to see. He needs to make those decisions. Right now what matters is what's best for him."

"You need to know that right now he's in isolation, and his immune system isn't the best. He's also contagious. Give it some time, and when he's ready he'll call you."

Conversations like that certainly represented many of the most difficult parts of our life. All around us were people living "normal" everyday lives. They didn't understand what it was like inside our world. Day in and day out we were doing our best to stay positive while making the hospital our home. We weren't being selfish, or trying to push people away. It was just hard for him to see people in his new found life. He needed time to be ready to face people. Once he was comfortable, then it would be better. Jamie mattered the most to me, and what he said I followed through with. When he couldn't speak, I spoke for him. When he didn't have strength, I would give him mine. I was flesh of his flesh, and I did whatever I had to do to care for my husband.

It would've been wonderful to have the kiddos and a lot of family there. But, the fact remained that Jamie wasn't ready. It was too overwhelming for him. He couldn't go outside with them. He couldn't sit up. He could barely speak. In light of all he was dealing with, we decided to keep our lives simple—just the two of us and our silly time in our new home…a hospital room on the 5th floor.

On a happy note—during the second round of PT and KT Jamie kicked butt! I was so proud of him! We even did a new exercise I'd made up to see how strong my sweet husband was. I asked him if I could "instaflate" his bed, which increased the air in the mattress. The staff did that whenever they had to roll him. We did it for four minutes. Then, I asked him to put his right elbow in the bed and push off to the left. After the right elbow, then the left. He was having trouble, so I asked his dad to cup his hand over Jamie's left elbow as I did the right (using our strength to provide more stability). He attempted this for five seconds on each side. Even though Jamie didn't immediate and direct control of his back muscles, we were trying to build up those muscles with an indirect approach! We did this ten times on each side. When Jamie finished he whispered, "I like that." I said, "Yeah, I know babe. I'm magic like that!" He smiled and said, "What's next?"

I knew I had his undivided attention. So, then we did his triceps, biceps, and curls with his arm band. Once he completed the reps and sets he was good to go! He did fifteen reps and three sets. He ended up doing over six exercises and he kicked butt! Sometimes he started falling asleep, so I'd have to put my cold nose on his face.

"No cold nose," Jamie said. "I'll do my exercises."

A little motivation was always good.

I booked Jamie's dad's flight today. He would leave on Tuesday to go home, and then it was only Jamie and me once again. I was happy his dad had come. He'd been a tremendous help and did what he thought needed to be done. It was 5:00 PM and time for the third round of PT.

-15-

Looking Forward to Denver

Jamie was taken off isolation. We were excited! Then, a day later he was put back on isolation. He had his swallow study done, and needless to say it wasn't what we expected. We waited for the doctor to come and let us know the next step.

Not knowing what would happen, or what would be next, made our emotions difficult to control. This was also a result of living life day to day at the hospital; sleeping at the hospital; and even dreaming about the hospital whenever I did sleep. There were those in similar situations who would go shopping regularly, or go out to eat in order to get away from the hospital. I found myself thinking, "What's the point? You have to come back to the hospital when you're done!" Jamie wasn't going to magically get up and get better because I went out to eat at Olive Garden; or, because I shopped at Old Navy. He was still going to be sitting at the hospital waiting for me to come back.

If I stopped and thought about it too long, everything we had gone through in the past three months would become very overwhelming. We lived day by day and hour by hour, always hoping that tomorrow would be better while at the same time praying for the outcome which had been determined for us. We also kept thinking all of this would be over soon.

It goes without saying the life we now lived wasn't what either of us planned. Even so, the fact that he was an incomplete quadriplegic wasn't the problem either. The difficult thing to deal with was not knowing whether he was going to be able to eat or even live an almost normal life—that was scary. After returning from Richmond, our lives had been turned upside down. We were both tired. It all took so much out of us.

Yet, being back at Bethesda was the best thing that had happened. It was nice having some of the same doctors and staff once again. On the other hand, our time in Richmond had left me skeptical. As a result, I found it difficult to trust some of the most incredible doctors—doctors who were next to none.

At Bethesda we were being told how the VA hospital had been wrong on so many different issues.

1) Allowing Jamie to be in his wheelchair "as tolerated" (which was clearly stated on his order and in his file). Jamie had stage three and four pressure ulcers, and it was due to the doctor saying it was okay! "Why didn't I stop this?" I asked myself. I saw it getting worse little by little. Why didn't they send Jamie back to Bethesda? They mentioned on several occasions that he wasn't a rehab patient—he was a medical patient. Why did they keep us there?

2) Taking Jamie off his oxygen and letting him dry up. He

barely had any humidity or oxygen for three weeks. Now, twice a day he gets mucous plugs. This is the same condition which put him into cardiac arrest less than two months earlier. Once again I wonder why they allowed that. They literally dried up his insides, and now he was dealing with the after affects.

3) They didn't start his antibiotics until the beginning of July even though the infectious disease doctors from Bethesda specifically told them to start the oral medication (on June 15, 2011). Instead, once they notified their infectious disease doctors at the beginning of July, we'd already requested a transfer. (Granted he did start the oral antibiotics, but it was too late.)

4) The VA representative told us before we went to Richmond that it was a great facility, and that all the facilities were the same. Then, when we got back, they informed us that she should have mentioned the prior complaints against the facility! So, who's looking out for Jamie's best interest?

At that point we simply wanted to live our lives like everyone else. We wanted to go to and from work. We wanted to drive our cars, make our own dinners, pray with our family, kiss the kids goodnight, and sleep next our loved ones. It didn't seem like too much to ask! Just to live life...

⁎

After numerous doctor visits, concerns, and questions and answers—Jamie was still in discomfort. He'd exhausted all his pain medicine the previous night. The nurse called me at 11:00 PM to tell me Jamie wanted me next to him. We waited for the pain management team to pay him a visit and help alleviate his pain. He said there was pain in the small of his back, but when the exam was done he didn't feel pressure. But, when they applied pressure to the area around the hardware in his upper back, he went from a pain level of eight to ten.

After an early morning run, my body felt somewhat better. The life, however, felt drained out me as I watched Jamie in pain knowing there wasn't much I could do. I massaged his hands, arms, legs, shoulders, and his head to try to relieve any pressure. He would feel good for about thirty minutes and then ask me to call the nurse. I gave him a warm bath to relax his muscles. There was obviously a lot going on inside his body!

We played a waiting game. Our goal was August 9, 2011. That was three months after the stent was put in, and also when it could be removed. At that point it was nothing by mouth and spit out saliva and just wait. At times I thought about the life we'd been given, and I knew we had a purpose. I tried not to think of the "why" because sometimes there wasn't a recognizable answer. Unfortunately, by the time many people are five years old they've already been jaded or tainted by life. We live, learn, and love. Each step we take we accept our challenges. It doesn't mean we have to like them. At that moment I would've given anything for Jamie to have his life back. Each day he breaks little by little, but we do our best to look forward to our future. We have our faith, but we also have our life of isolation.

Despite everything today, it was a good day. When the doctors came in, they asked us how we were. We smiled and said, "Well docs, we're playing hide and seek, but now we have to figure out our spots again since you interrupted our game. Darn it!" The look on their faces was priceless. It was a good day...

The next morning (about 6:30 AM) I thought, "Today is *our* day!" We had already accomplished so much! I got their super early to check Jamie's vitals. Everything was perfect just like him! His temp. was 97.3, his O2 was 100%, and his heart rate was 82. I smiled wanting to kiss him, but I couldn't kiss him through the mask. I asked the corpsman for our nurse, and if he would get the suppository so I could begin his bowel stimulation. After reading, watching, and discussing it with the medical staff, it would be good to get him on a consistent schedule in order to clean out his colon. This would help insure that there wasn't any incontinence.

The nurse came in and started putting in the pill.

"May I please do that so I can complete the stimulation program?" I asked.

"What program," she responded.

"The program we'll be doing for the rest of our lives. It begins today."

Smiling she said, "Yes sweetie."

I shut off his tube feeds and propped him up on his left side to ensure he was comfortable. I put a nice pillow under his head. Then, I put on double-gloves and began the process within twenty minutes. I was excited! I jumped up and down as Jamie laughed at me.

"I don't understand why you're so excited," Jamie said.

"This is a success," I told him.

He nodded his head and laughed. For me it was nice to know that he had a choice in his life. He feared he would have to depend on others every day for the rest of his life. If this were to occur, I knew that each time it did a little piece of him would die. I could not let that happen! So, as I told him before, as we move forward he's the boss. He needs to control his care. Of course nothing to abrupt. But, if he needed turned, he should press the call light. If he wasn't comfortable with a nurse, switch that person out. If he needed more clarity about something, he should feel free to ask!

I sat and thought about how great it was having Jamie stable. Just yesterday his heart rate and blood pressure had shot up. His calcium, potassium, and electrolytes had been completely off. I wondered how that could be. He'd been dehydrated, his stomach wasn't digesting, and the doctor wasn't sure what was going on. He wanted an EKG. As all this was occurring, I sat monitoring Jamie, the nurses, and the doctors. I needed to understand what was going on. I was with Jamie each day, and I needed to know the in-and-outs of his body.

When his heart rate shot up earlier in his care, it was because he had a lung infection. But, yesterday his lungs were clear (according to the chest X-ray). I "Googled" for answers about the imbalance of his electrolytes, potassium, and calcium. I checked his tube feed (which he'd been on for awhile). Then, I checked his new tissue builder they just started two days earlier. I found it had over 200mg of the items which were elevated in his body. I asked the nurse how often he got this, and what procedure she used. She said, "Um, I follow what the doctor said." (Smart girl...)

I was told that three packets were administered in the last twenty four hours with 150ml of water each time. So the package (which was very thick) was only given 5oz of water. On the packet it clearly stated it needed 10ozs of water. A simple fix. Stop using the Juven (a therapeutic nutrition drink), or use water to dilute it. It was no coincidence that he hadn't had any Juven since yesterday at 10:00 AM, and today he was in perfect condition. The doctor came in and said everything looked stable. I asked him how it happened. The doctor looked at me and smiled saying, "It was a little birdie." Well...tweet tweet!

Today I had Jamie's blood pressure hose on his legs and his abdominal binder on his stomach to help keep his blood pressure up. Physical therapy was talking about putting him on the tilt table to get him up and going. We were hopeful that today he would be up and out of bed.

(To answer some peoples questions…yes I kissed Jamie with my mask on. The silly stuff I would do through the day to make his life better *was so worth it!*)

෩

We said a prayer for the American soldiers sacrificing their lives every day for our freedoms! We prayed for the 4-4 Cavalry—Jamie's brothers and sisters—to be at peace and follow the Lord's path on their great journey!

> "Father God, thank you Lord that we can freely come to you at anytime in prayer. We praise you Father for you are the only One who can heal. You're the only One who can restore and transform us into something beautiful and perfect. Forgive us for anything that we've done or said that will cause a separation from You. We ask you Father to protect and heal our American soldiers. Only You know exactly where healing and restoration is needed, for You are the Creator of our bodies. We believe Father that only You have the power to heal, for You said that 'by your stripes we are healed.' So we pray Father that You will put Your powerful healing hands on our soldiers and their loved ones they protect. We pray all these things in the name of Jesus."

We had many friends and family following our journey. We asked them to also say a special prayer for Jamie's brothers and sisters—*our brothers and sisters* that protect us while we sleep. We considered ourselves to be doing well because we were on American soil surrounded by a medical team, and we had the comfort of a loved one—one another.

There were so many days when all I wanted to do was

journal about our life. That way I could read and reflect on everything that was happening. Many times I felt things were going smooth because I was there. I watched as the nurses tried to understand everything that was wrong with Jamie. However, they were usually unable to look through his charts thoroughly. Twenty thousand pages were a lot to comprehend!

Even at Bethesda, our days normally began very early (usually around 5:00 AM). Jamie got up and I encouraged him to stretch his arms, do his neck rolls, and then I massaged his hands. If he didn't use his hands for a few hours, the muscles would tighten up and he couldn't move them. Giving him a massage four times a day helped so much. After the massage, and with the nurses assistance, I would roll him on his left side. This was in preparation for his bowel stimulation. I made sure his head was comfortable, and I put his right leg on a pillow to give it support. Then, I got the suppository and lubrication to complete the process. Jamie's body was getting use to the process. He usually had a bowel movement within five minutes after the first stimulation. The nurse and I would clean him up, and then after fifteen minutes of the first stimulation I repeated the process each fifteen minutes for the next hour.

The process takes patience, and it was good that we'd learned to use our time wisely. In between stimulations, I would assist Jamie with brushing his teeth. He tried to do a little of it himself, but he was unable to grip the toothbrush. I also brushed his hair, shaved his face, clip his fingernails, toenails, and gave him a bed bath.

After the stimulation was complete, we rolled Jamie onto his other side to begin stretching his legs, hips, knees, ankles, and arms. It was nice to get the blood moving early in the morning. After his morning KT, I would give him a massage to loosen up his muscles and make sure he was getting moisture on his skin. His skin broke down so easily that it required daily care.

The nurse would bring in his medications around 8:00 AM. This included calcium water, muscle relaxers, spasm control medications, and a few others. Then respiratory care came in to do his trachea cleaning and inner cannula cleaning. Jamie had been having green, yellow, and red mucous discharges up to four times a day.

Around 9:00 AM we would begin stretching and moving his arms more. We were now trying to *build* muscle. We would get the bands out that I'd purchased for him. Typically he tried to do fifteen reps three times each. In the past week he hadn't been able to do that many because he was in so much pain. We found that his methadone expired the previous Monday, and no one realized it had expired. As a result, he wasn't receiving the methadone which was necessary in creating a "baseline" for him. Concerning his exercises, we did triceps, biceps, and anything else we could think of that would help him! At 10:00 AM the PT and OT therapist usually came in. We also had mental wellbeing, which included the doctor Jamie was comfortable with discussing many things with him. It was nice for him to talk with his speaking valve *and be heard.*

Throughout the day Jamie's vitals were checked three to five times (depending on the corpsman). His vitals had been perfect! He was improving *and advocating* for his care. For instance, we discussed when his ortho boots were to be put on, and how long they should stay on. The answer was that we put them on when he wakes up, and then take them off two hours, and then put them back on. We discussed how often he should wear his oxygen. The answer was all day long because it helped keep humidity in his body in that area. We discussed how often he should be rolled on each side. The answer was every two hours, but never on his back due to his stage three pressure ulcer. We talked about who does or doesn't have to wear a mask, gloves, and the banana suit. The answer was that anyone walking into the room must have them on! Jamie's immune system was so weak that even the stomach flu would set him back.

Other medical issues discussed:

- How often his JP drain needed to be emptied? It needed emptied once a day. Prior to last Tuesday it had been draining less than 1cc. However, lately it had been 7-10ccs per day. This concerned his general surgery physician.
- When should the bandage on his backside be changed? It should be changed when it was dirty, contaminated, or compromised. If it was clean, keep it on, unless it's been longer than three days.
- When should his IVs be changed? Typically, the standard was every three days unless they've become blocked.
- He should never swallow his spit. He must spit it out every second of the day. I told Jamie it was good for his physical therapy to move back and forth with his hands.
- His gastric outtake bag should be emptied once a day. It wasn't draining that much anymore.

We were opting to move toward straight-cathing right away to train Jamie's bladder every four hours. These were some of the little things we did together each day. Each day his body was healing and he was getting better. Even with the infections, his vitals were maintaining great levels!

I would be leaving the next day to go home and look for apartments. I would also be looking for a new SUV for Jamie, getting maintenance done on our cars, and spending time with

Celesteal and Alexa. We would pack up some of our items in preparation for Denver. We were looking forward to being there by mid or late August (pending Jamie's surgery on August 9, 2011.)

The past week had been a long one. Jamie and I pushed through to see something positive in each day. Even though it had been some of the most emotional times, he felt bad for me having to take care of him. But, then he would say he had tears of happiness knowing that I took such good care of him. I told him I treated his body as if it were mine, and the things I did, I would do regardless. This was our life, and I loved it. There were moments during the day when Jamie was asleep that I would look at him, touch his legs, and give thanks to God for his return.

I'd waited my whole life him—a husband who understood me, supported me, and loved me inside and out. He was the man who played his guitar outside my bedroom window for three hours to ask me for another date. He was the man who brought me a Teddy Bear on that date, and would lead me in the right direction in my life.

191

-16-

Just Live, Laugh, and Love

Daddy Jarboe will be flying here to stay with Jamie for a couple days while I'm gone. It would be a quick trip for me, and I'll return the following weekend.

Neither of us slept well last night. We kept waking each other up talking about our future. I'd seen a change in Jamie this last week. He seemed to get irritated easier. It's obvious he's tired of breathing through his neck and not being able to talk or eat on his own. Most of my time is spent listening, loving, and learning about our love we've been blessed by.

I do my best to empower Jamie with decisions he can make on his own. I see it build him up day by day. I never want him to break or feel insecure with his new life. Seeing him each day, whether he was in a wheelchair or lying on the operating table, the word "handicapped" has never crossed my mind. Until last night when a nurse mentioned a *handicap parking pass*. It really struck Jamie and me. That was now a part of our life. We both sat there looking at each other. However, my thoughts were still the same. I was thankful my husband was here, and that I didn't have to bury him. I'll take the "handicapped" sign and life within that framework any day.

Jamie stares at me with puppy dog eyes as I pack. He says he doesn't want me to go, but he's happy I'm going to be with our girls. I remind him that I'm always with him. He just has to close his eyes and I'll be there. Or, he can Facebook, text, or call me. We love technology! Either way life is beautiful.

Last night he posted our prayers for Sgt. Jamie Jarboe on our Facebook page. The response was overwhelming! Our friends and family (and new found family and friends) are beyond anything we could have wished for! We are so thankful for life!

ஐ

What a beautiful Saturday morning! I woke up early to head into my office to pick up Jamie's footlockers. I wanted to take pictures back for him, and also see if there was anything else he wanted brought to Bethesda. I'd also planned to drop papers off at the bank, and then drive by some property I found that would make a great place to build our home. It was six acres of land, and it was gorgeous! Jamie would love the land and the trees!

"Is there anything in particular you want from your footlocker?" I asked Jamie when I called to check in.

"No. I can't eat or drink, so what does it matter?" came the reply.

Whoa! He was awfully negative this morning!

"Yes, you're right. You can't eat or drink, but I'm happy you can see, smell, hear, and touch."

"Okay," he said calmly, "I get it honey."

When something like that occurs, it's easy for people to see only the negativity of the statement. Not me. I wouldn't allow that emotion to take over my life. I wouldn't allow myself to feel as though my life was over because the man I married was no longer able to take care of himself physically. That didn't matter to me. I told Jamie when we were dating, "I don't need a man who can support me financially, physically, or monetarily. I need a man who will support me emotionally and love me for who I am."

Jamie hadn't changed from the man he was years ago. He still swore and talked a lot of crap. He was still *the big bad guy*— *"hear him roar."* But, he was also at peace inside. I knew each day would be a struggle, and that people would tell us, "Oh you have such a long road ahead..." But, doesn't everyone? We all have a long road ahead of us. Jamie won't be able to *walk* down that road, but he'll find a way to keep going and I'll be right beside him.

I woke up at 2:30 AM the next morning, and it was the best thing ever! I woke up Celesteal and told her she didn't have to go to the airport with me. She could sleep in. She said, "Yeh right. I'm going and so is Lexi." We went in to wake up li'l Lexi Lou with a kiss and hugs. She asked to awakened so she could say bye bye to mommy! Melissa (one of my friends) showed up at 3:30 AM, and we loaded the kiddos in the car. We were on our way to Kansas City. It was nice to know I had such a great person in my corner. She wanted to do anything she could to help me. Though I had such a difficult time asking *anyone* for help, it was nice to be able to ask and know she would be there!

Getting to the airport that morning and saying goodbye to my gorgeous daughters wasn't sad. It wasn't sad because I knew

195

when it was time we would be a family again. They would be strong, and they would value the times we would have together in the future.

&

It was great being back at the hospital to see Jamie and give him a kiss to wake him up! I got out his aloe vera socks and showed them to him. He asked me to put them on. When I began putting the socks on, I noticed his feet were pressed against the base of the bed and his toes were stuck with a pole in between them. At 10:25 AM I went to the nurse's station and asked for his corpsman or nurse. at 10:50 AM I pressed the call bell in his room. Finally, at 11:15 AM I walked into to the hallway and stood, and there I was met by his nurse.

The nurse walked into the room without a mask.

"Would you please suit up?" I asked, "Jamie is on precaution."

"No. It's fine as long as I don't touch him," she answered.

I said, "No, it's not fine. The note on the door says if we're within eight feet we have to suit up."

She stopped, gave me a look, and then kept walking toward Jamie's bed.

"Would you please leave the room and get the appropriate equipment," I told her in a firm tone of voice.

As she ignored my request, I took my camera out and took a picture of her standing over Jamie's bed. I thought to myself, "Why do I have to take this measure? It's clearly posted outside of his door by professionals who are doing their best to take care of him and stop the spread of infection. But, here she is taking it for granted!"

Needless to say, things went downhill from there. I showed her Jamie's toes. She couldn't explain why his toes were jammed between the posts in his bed. I asked her if she'd seen the order for his ortho boots every two hours. It was 11:30 AM—four and a half hours after her shift had started. Jamie's boots were not on. She said she took them off at 7:30 AM. She had no explanation as to why the boots weren't put on.

"Are you married?" I asked the nurse.

"No."

"Do you have a boyfriend?"

"Yes," she replied.

"If your boyfriend was in the condition my husband is, looking the way he does, how would that make you feel?"

The nurse replied, "Ma'am, I've been a nurse for eight years, and in my medical expertise I would say he's fine."

"Like I said, if this was your boyfriend laying in this bed in this manner, how would you feel?"

"Ma'am, I'm a trained professional. I understand the nature of his injury."

She went on to tell me she'd bathed Jamie that morning from head to toe. Jamie started shaking his head no saying, "No she didn't."

"You bathed him from head to toe," I asked the nurse.

"Yes."

I pulled up the towel across Jamie's body to show tube feed from his hip down to this thigh on his right side.

"That's not tube feed," she said, "That's dry skin."

"What?" I said astonished. "Dry skin? Just in that area?"

"Yes ma'am."

"All right. That means if I wipe it off with a wet cloth it will dry out by the end of your shift."

I got a towel and wiped down the right side of his body. It created yellow stains on the white towel—the same color as the tube feed dripping. I did this across his body as well.

"Maybe if you were here more often you would understand what we're doing here," the nurse told me.

"Who do you think you're speaking to? I've been next o my husband's bed for almost four months! I've been here every morning at 5 AM and have left around 9:00 PM. Many times I've spent the night next to him in his room to comfort him."

"Perhaps you need to speak with the nurse in charge. I'll get her for you when I'm done in here."

"Why wait," I said as I pushed the call button.

I met the charge nurse at the door and explained my concerns. She said it was her first day and that she understood my concerns.

"If you understand," I said, "then put yourself in his position. Each day he lays there, his concerns are not being heard. People are not assisting him, and he's being ignored. Each day this happens it breaks down his mind, his pride, his livelihood. It tears away at his resolve to hold on. He's a strong man, but he needs to be heard and he needs to be cared for. What are you going to do for him to care for him and ensure his needs are being met and not overlooked?"

"I understand," the nurse relied.

I asked her to come in the room. She began to ask Jamie what she could do to make his stay more accommodating.

"I requested a bed four days ago. It hasn't made it here," Jamie said.

"Let me go check on that. We'll get it taken care of."

She left and we were in the room alone. I told him I would be right back. I walked up and down the hallways, and I found a bed labeled "Jarboe"—delivery date July 22, 2011. Ten minutes later the charge nurse came in to let me know the bed was on its way.

"When did it arrive?" I asked her.

"It just got here."

"Really," I replied.

I showed her my camera with the picture of the invoice and the delivery date. I asked her if she wanted to recant. She looked at me and said she would look into this issue for me. *Then* she was on it! She brought the bed in and got it situated. She made sure Jamie was comfortable and happy, and then left.

Jamie finally fell asleep around 1:00 PM. He slept comfortably until a man knocked on the door saying he wanted to visit Jamie.

"Who are you?" I asked.

"Ted Nugent," he replied.

"Are you a personal friend of my husband's?" I asked.

"No, but I'd like to be," he replied.

At the time I didn't know who Ted Nuggent was. But, it was nice that he was there visiting soldiers! Jamie had his picture taken with Mr. Nugent. That was pretty awesome. And, we discovered that he's just a good old boy!

After Mr. Nugent left, a substitute doctor arrived to talk to

Jamie about his drain. They wanted to put a new bulb on it. I'd mentioned to the charge nurse that his JP drain wouldn't stayed suctioned. She said they were going to do a CT scan to see what was going on with his body. At 3:00 PM the nurse came back to put the contrast into Jamie's body. They put one liter of contrast through his feeding tube. It looked and smelled like Tang. She said to keep an eye on him because he could aspirate, or it could come out his trachea.

At 3:15 PM she said she told us they would return in an hour to take him down for a CT scan. At 4:30 PM I ran into her in the hallway and asked what time she wanted to go to the CT scan. She said she was working on it. Just then, I walked in the pantry to find four corpsman hanging out and eating some of the food the Blue Star Mothers had brought for the families of wounded. Needless to say, they ate the last of the meal, which was fine. I was going to have my Nutrisystem (trying to lose a few extra pounds).

We went into the room at 5:30 PM. The nurse came in with a corpsman to get Jamie ready for his CT scan. She started to roll Jamie because she needed to change his bandage. I got out the medicine that wound care staff told me to ensure the nurses to used. I gave it to the nurse, but she put it to the side. Then she took off Jamie's bandage. I was shocked to see that his wound had gotten worse! The redness was now three times the size it was on Wednesday morning (I knew because I had taken a picture).

"I don't see anything in the notes or orders about using the medicine," said the nurse as she continued to ignore the medicine I'd given her.

"I've kept in contact, and I've been instructed by the wound care team to ensure that this powder is used," I explained to her.

"Ma'am, what you're telling me today *is not backed up*,

therefore there's no orders and I'm going to do what I'm going to do."

"If you want to play magic," I said adamantly, "do it with your own family and friends. But, I will not allow you to be inconsistent with my husband's care and then cause him to have to deal with the brunt end of the force."

"None of the doctors have told you what to do. It's not in the system. There isn't an order," she replied.

"Jamie's charts are over twenty thousand pages. I hope for your sake you took time to read it thoroughly, because when the doctors come in tomorrow and show me the orders they've written up, I'll proceed to tell them about your inability to follow through. I'll show them pictures of your inconsistencies as well hold the nurses accountable for my husband's inability to progress."

Perhaps I was too harsh and expected too much. Maybe I was tainted from the abuse Jamie suffered in Richmond. What I can tell you is, he doesn't want me to leave because he fears repercussions. He says the nurses and corpsman talk about him "wanting too much." He's fearful of retaliation. However, I know Bethesda Hospital is not like Richmond. However, the damage Jamie sustained in Richmond and the medical state he's in right now doesn't help matters. He's very ill and it seems people just take it all for granted. They don't suit up; they don't follow orders; or orders are not written. At this point I see why wives and family members stress out and leave. It's not hard to be in the hospital, watch movies, play games, and do PT. The difficulty lies in the fact that you have to deal with antagonistic nurses.

℞

It had been a long night. I was so grateful for my bed in Jamie's room. His CT scan revealed some concerns. His esophagus and trachea had became one. The doctor visited and gave specific orders to hold his tube feed and monitor his blood pressure. Credit must be given to Jamie. He told me that he and daddy were having problems with his JP drain staying shut. It kept filling with air. I had get the attention of three doctors in order to get them to act.

They changed the bulb, but the problem continued. We were now waiting for general surgery to get in ASAP. We needed them to make the decision whether or not Jamie would go into surgery, or to give us a plan of how they were going to fix his airway and his esophagus. They needed to separate them somehow. Thankfully, the *new nurse* was doing her best. Her attitude was that there was a lot involved with Jamie's care. But, she had no problem letting me assist with moving him and helping with his bowel schedule.

We also had a meeting with the hospital commanders and the patient advocates. It was unfortunate that we had to go through and regurgitate all the issues. Jamie and I agreed that there were so many politics there, especially in the transition between Bethesda and Walter Reed. The main concern voiced was that Jamie was a high medical need patient with both new and old issues. They would be transferring us out of the 5C area, trying to get us in the medical ward. However, they were all full at that time. The wounded warrior floor (4) was completely full.

It was even more unfortunate that nothing was resolved in the meeting. If anything, Commander Vernon was especially antagonistic after I mentioned the fact he also failed to follow procedures at one time. It happened when he was training his corpsmen and nurses on how to complete trache suctioning, and in the middle of teaching them *he forgot* to use the sterile gloves provided in the kit. Instead he used *the same gloves* he'd used when he helped moved Jamie into the bed, and the same gloves he used to move the trash can after he cleaned up a bowel movement. Furthermore, while completing the suctioning he laid the hose going into Jamie's trachea on his blanket. I brought my concerns to Commander Vernon the same day, and he argued with me. Thirty minutes later he returned and apologized saying he was mistaken. It was unfortunate I had to be put in such a hostile environment when these were supposed to be qualified individuals. What was *not* unfortunate was the surveillance camera I'd purchased in May to keep in Jamie's room.

కు

I woke up at 5:00 AM and walked to the hospital to wake Jamie up for his morning bowel stimulation, bath, and physical therapy. He was a little combative, which was understandable. Once he vented his concerns about never eating again, never walking again, and not being able to sleep next to his wife at night, I kissed him and told him I couldn't begin to understand his frustrations.

But, I encouraged him by telling him the doctors were hopeful they could fix his esophagus. It might be a few more months that he couldn't eat, but when he could it would just be that much better. I reassured him that I would do everything in my power to make sure he didn't just sit in a wheelchair. Between muscle stimulators and the Easy Stand 5000 machine (that helps build leg muscles), he would stand straight and proud. I told him how all these concerns he had now were such a small part of life because seven miles away in Arlington Cemetery were some of his friends who were not as fortunate.

One of Jamie's best friends was laid to rest only two months earlier. His friend never got the chance to feel a kiss from his wife before he left. He never got to feel the simple things in life we took for granted. So, even in the most darkest moment, I could see the light and I needed him to see it as well. We couldn't lose hope. We couldn't lose love. Most of all we couldn't lose *us*.

After speaking these words of encouragement to him, he looked away for a moment and then asked, "Why do you love me so much? Each day I get mad, rude, and I don't understand the medical terms like you. But, you still put up with me. Why?"

"Because we were created for one another, and to go through this challenge together. I might love you *a little bit…*" I said smiling.

He smiled and laughed saying, "I love you more than anything. I know if it wasn't for you caring for me each day, I would've given up a long time ago."

I laughed and said, "Oh, you can give up and quit life, but you couldn't quit smoking cigarettes before you deployed? You're silly. Let's get you stretched out baby."

Each day I felt emotionally drained. Whether it was a result of Jamie and his justifiable emotions, the nurses trying to understand what was going on, or the doctors doing their best to find solutions for all the damage that 762 bullet did to Jamie's body. All I could do was hope, love, and learn. I believe we go through challenges in our lives to give us an appreciation of the world we've been blessed with.

People say they're concerned for me—for my wellbeing. The staff told I needed to get away for awhile and care for myself. But, I do that each day. I left for nine hours a night to get some sleep. Most of what Jamie and I did together was stuff we'd do at home just being silly. The only difference was, he was in a bed. I could work around that. We'd watch movies, play angry birds, play board games, and we'd talk about our future. We were all right. We were alive, and each day we would triumph over the trials we faced. (It only took thirty-six chocolate bars for me to feel better. I was ten pounds heavier, but I felt good!)

X-ray after X-ray, and specialist after specialist, they were doing their best to find the least evasive procedure to deal with Jamie's esophagus and trachea. We told them how it's not a big deal to us. We knew they were doing their best and we trusted and had faith and confidence in their abilities. We had tons of patience, especially since his vitals were all stable and his blood work looked good. The doctor said he'd been contacting specialists all over the world to find the best fix for Jamie. That was encouraging! I was very thankful for the general surgery team. They were on top of it, and wanted what was best for Jamie. Most days Jamie would sleep for twenty hours, and I would stay vigil next to his bed waiting for him to open his eyes. I would just think of our future.

∞

We were eager to make our way to Craig Hospital in Denver when it was time. We had so many people tell us our therapy at Craig would be brief because our insurance wouldn't pay for it. We were told we would end up at the St. Louis VA, and that we should be thankful we could get care there. Jamie had made his mind up he wanted to go to Craig. After reading reviews, talking to staff and ex patients, I wanted him to go to the hospital of his choice. If Craig was that hospital, then so be it. I told Jamie if our medical insurance didn't pay for it, then I would work full time, sell everything we had, and work a second job to make sure he got the medical treatment he needed. We'd come too far to be stopped. We'd made calls to Tricare and Craig Hospital. They reassured us there should be no issues. Either way we would make it work. We had to keep on believing.

There was the possibility that I might be going to lunch the following day with one of the mothers of a wounded warrior down the hall. Just a little getaway for some "real" food. It's crazy all the little things I took for granted until I didn't have them! I'd been eating my Nutrisystem. It was interesting how Jamie wanted to smell the food, but he didn't get hungry because he didn't have feeling down there. He just enjoyed the smell—everything from blueberry muffins, pound cake, lasagna, and mashed potatoes to chocolate brownies. He would ask how it tasted. I would tell him it tasted like cardboard. I fibbed a little bit, but I didn't want to hurt his feelings by raving about how good it was to eat when he didn't want me to leave the room. He always wanted me to stay in the room and eat next to him.

&

It was time for PT again. The two of us doing PT together was going very well. In the past he would often say, "I don't want too," or he would say, "later," and then we would never do it. What I noticed is that now would he say, "Hey, I want to do a few more reps!" That was all I needed—to see him pushing harder and harder!

During PT he was only able to do 20 reps. I really wanted to push him harder, but realistically he just wasn't ready. He told me he was tired and wanted to rest. So, I went to get dinner. When I leaned down to kiss him goodnight, I could feel his head was hot. I felt under his shoulder and behind his head. He was sweating. I grabbed the machine and took his temperature. It was 100.7! I pressed the call button for the nurse. She came in and took it again. Within ten minutes it jumped up to 101. She left to call the doctor. Next, I received a phone call from our doctor who said they were going to transfer Jamie to the ICU for observation before his procedures tomorrow.

While getting him situated in bed, the other doctor came in to do a body assessment and see what was going on. I noted that his stomach was hard, which was not typical. His breathing was also shallow. The doctor ordered some labs and an EKG as he started examining Jamie. I moved the towel across his groin area as the doctor pressed on his stomach. As I moved the towel, we both saw the same thing. His catheter was kinked! He moved it and I took it off the catheter holder allowing the blood and urine to flow through to the bag. At that point the nurse came in and started emptying the bag which had been empty moments before we un-kinked the catheter. Jamie's body drained 1400cc's! Jamie slept well that night, and his fever broke around 3:00 AM.

ॐ

When we woke up, it was time for surgery. The doctors had so much they wanted to do with him, and he'd been in surgery for quite some time. I was patiently waiting for answers. I walked around and lollygagged through the hospital.

I went back to his room where I was met by one of the doctors. They said they were taking Jamie back in at 1:30 PM.

"What does he have to go back in for?" I asked.

"We need to do a bronchotomy."

"May I be part of the procedure?"

"Do you have a different pair of shoes," he asked.

"Yes."

"Okay. We'll provide you with the other necessary items."

Wow! They were going to allow me to sit in during his decannulation and bronchotomy! It started with a camera down his nose. At first they had to stop because Jamie kept waking up and asking for more pain medication. Finally, they were able to get it inserted to see what was going on in his body. Before they were able to pass it through his vocal cords, they had to make their way through extensive granulation and scar tissue. They called in an ENT ASAP. Finally they went past his vocal cords confirming they were as severely damaged as they suspected. One was so bad it looked like only half of it was there.

They went further down to his trache area. We were able to see his tracheostomy. As they looked around near the walls, everyone in the room went silent. The doctor looked at me and said, "Mrs. Jarboe, it's not good. At that point everyone started barking orders to their assistants. The tech couldn't get the camera to work on the hook they were using to go down Jamie's nose. No one had their phones on them except me, and of course I had to take a picture! I sent it out to whoever needed it.

The next step was Jamie staying in the ICU. They couldn't pull out his trachea because that was the only way he could breathe due to all the scar tissue above his tracheostomy. So they decided to move forward with more surgeries. They removed the scar tissue from the area around his vocal cords. Then they tried to close off the tracheostomy. They wanted to take a piece of his femur bone from his leg and put it near his T2 in his back. Then they would try to figure out what they were going to do with the confirmed tracheostomy esophageal fistula. One doctor told me that wasn't typical. However, they were confident they could find the best way to ensure the problem was corrected. Once again, I waited knowing there was a hole in between Jamie's airway and esophagus that was created by his tracheostomy and esophageal stent.

༄

As the sun set today, I made the call for my great aunt Esther to come and visit. What a huge difference she has made! She'd been here less than twelve hours! She got up early with me (at 5:30 AM) to go up and see Jamie. He was happy to see us and the energy was high! He could feel our love, and he said he still didn't know what he did to deserve me. I smiled and told him, "You put up with me babe."

Around 9:00 AM, after Jamie did some PT with his arms and bands, I stretched out his legs, knees, ankles, and hips. Then, he began to fall asleep. I gave him a kiss and told him we were going outside the gates to do some shopping. I asked if there was anything he wanted. He said, "No not really."

We went to the mall and walked through Target. We found Nerf games and a few guns for him to shoot in order to work his fingers. He still wasn't able to write or pick up certain items, so we needed to build up those muscles. Then we got him the Nerf basketball and hoop to work his shoulders and range of motion. We also got a Nerf football so we could throw it around. Then we went hog wild and got him a remote control helicopter. To fly it he would have to use both hands and two fingers (index and thumb) to move the controls. We also got him some speakers for his iPad because he could barely hear it. It was so awesome! Nothing like the Nintendo DS to help him with his fine motor skills. Last, but not least, we got him a softy microfiber blanket. Jamie loved all his presents! He couldn't quit smiling when we got back and showed them to him.

After being back in the room for ten minutes, Jamie said he burped. Typically, that would be funny. But not in Jamie's situation. He hadn't had anything in his stomach for over three months in order to protect his esophagus. He had a gastric outtake in his stomach to drain all the acid. In his condition, any little reflux could cause major damage.

"What do you mean 'burped'," I asked him. "Did you feel anything come up?"

"No."

I pulled his blankets off and saw that his gastric tube was disconnected. Only his feeding tube was connected. Immediately I pushed the call button for the nurse. I tried my best to not look fearful.

"The feeding tube is jammed," the nurse explained.

This had happened six times in the last month. They said it wasn't unusual since he'd had it for a while. She called the doctor who told her that with the jtube she could push his meds through his gastric.

"What? Has the doctor looked at his chart?" I asked.

"Ma'am, the doctor had a demonstration in here to show how to do it."

"That's fine, but did the doctor look at his chart?"

I walked the nurse through the reasons he had the gastric outtake, and explained why he had a tracheaesophogial fistula, which is where the food tube and air tube had a hole. The concern had to do with the fact that the doctors couldn't stitch up the hole because Jamie's esophagus was too vulnerable. It would be like tying a knot in your scrambled eggs. That was exactly how our doctors explained it.

Immediately they called the doctor. As it turned out, the doctor hadn't even come in to our room. It had been an on-call doctor, and after she read his chart to him, he immediately changed it back. They decided to flush his feeding tube after putting in meds to ensure there was no continued blockage.

The nurse asked me, "How do you remember all these medical issues Mrs. Jarboe?"

"It's easy," I answered, "It's my husband's life, and if I have to forget my own name to retain more information, I will!"

I did feel as though I had to keep track of all the dramatic issues and medical concerns. I couldn't understand why it was so difficult for them to keep up with Jamie's chart. It was sad to even have to explain to people that from day one I was the one who had to do Jamie's PT and OT three times a week. One reason was the hospital didn't offer two hour time slots for the quadriplegic wounded warriors to get out and about. It was all left up to me.

In the end, all was well…so we thought. Except for Jamie's JP drain that was in his back. It filled up to 15-20cc's. It had been empty for the past few days. That meant something had come up his esophagus, and some of it drained out his JP drain. Now the question remained—was there more damage done to Jamie's esophagus? At that time we didn't know, and we wouldn't know until the tests were complete.

℥

The politicians don't understand why soldiers are having to stay longer in the hospital system. Why is it taking wounded warriors so long to heal and be released? I wish I could raise my hand and tell them why! It's because we wouldn't be there if adequate funding and proper training were given to the medical staff. Of course not everyone is to blame. But, even ten percent of failure to comply can cause enormous setbacks resulting in massive amounts of taxpayer dollars being spent. The average age of a corpsman on a medical floor was nineteen to twenty-four years old. There were students who came in directly from basic training. One of those young men threw up in Jamie's room when he had to empty his gastric bag.

For some reason I woke up at 3:30 AM, so I decided to head up to the hospital. When I arrived Jamie was awake. He was watching the History Channel, something he frequently did. We both found world history exciting. His nurse came in, and I asked her what time Jamie would be going down for surgery.

"Ma'am, he doesn't have surgery today," came her reply.

"When the doctors did their rounds they said his surgery was first call this morning."

The nurse smiled and said, "Sorry, it's not now."

"Are his tube feeds stopped?"

"No. Ma'am, there's not an order for surgery, so why would we?"

Assuming his surgery wasn't scheduled after all, Jamie and I started our routine around 5:00 AM. We did range of motion, PT, and then daily hygiene. The doctor came in his room at 6:30 AM and asked why we weren't downstairs. We told him the nurse informed us that there was no surgery today. He said, "Yes there is! Then he walked out the door." He came back a short while later and told us how that typically doesn't happen, and that he would look into it and get back with us.

By this time we had learned not to let inconsistencies or inabilities get in the way of our routines. If it happens it happens. If it doesn't, we move forward. Crying about our problems never helped. It only breaks us down.

Aunt Esther came up to the hospital shortly after all the confusion. By the time she got there, Jamie was fast asleep. Normally I did my best to fatigue his muscles and wear him out. That way his muscles were contracting and he would get great blood flow as he took a nap from 7-9:00 AM. I never worried, and I knew why. His wife just "smoked" him in PT (as his Army buddies would say)! Esther and I began playing Angry Birds, which was hilarious. The skill and precise measures it took. My goal was to beat Jamie's high scores (he was pretty good at the game). We were only able to beat one high score out of four boards, but...hey, we tried.

The doctor came in and said, "I swear on my life he was scheduled for surgery today. But, we're going to reschedule for tomorrow. We'll get Jamie in for the afternoon." Jamie woke up a short time later, and we did more stretching and talking with Aunt Esther. It's was so calming having her around. She had seen the inconsistencies, and she complimented Jamie and me for our actions. It was nice to have someone encouraging us—someone who was a selfless person. That was our philosophy. We believed in giving to others before ourselves. We'd been blessed with so much, so why have an entitlement attitude? There was no point to it. We just lived, laughed, and loved.

I snuggled onto the bed next to Jamie and started drifting off. Aunt Esther went back to the Fisher House. Jamie and I fell asleep for a bit. When I woke up I went up to the ICU to take another Army family some gifts the Army provided. The gifts were from CSM Greco and the 10th Mountain Division. While the gifts were nice, we really didn't need any more shirts, bathrobes, or flags. I asked Jamie if we could give the items to another wounded warrior who had just arrived the Friday before (including the Spartan poster that was made for him). He said yes. Even though Jamie doesn't completely remember the first two months, he knew he was loved and he could feel positive morale his dad and I portrayed. I had to find a marker to mark out "Sgt. Jarboe" that was written on some of gifts. But, I wondered if it was really worth it? We knew the PFC would love to see Jamie's Spartan poster with all the get well wishes that meant so much![2]

When I arrived in the ICU, I met with the wounded warrior's mother, father, and seven other family members. Hearing the mother's concerns and witnessing her overwhelmed emotional state was concerning. I remember being told the first hour I was with Jamie that my feelings no longer mattered. My soldier needed me, and my life was now on hold. Each day I thought of those words. While I remembered to care for myself (eating and sleeping), everything else except Jamie was irrelevant. If my feet hurt, I felt blessed to have the pain because I knew my husband

---

[2] CSM (Command Sergeant Major); Sgt. (Sergeant); PFC (Private First Class).

no longer felt those things. If I was tired from having to walk outside, or if I felt it was too hot, I embraced those feelings. After all, Jamie didn't have the luxury to feel burdens.

I paused for a moment and reminded the soldier's mother of what the nurse told me. She smiled and agreed. However, her actions spoke louder than her words. At that point, I felt it was necessary to leave the ICU. As an outsider looking in, I had my opinions, but this was their path and I didn't want to invade it.

As I was leaving, Jamie called my phone from his iPad. He said there were visitors in his room. I asked if they had masks on. He said no. I ran down to his room where two women met me outside and introduced themselves. One lady was the mother of a soldier who was injured last August and would be going home that weekend. They'd been there for almost a year when I met her. She told me about the ups and downs with her son, his care, and the new life he was leading.

It was so uncanny because Jamie and I found out that very day that we might be there for another two to four months due to the severity of his fistula (the hole that went from his airway to his food tube). Even though physical therapy was so important for para and quadrapalegics, so was Jamie's medical treatment. We'd decided to put Craig Hospital on hold until Jamie was completely cleared. There was no sense in hurrying something that might injure Jamie even more. He was so fragile.

The mother of the soldier told me she was from the same town Jamie's family was from. She mentioned how saddened she was to hear about the people taking money in Jamie's name (a scandal which occurred in the first two months of fundraising). Donations had been collected by a relative that never made it to Jamie. I told her, "To each their own." I also let her know that we intended to pay the money back to the businesses and individuals

214

who donated. We appreciated them so much, and no one should take them for granted!

She also mentioned how sad she was that her son was going home that weekend, and no one really knew about what an amazing hero he was. That broke my heart! Every soldier, wounded warrior, and man or woman who has put their lives on the line for our country deserves a hero's welcome home! The soldier's mothers left their contact information. Jamie and I spoke with Aunt Esther about creating a Facebook page for this soldier. Twenty minutes later we had a page up online, and an hour after it was created nearly one hundred people had posted a "thank you" showing their support for the amazing hero!

I went back to Jamie's room and opened his iPad to show him the results. He smiled and said, "Great job honey!" I told him it was only fair. People wanted to take care of us, and we needed those overwhelming responses of love and the words of encouragement. We needed that so much! We wanted Eric Braman to feel the same. Around 6:30 PM, aunt Esther and I decided to head to the Fisher House for the night. She was leaving early the next morning. She said her goodbyes to Jamie. I told my husband goodnight and we started walking home.

On the way home we decided we needed a diet Coke. We got in the car and found a nice little Mexican restaurant. We had some diet Cokes and great dinner!

Today was a good day.

-17-

Waging War at Home

Just walked Jamie back for his surgery this morning. We sat in the PACU for two hours before waiting for the operation room to be ready. Aunt Esther came up before her plane left, and we had tons of fun. We joked and laughed, and we talked about the beautiful life we had. Jamie and I decided that when he started coming out of the sedation, we would discuss our family vacation to somewhere tropical. We would talk about beautiful sunshine, great fruit, and the loving smiles our daughters faces!

Jamie's surgery wasn't rescheduled until that afternoon. However, throughout the night the "plan" changed. His JP drain increased output from nothing to 25cc's in only a few hours. He called me at 4:30 AM to tell me they were taking him down ASAP.

Within in nine minutes I'd brushed my teeth, dressed, and ran a block to the hospital.

Then I waited.

⁊

Jamie made it out of surgery, but no report was given. The next day we had many things organized, stretched, and we were able to get moving a little bit. Then, a doctor stopped in and said they were concerned about Jamie's left elbow. Apparently that was why he'd been so sore. When he was being transferred in ICU, something happened to his left arm. I wondered why wasn't I notified beforehand? I was waiting for the general surgery doctor to make his rounds to explain what may of happened. It would explain why Jamie had been in pain (more than ever) for the past few days. Once again, I was frustrated at myself for not noticing. Jamie said he didn't know anything about it either.

Now we played the waiting game...*again*. We were going to start reading our *Love Dare* book, and then watch some funny videos to get us up and at it.

Jamie was able to get up in his wheelchair, but he had a difficult time using the power control. It took us an hour to get from his room downstairs to McDonald's (a block away). Jamie got so flustered trying to cross the road in his wheel chair. He couldn't steer, and he almost steered it off the curb. He was so mad and frustrated! I told him, "No worries. There's no one here that's man enough, or hurtful enough, to complain about him being slow."

Even though it had taken almost five minutes to cross the road, I could see the hurt in his face. His nightmare was coming true. He literally stopped traffic and had so many people looking at him. He worried what they would think and how he wasn't able to be self sufficient. I told him he was doing great. I encouraged him

218

to be patient and told him how much I loved him. He looked up, smiled, and said, "Why do you put up with me?" I told him it was because I loved him and I've always looked forward to a good challenge. And, above all he was created for me.

He smiled and tried to focus on the wheelchair. We had to shut it off and I had to push it manually because it was just too much for him to endure. He was so scared of people laughing at him. He didn't understand—everyone there knew what it was like to get up and out for the very first time. Plus, if someone did have a moment when they wanted to say something to him, I knew in my heart it would be, "Thank you soldier for your sacrifice."

Overall, the rest of the day went well. Jamie fell asleep. He took a nap while I went to help another soldier watch his two beautiful daughters. He was a double-amputee, and his parents wanted to go have lunch. They asked me to help their son. It was so nice being around his beautiful daughters! It was hard to see him in so much pain. He'd lost both legs and half his pelvis. He'd been in and out of surgery as much as Jamie had. When I got back to the room, I hugged and kissed my gorgeous husband. I was so thankful for the fact that he was still alive. No matter what happened medically, he was there and he was alive.

The doctors made their rounds yesterday. They told us Jamie had a slight dislocation or sprain in his left arm. We were waiting for the main doctor on Monday to find out who, what, where, and why. I was hoping there was a procedure in place to notify us when something of this nature happened. Either way, we still kept moving forward. Today was going to be a beautiful day.

We both cried this morning while watching a video a friend had made of us. Lucy was another amazing Army wife, and to view the video and read her words of inspiration was amazing!

ଔ

It was a busy day in the world of the Jarboes! Starting early again (at 5:00 AM). Since I'd spent the night, I got up and started getting Jamie freshened up. I brushed his teeth, I gave him a bed bath, and then started his stretching with his legs. I'd noticed Jamie was requesting more pain medicines due to the tingling in his hands. I ask him if it was pain, or if the tingling was annoying. He said it was very annoying. He took two Percocet at 7:30 AM, and then slept for two hours.

The pain management doctor and team came in to do a neurological exam on Jamie. They wanted to check his strengths, and then attempt to get a baseline for the extent of his injury. We'd been told Jamie was an incomplete quadriplegic. But now the doctor said it was final—Jamie wouldn't have any further progression. The fact that he could move his arms was good news. However, it was very important for him to stay consistent with exercises because of his joints, muscles, and body wearing down during the past two months when he wasn't able to do anything.

We talked to the kiddos today. Wow do we miss them! They said they missed us every day, but knew we would all be together soon. We couldn't wait for that day. I was also able to get to Sam's club where I spent a couple hundred dollars on care packages for Jamie's fellow soldiers! I couldn't wait for us to pack all the goodies in the boxes and send them to his friends. He missed his friends so much! There were a few soldiers who kept in direct contact with me. We talked about some of the guys who e-mailed me. I felt so bad for them. I knew they were aware of what I did for Jamie. The problem was they compared their wives to me. In love, there should be no comparisons. The guys now wanted their wives to do what I did.

When I think of what I'd been through; the obstacles I had encountered in my life (which made who I am); I surmised that many people couldn't have lived a moment in my shoes. I'd never met my father. Until I was sixteen I was raised by a single mother who worked numerous jobs to put food on the table. My family was full of alcoholism, habitual drug users, and consequently I'd been in and out of foster homes. On top of that, I was pregnant at seventeen and lived on my own. But, I desired to give my daughters the life I never had. So far, I had accomplished so much. I did it because I was motivated to do so, and not because I wanted people to be proud of me or approve of my life. I learned early on that the only person who needed to love me was myself. Once I was able to love myself, I was able to learn to love others. I gave to others because I was so happy with what I had—*even the life I had now.* My husband, my children, and my happiness—nothing could make life better than the love we all had.

I walked into Jamie's room the next morning to find machines, nurses, and doctors hovering over him. His feeding tube was jammed the previous day, and I'd made mention of the gastric outtake not coming out. The nurse said his colon was backed up. I agreed because his body was starting to get into a routine as a result of the bowel stimulation.

Then I looked at his JP drain that was inserted near the leak in his esophagus. It was draining his gastric acid. Dang it! This meant his input for tube feed and gastric outtake have detached and his stomach was full of acid. Once the acid came up through his esophagus it eroded the leak, making the leak and hole bigger.

Once again, I would wait.

಄

General surgery and CT doctors had been up. In the last thirty minutes Jamie had hiccupped and felt fluid coming up. His JP drain now had 25cc's of fluid in it. This JP drain was under the leak in his esophagus below the stint. That meant the leak was still in his esophagus. I was hoping none of the acid was going through the hole in between his windpipe and his esophagus. Once it reached that point the acid would go right into Jamie's lungs. The doctors told me to go ahead and do his stimulation to help clear out his colon. At the moment Jamie was asking me to get the bugs off of him and feed the dogs. I was just rubbing and scratching his head. I told him about the girls going school, shopping, and I asked him to tell me what he was thinking the day we were married. *Good happy thoughts!* JP drain 30cc's at 8:03 AM. At this point Jamie was becoming delirious, nonresponsive, and he was sleeping twenty-three hours a day.

ℒ

My first and foremost concern was Jamie's health and well-being. Right now we were both at a loss. We had just been told by a First Lieutenant that there was nothing to worry about regarding Jamie's gastric outtake from the JP drain. Its output was only 10cc's in the last eight hours. Normally it could range from 300-800cc's per day. Not to mention the blood coming out of his catheter mixed with urine (bright red and dull red depending on the quantity). Urology was called at 7:30 AM that morning, but we still hadn't heard from anyone. I had requested that someone check for a UTI (urinary tract infection) almost two weeks ago (at the end of July). Nothing had been done! His temperature was ranging back and forth from 94.7 to 101 all day. His blood pressure dropped down to 85/62.

Yesterday, when I arrived at 6:00 AM, the nurse was doing an ultra sound on Jamie to see how much urine was in his bladder. His stomach was rock hard. According to the machine, there was nothing in his bladder. Jamie had four bowel movements within three hours. Then, he said he felt fluid coming up his esophagus. Moments later we looked at the JP drain that's located below the stint in his esophagus, and below the leak that he had in the back of his esophagus. There was a black and green fluid coming out his JP drain amounting to 30 cc's within in an hour.

General surgery was called. The resident came up and said there were no concerns at that time regarding acid reflux. Then I mentioned my concern regarding the acid reflux coming up his esophagus.

"Well, the JP drain is draining it," the resident told me.

"Yes, but that's not the JP drain's job. We're trying to get the hole or leak to heal. With more fluid, especially gastric acid fluid, going through the leak, the probability of it healing is slim. My concern is that the acid will reach the fistula and go into his lungs and he'll aspirate."

"When was he diagnosed with a fistula?" asked the resident.

I literally had to count backwards from one hundred. As it stood at that moment, Jamie had a fever, he'd had three bowel movements that afternoon, 10cc's of fluid drained out of his stomach in the last eight hours, blood in his urine, and his stomach was firm and getting harder by the hour.

A nurse told us, "Don't worry, we know what we're doing."

Why did we feel like Jamie was being used as a guinea pig? He had a stent put in his esophagus three months ago to heal a 1 cm leak. It didn't work. He'd been NPO for three months, and now they were telling us they wanted to use another stent for another three months, and perhaps as long as six months.

To top things off, PT and OT told us they only had time three days a week to see Jamie for fifteen to thirty minutes a day. Oh, but they were proud of me! But, little by little I was wearing down as I managed his care. I had to manage nurses, beg for the doctors to read inaccurate charting, and hope PT and OT would show up to help keep him mobile. Things shouldn't be *this* stressful. They told me I should get out more and let them do their jobs, *or lack thereof.* What was I supposed to do? Go and live my life and just hope for the best?

Where did this leave us? We were already dealing with the fact Jamie was a quadriplegic. That was all right. We could deal with that. But, being pushed backward in our lives because people were "too busy" to manage his care wasn't fair or acceptable! The doctors, nurses, therapist...they all got to go home to their families. Meanwhile, we sat there and waited for them to *make time* to correct Jamie's esophagus with another procedure that may not work. What if it was one of them? What if their life was on the line?

People would tell us to contact our local congressperson. Why should we have to take it to that level? Why couldn't this process be easier for our family? We were told that it wouldn't be a problem if this were the first stage of his surgeries and corrections. But, the fact that it was months down the road, specialists would have to be called in, and right now they weren't sure about the best fix for Jamie.

How about we find a hospital that's familiar with these issues? How about we go somewhere where they're familiar with the care Jamie should receive? Why don't we find a place where we can receive care from nurses who been working in their field longer than a year? We had a twenty-one year old nurse in our room caring for Jamie, and a twenty-three year old supervising. We literally felt like we were at Sonic and they kept messing up our order...over, and over, and over again!

ℳ

I spoke with the doctors, nurses, and the NCM (Nurse Case Manager) regarding transfer to Craig Hospital for assistance with Jamie's tracheaesophogial fistula. The doctor said she would make phone calls immediately to Craig to discuss the options of doctors and care. She said she understand how we felt, and would take care of the transfer personally.

It was kind of the doctors to be upfront and honest with us regarding the fact that they had never dealt with such an extensive esophagus injury. That was scary and comforting at the same time. Now we waited and were hopeful of a positive outcome. What was meant to be will be.

After meeting with the doctors, I met one of the soldier's mothers for lunch. It was so nice to see her. She had been a strong support for me. She understood everyday life inside the hospital walls. We discussed many things, but we always came back to one particular topic—how some soldiers weren't being cared for by their families or spouses. I understood better why the hospital staff wasn't very understanding of me or the care I gave to my husband. They were used to the *absence* of family members. Then they had to deal with the abrasive comments and complaints about the care as these family members showed up for a once-a-week or once-a-month visit.

I saw this at Walter Reed, but I witnessed it at its best at Bethesda. Especially with the younger soldiers (typically eighteen to twenty-five) who got married right before they deployed and gave their POA (power of attorney) to the new found love of their life. Relationships that often had a whopping two week commitment before deployment. Then, when the unthinkable happened, the wounded soldier had to rely on a person they barely knew to make life-altering medical decisions. From what I could discern, it was only about one spouse out ten that could handle the stress, the extent of the injury, or the physical appearance of their spouse. Another common scenario was a family member coming in, but then leaving it up to the medical staff to care for their child because they couldn't handle the stress.

Divorce papers came each week to new wounded warriors on the floors from spouses they thought were going to be there to care for them. It was easy to feel sorry for them (as many of do). The question that rolled over and over in my mind was: What was that soldier thinking! Why wasn't someone there to stop them? Getting married is a commitment. When did the commitment to wedding vows diminish to the point where they're not taken seriously? Don't we promise to stay together "for better or worse"? What if the "worse" comes before the "better"? What gives them the right to leave?

Even with my faith and love for God, I knew I was being tested time and time again. While I missed my children, and the life I once knew, I knew my place was next to my husband. Even if he didn't know I was there next to him. I knew! I treated his body as if it was my own. We were one. When he was hurting, I was hurting. When he smiled, I smiled. Our lives were created for us before we were born into the earth. I accepted that.

I'm a firm believer there should be a questionnaire for those considering marriage—especially when marrying a soldier. They should know what they're signing up for. The soldier should be questioned as to whether he's confident the one he's marrying is the one person in life he can depend on to care for him and keep him alive. If he cannot answer that in the affirmative, then he should leave for deployment and write to a stranger. He can tell that individual his fears, but *don't marry them*. The fact is, if he married an uncommitted person, that person could hurt him more than a bullet, IED, or the enemy ever could.

The battles weren't just overseas, many battles for the life of the soldiers (mentally and physically) were being fought on American soil. I knew because I was engaged on a daily basis.

-18-

One Step Forward, Two Steps Back

I woke up at 5:00 AM, even after getting back to the hotel late after checking on Jamie the previous night. I'd returned from the Blue Star Mother's Dinner and he was asleep. The nurses said it had been an eventful evening. Jamie's nurse told me she'd called the doctors to evaluate Jamie and his mental stability. Since he was sleeping, I told her I'd be back in the morning for his bathing, stretching, PT, and stimulation. By this time (for accountability purposes) I was keeping daily logs and communicating only by e-mails to the nurse case manager, AW2, and the federal recovery coordinator. That way, all correspondence was time stamped and read receipts were sent. Each night I would go back to my room and transfer my notes and video or voice recordings to my files and BizNet the information on our CaringBridge and social media pages. This was my way to break up hospital "psychosis" and document our lives for the day Jamie would be able to wake up and read everything he had endured.

When I arrived at the hospital (around 5:30 AM) the next morning, the nurse and corpsman were in Jamie's room. They were cleaning off his catheter. Apparently, he'd pulled it out sometime during the last hour. Within the last twenty-four hours, he'd pulled out his catheter, his feeding tube, and he caused severe damage to two corrective surgeries. I also learned he told the corpsman to sit him up and get him dressed because he had appointments that day. (It was Sunday, and Jamie didn't have any appointments.) Not knowing any better, the corpsman began to sit Jamie up (around 4:30 AM). When Jamie told the corpsman to quit holding him up because he could do it on his own, he began to fall slowly backward. He couldn't hold himself up due to the fact he's paralyzed from the chest down. He told the corpsman something's wrong with his body—it's wasn't working. Jamie asked, "What the hell were you thinking dropping me?"

The corpsman called for the nurse. She came immediately and began to lay Jamie down due to his blood pressure issues. They took his blood pressure and it was 73/44. The nurse gave specific directions for the corpsman to listen and communicate with Jamie, but don't follow any of his commands. Just tell him he needs to get the nurse or his wife. With the recent surgeries, medication, PTSD, and traumatic brain injury, Jamie was in his own world.

After that, another corpsman was sent in to assist me with Jamie's care. The nightshift corpsman felt ashamed of what had happened even though I told him understood that accidents happen. Nevertheless, he still felt responsible. The nurse and I discussed a few issues with Jamie, and she said that he would be alert, talking about life, and then a second later he would be back in theatre giving orders to throw a grenade, take cover, or to move out. I didn't know if I should believe the nurse because I'd been with Jamie everyday in the last four months, and I hadn't seen him act as she described. I had witnessed inconsistencies in his dreams, yelling out, or acting out movements. But never while he was wide awake.

The nurse left us a for a few minutes. While she was out, Jamie asked me if the water was clean enough to drink out of his camel pack? I told him yes. I was sure it was. Then he said, "Wrong private! The water is contaminated. None of the water is clean. Only drink water from the distributed water on base. Even the water through the purifier is contaminated."

I left the room to get some towels. When I returned I sat down next to Jamie's bed. I asked him if he liked his bath. He said, "Yes, I feel clean." Then he said, "I got an e-mail from a friend at Fort Campbell. He wants me to spend New Year's Eve in Kentucky. But, I don't want to leave home." Then he went on to say, "I should go over to his house and meet his wife and children. His wife takes such good care of him. If I'm lucky, someday I'll meet someone like her." Then he said, "But she's mine, and if you try to take her away from me I'll kick your ass."

I sat back in my chair next to his bed with tears in my eyes. I wondered when my husband would come back to me. It hurt so much to see him in this condition. For him not to know who I was as I sat next to his bed talking to him as he looked right at me and listened to my voice left me at a loss for words.

Jamie's nightmares were getting worse. I got up to put a

towel over Jamie's feeding tube and groin area because he had the blankets off and he was tugging at his tubes. He told me there was a sock on his chest from the laundry. I told him it was his feeding tube. He said, "No it isn't." I'd been told by the doctors that since Jamie was having difficulty in the area of mental stability, they were going to put him on more anti-anxiety and depression medications hoping it would reduce the dreams and hallucinations. Jamie had become aggravated and very hostile. He refused to work through those struggles. Even though he may not like them, at some point he would learn how to get use to them.

∞

Tears filled my eyes when I saw a cavalry soldier at the Blue Star Moms national convention. I missed seeing my husband in uniform! He was my best friend and man who had loved me unconditionally. I wanted him there to look at me, smile at me, and to love me. I knew we would get there in time, and I was thankful he was still alive. I would be lying if I said it wasn't torment—this twisted nightmare of life I watched him go through each day. I watched him hurt, suffer confusion, and get depressed to the point where he wished he would've died so he wasn't making my life harder.

He told me he would no longer wear his uniform. He said he wasn't a soldier anymore. I listened to him tell me how he felt. I told him there were so many people that loved him and supported him as a soldier. They were proud of his selfless sacrifice. He was a hero. His reply was, "No, I'm the guy who got shot and can't walk next to his wife."

Each day I had to stay alert for Jamie's sake. I listened, loved, and understood his frustrations. I let him have as many moments as he wanted, but in the end it was all the same. I loved him and there wasn't a day that went by that I wasn't thankful for him coming home.

જી

The past couple days had been a trial. The medications hadn't been changed. I was running out of options and needed help. I reached out to a friend from high school who was now a pharmacist. I asked her if she could look at Jamie's medication list. At this point I needed someone to bounce ideas off of, and Natalie was that someone. The doctors thought he might have an infection in his lungs or chest area. Yesterday they asked if I wanted him on anti-depression meds or anti-anxiety meds. I told them I didn't feel we needed more meds. I wanted to try good old fashion love from his wife as a treatment. I requested a list of his medications. They refused to give it to me. I was told that I needed to speak with their supervisor at patient administration.

I spoke with a doctor from pain services, and expressed my concerns about Jamie's symptoms. I showed him a video of Jamie, and he asked why he was removed from Percocet, Roxie and Valium. I told him I wasn't sure. He said perhaps the order expired and it wasn't put back in, and he was concerned about withdrawals.

Later that day I completed his bowel stimulation and got him dressed. I was going to try some PT to get his blood flowing for the day. I was hopeful the doctors could find what they were looking for so we could move forward a little bit.

It was Wednesday, and Jamie signed his consent for surgery at 4:00 PM tomorrow. (Yes, another surgery!) This is only the second consent ever signed and Jamie had had nearly sixty surgeries or surgical procedures. My issue with this was, he had a TBI and was on medications, so why were they allowing him to sign a form? This one was for the removal of the stent in his esophagus. Even though I met with all the doctors that morning, and they stated how the procedure would be done in the ICU, they reset his surgery for tomorrow morning at 8:00 AM. They are placing *another* stent in his body. The first one had been in his esophagus for over three months and had not healed a 1cm leak in the back of his esophagus, and now they expect it to correct *two* leaks.

Jamie was still NPO and not eating. He was getting fed through a tube which would do its best to maintain his weight. However, the scale on his bed showed us that Jamie wasn't even 117 pounds. He was still 101 pounds. It was senseless to go back and forth and point out inconsistencies and nothing being corrected. At this point I felt that Jamie was a guinea pig for them to practice on. Each time a new medical student would come in we would have more issues. Yet, we were determined to move forward even if it meant letting them practice on Jamie as they saw fit.

We requested an immediate transfer to Craig Hospital in hopes they would accept us and be able to assist in the correction of the fistula and leak. But, now we are being told it wasn't going to happen. We were told they were working on correcting the situation. At the same time, we were being visited by Wounded Warrior representatives encouraging us to look into transferring to Texas so we could stay inside the DOD guidelines and not lose benefits. *That's right*...a representative of a non-profit came to Jamie's hospital room and told me to sit down and listen. And, if I wanted to help my husband I would do "what a wife is supposed to do" and follow commands. I was told that if I removed Jamie from a military hospital or VA he would lose benefits, his ability to get equipment from the VA, and maybe even his retirement.

After RJ enlightened me concerning his personal opinion, I politely let him know I didn't appreciate him lying to me or using a scare tactic. I told him that even if I had to sell everything I have, my husband will receive everything he needs. Then I told him he could take his projects backpack and his scare tactics back to his office. I also suggested he check his e-mail for a video of our conservation (recorded on the camera in Jamie's room), and that he should never set foot in Jamie's room again.

My suggestion to the doctors (as they would come to Jamie's room meetings) was to be cautious of placing another stent in his esophagus or trachea because it had failed for three months prior. He weighed 101 pounds, he was full of infection, and his immune system was weak. He was in the beginning stages of AD. At that point no one there knew how to care for a quadrapalegic, parapalegic, or someone with a tracheoesophigial fistula. So, I was left doing his bowel stimulation, assisting with managing his medications, straight-cathing, bathing, PT, OT, RT, and KT.

Not only was Jamie being neglected, we were being abused by the very people who should've cared for his wellbeing by being proactive to issues that could've been stopped before they began. Preventative measures were certainly minimal.

ᔥ

It was an early day. For some reason I woke up at 3:30 AM. I was at the hospital by 4:00 AM. Usually when they took Jamie down to surgery, they took him to the PACU (Post Anesthesia Care Unit) first for assessment. After that we would consult with the doctors. However, today at 6:00 AM he was taken immediately to the operation room where it's restricted access: *surgeons only*. I had to kiss him and tell him I loved him at the door, and then they wheeled him into the surgery room. We were told by a thoracic doctor the night prior to Jamie's surgery that it would not begin until 8:00 AM, and that all the doctors were meeting at 7:30 AM.

We'd also spoken to a medical student from GI who had us sign a consent with a picture attached. The medical student assured us that they would only be doing the camera portion to see the progress (or lack thereof) of the stent that was put in his esophagus over three months ago. Then, he told us that the two main doctors would be there; the doctors who originally put in the stent. My question was, *why* would those doctors be there just for a scope of the stent and area surrounding it?

Then he said, "If there's a 'game time' decision, they'll perform the stent swap at that time."

"Why isn't there a consent for that procedure?" I asked.

"Well, we're not sure at this time if we'll have to do it."

"So, you're telling me the doctors are going to be there, but instead of doing the cam in the ICU, *as you have previously planned*, you're moving forward and he's going straight to the operation room? And, the plan to do a swap of the stents was already underway without any consideration to our feelings with regard to the possibility of no longer utilizing the stent (which hasn't worked).

"Why would we want to move forward with the stent when it has been proven unsuccessful?" I kept pressing. "Less than forty-six percent of surgeries were successful using a stent whether it was metallic, plastic, or silicone. The bottom line was, it wasn't working so try something else! My husband now weighed 101 pounds!"

"Ma'am," he replied, "I didn't say we *were going to do* the surgery..."

"You didn't have to! You're telling me it's going to be a 'game time' decision, and you're trying to fly below the radar because we've voiced concerns about doing this surgery. So against our desires, the decision was being made behind our backs—*in a deceitful way.*"

"How many stent placement operations within the

esophagus have you participated in?"

"Ma'am, you'll have to ask the GI doctors."

"I will," I assured the medical student, "and their answer will be *zero*. And yet, they'll practice on my husband again, against our wishes, to try to make medical breakthroughs at the expense of my husband's wellbeing."

I was allowed to be next to Jamie's bed in PACU prior to surgery. I requested to speak with all the physicians who would be attending his surgery, which consisted of an EDG (esophagogastroduodenoscopy) and a bronchostomy. They had close to thirty people involved in the surgery. The main "game time" decision about the stent removal was apparent. GI surgery stated they didn't know if they were going to have to replace the stent after they moved it. As they completed the EDG, if the leak was still there, they would have to insert a new stent. That was the information I wasn't being told.

The information I was being given was vague. In truth, there were thirty professionals getting ready to do surgery that had never been done, and was outside their scope of practice. It wasn't going to be a quick ten minute procedure. The procedures were being done in the OR and it wasn't because the ICU was full. The stent had been in place for over three months and needed to be removed regardless if there was a leak.

We met with the doctors and voiced our ongoing concerns. We needed to know what kind of stent was being put in—plastic, silicone, or metallic. We wanted to know if it was a "z" stent, an ultraflex, or a wall stent. We felt these were questions we should have answers to. When I spoke with the doctor I told him my husband and I needed to know: 1) facts not fiction; 2) *his* track record; and 3) the plan of care. I wasn't trying to make anyone's job more difficult. I certainly didn't want to waste taxpayer's money on invalid concerns. However, at that point, answers were needed.

After we met with all teams, I shook their hands and wished them the best in surgery. I was sure they had the best intentions for my husband who was a soldier much like they were. They were soldiers who loved their country, their families, and the life they'd been blessed with. After all that, Jamie was finally taken in to surgery at 10:00 AM.

I spoke with our NCM who told me they were working diligently to get us to Craig for several months of physical and routine therapy in order to get Jamie's body ready for his new found life.

ॐ

I arrived at the hospital early to check on Jamie. He was awake, but when I kissed him I noticed his head was hot. The medical student came in from general surgery and I asked him what Jamie's temp was.

"It was 98.2 at 4:00 AM."

"He feels warm," I told him.

I called the nurse and asked him to take Jamie's temperature.

"He was fine all night."

"I appreciate the information, but I'd like for you to check," I told him.

He checked Jamie's temperature. It was 101.5.

"Did you do a full body inspection?" I asked.

"Yes," the nurse assured me.

I examined Jamie's groin area. The nurse told me he'd

thoroughly cleaned all the blood up twice during the night. I showed him a picture I'd taken the previous night showing how I'd marked Jamie's inner thigh with my red lip gloss.

"Before you answer that question again," I said, "I'm going to wipe him down."

"Ma'am, I can do that," he said.

"Watch what I'm doing," I told him.

I took a wet wipe and wiped Jamie's leg. Then, I took another cloth and wiped his other leg and his stomach. I laid all the wipes face up (which had the previous night's lip gloss on them) and asked him to answer my question again.

He said, "I did try to wipe his legs."

"That's fine, but if you did such a thorough job, then why would there be lip gloss on my husband's inner thigh that I put there last night before I left?"

"Yes ma'am," he said, "I'll get him cleaned up right now."

"I appreciate you and the work you do," I told him. "I know you're understaffed and overwhelmed, but please don't lie to me. I'll be glad to help you if you tell me what to do."

The PACU commander stopped in.

"Good morning," she greeted me. "How was your day yesterday?"

"It was a training day of what *not to do* with a catheter." I answered her (referring to how a nurse wrongfully adjusted his catheter the previous day).

"No," she said, "I'm asking how *you* are?"

"I'm *constantly* protecting my husband," I explained. "The accountability here is limited, and I'm hurt at the fact that my husband was injured yesterday and it could've easily been prevented."

"I understand," she replied. "I'm working to ensure these things don't happen again."

The bronchostomy procedure had revealed an excessive buildup of fluid (ten to twenty-five percent) in Jamie's lungs, which was removed. Now, chest X-rays were ordered and lab were requested to find out why he had such a high temp. Once again…we waited.

They found Jamie's blood count had gone up to 13, 000. His colon was enlarged and there was excessive air around his colon and intestines. They were concerned about a possible perforation of the stomach which occurred during the EDG.

The following Monday I discussed all of this with the doctors. We also discussed Jamie's ability to make a competent decision since we were constantly having to tell him what was going on. We voiced concerns to the medical team about Jamie turning off his tube feed. He hadn't received adequate nutrition since the previous Wednesday. The general surgeon confirmed Jamie's nutrition level was at seventeen, which was alarming! They were trying to start the TPN (to feed him intravenously), however the batch made for Jamie wasn't made with fat. They decided not to hang it at 2:00 PM and instead they waited until 9:00 PM so he could receive nourishment. His tube feed was able to go at 20cc per hour, but Jamie had the nurse turn it off four to six times a day.

Two days later, Jamie had been in and out of his dreams and most times he wasn't aware of who he was talking too. I begged the doctors to look at his medications. I told them the man in the bed wasn't my husband. He was aggressive, overbearing, frustrated, and unhappy.

The contrast showed up the next day in Jamie's JP drain from the previous day's barium. His bowel also had a reddish tint which was something new. This was due to lack of nutrition. Previously it was black with a green tint and now it was brown with a red tint. All of my concerns were conveyed to the doctor, who in turn said he would convey them to the primary team. The general surgeon came in shortly after the ICU doctor left. Jamie was in and out of drowsiness, and the doctor starting speaking to him. Jamie told him to move the car out of the garage out back next to the shed. Even though Jamie's eyes were open, he was almost in a daze. I asked the doctor about his JP drain and whether there was contrast in it. He said no, and then looked at the drain.

The doctor dropped his head and examined the JP drain thoroughly. I asked him if we could start giving Jamie Kool Aid (grape, red, or blue) to see if it shows up in the JP drain. The JP drain was attached outside his esophagus in the back area where the 1cm leak was found in May. Dr. Rodriguez told us he would order a color test for Jamie and see if it comes out the JP drain. He would also order an X-ray to see if it was the barium or something else.

I discussed Jamie's mental status with the doctor—again voicing concerns regarding his medication and the dramatic change in him the past few weeks. I also explained how the psychologist mentioned that Jamie may have delirium induced by the medications he was on. The doctor said he would look into getting Jamie to the fourth floor soon in addition to moving him on to rehab. I expressed my concerns about moving him to rehab so soon. In his condition, I wanted to ensure there would be someone to follow him. They needed to be fully aware if anything changed with his stent and JP drain.

The psychologist came in after the general surgeon left. He

tried speaking with Jamie, asking him what day of the week it was, and if he knew *where* he was. He wasn't able to answer correctly as he drifted in and out of a conscious state of mind. Finally, the doctor said he was worried about him being over medicated. One of the medications mentioned was Valproic, which was commonly used for seizures. He didn't need to be on that medication. The psychologist was going to consult with the general surgeon regarding Jamie's medications. If the intent was for Jamie to go to rehabilitation in a few weeks, then it would great to go ahead and decrease his medication so there wouldn't be any issues concerning withdrawals once he's at rehab. Meanwhile, I was waiting for Natalie to review Jamie's list of meds and then educate me in how to taper them down.

The GI doctor came in to check Jamie's status. He was glad to see Jamie was able to eat clear liquid after the swallow studies the previous day. He wanted to see if Jamie had any sever discomfort in his chest or neck. Jamie only indicated a slight discomfort when he swallowed. He said the goal was that in the next three months they would do a bronchostomy to check status of the TEF fistula, though they were unsure the stent would repair the tracheaesophogial fistula. He knew the other doctors were exploring other options.

I asked the doctor why they put the stent in the first place if it was a blocker and wouldn't heal Jamie's first esophageal perforation from the surgery in May. His reply was simply, "No one knew how to do the surgery, and the thoracic surgeon wasn't willing to operate." Finally I understood they had no idea what to do with Jamie or how to fix his injury.

When Jamie woke up I wanted to start him on PT. But, his aggressive demeanor was terribly frustrating. I had to tell him that his exercises were an important way for him to improve and get up out of this bed. It would help him fight infection and get better sooner. He listened and seemed to understand. However, the problem was that due to his meds he would forget, and then I would have to repeat everything two hours later.

The mentha blue die was given to Jamie around 7:00 PM. By the time daddy and I were ready to go, it was already seeping out of his JP drain in his back. I couldn't help but think that it wasn't the hole in his upper esophagus, but rather a hole in his lower esophagus that hadn't been discovered. Otherwise, why would we be able to see the contrast drain into his stomach and then see it in the JP drain? Or, perhaps there was a leak or perforation in his stomach. Something was wrong, and it was hard to watch it happen to my husband each day.

ॐ

(Friday, August 26, 2011)

Walking up to the hospital at 5:30 AM, I got to Jamie's room to find his lights on and the curtain pulled. I walked in to find two nurses laying Jamie on his side.

"What are you doing?" I asked.

"I'm putting in a flexi seal," said Julian.

"Why?"

"Your husband had loose stools last night and he needs this."

"No, I'm here to do his bowel stimulation, and once that's done he won't need the flexi seal because we'll stimulate his colon."

"The doctor ordered it," Julian interrupted.

"Who asked the doctor to order it?"

"I did," he answered.

"You're setting my husband back from his independence! If you're so worried about his loose stools, then you should check on him more to ensure that there's no stool. The answer isn't putting a flexi seal in simply because it makes your job easier. You're taking away everything we've worked for with his bowel stimulation. The goal is to make him independent.

"I was not consulted concerning this, and I would like for you to stop."

"No. We're keeping it in," he answered. "I asked Jamie if I should call you, and he said, 'No, go ahead and do it.'"

"Jamie, did you know Julian was going to put a hose out of your butt?"

"No. I thought they were just going to clean me up."

"Don't speak to him like that when you're asking him questions," said Julian.

"Why?" I asked. "I'm not yelling, cursing, or raising my voice. I have questions, and I want answers."

As Julian continued trying to move Jamie around, he said, "I want you to leave the room. You don't talk to my wife like that."

Jamie was laying flat on the bed with the pillow at the top of his head pushing his chin into his neck. He said his neck hurt and he wanted to be adjusted. Julian left, and Katrina came in and gave Jamie his insulin. He also assisted me in moving Jamie around.

By 5:50 AM, Jamie's blood pressure was good. His heart rate was 122-129, and his 02 stats had been less than ninety percent for the past forty-five minutes. Nothing had been done by the nursing staff to correct Jamie's 02. His machine kept beeping and Jamie was in pain. How could they let my husband get like this?

Much had happened since yesterday. This morning the doctors starting coming in as Jamie's heart rate went up to the 130's and 140's. His respiratory also increased from 44 to 48 per minute. One doctor came in and felt his stomach saying it was distended and perhaps he needed to have a bowel movement. He requested the order to have the flexi seal removed. He asked why we didn't want it. I explained to him how the nurse asked my husband if he wanted a flexi seal, and my husband said, "Sure why not?" But, when I told him what a flexi seal was, he said he didn't want it put in. Jamie looked at the doctor and said, "If I would've known what it was, I would've never agreed."

The nurse removed the flexi seal, and I started his bowel stimulation. We were able to get about two small movements from Jamie when his respiratory started increasing. We decided to lay him on his bed and then sit him up. Right when we sat him up he had another bowel movement. However, we didn't want to move him without the nurse present (it was just myself and the RT girl). The doctor came in and said he wanted to put the artery line in for Jamie's pulse blood pressure to ensure it was accurate (since he'd had the menthalene blue, the numbers could've be off). Then the X-ray Jamie had done at 5:00 AM came back and showed both of Jamie's lungs had collapsed. At that point, the doctor said they needed to ventilate Jamie to help him breathe. For the past few hours his body had been doing so much by itself it needed to rest before it broke down.

I told the doctor I understood, and then the doctor communicated to Jamie what they needed to do. Jamie said, "No, I'm fine. I don't want to be on a ventilator." At that point I walked over and calmed him down. They were able to administer the necessary drugs to relax Jamie and put him into a sedative state. The room was filled with doctors and medical students. Before I went to the corner of the room I was able to kiss my husband's lips and whisper, "I love you." Then, I watched my husband with twenty people around him doing their best to take care of him.

When they took off the oxygen and tried to place the ventilator, Jamie's heart rate slowed down significantly. The doctors moved closer to the bed. Thankfully, the medical team followed the proper procedures and were able to manage the situation. They quickly got his heart going in the right direction.

Daddy came in room after the procedure was done. He'd been taking some boxes to the Fisher House. Since everything happened so suddenly, I didn't have the chance to contact him and tell him to hurry. After he came in the room he just sat and looked at his unconscious son. That was one of the hardest days for all three of us. We didn't talk. We both sat in our chairs watching Jamie sleep while knowing the machine was doing one hundred percent of the work so his body could rest.

The main doctor came back in and told us about Jamie's lungs. He walked us through the procedure they did, and then he asked if we had any questions.

"Yes," I said, "Is my husband septic?"

"Yep," came the doctor's reply. "Any further questions?"

"No. I have nothing more to say to you," I replied.

-19-

Difficult to Fix

I met with a Master Sergeant regarding the ongoing lack of communication. To us it seemed as though new orders were put in, new medicines were being administered, but we were never informed. After making them aware of my concerns, I was greeted by the primary physician (once again) between three and four o'clock in the afternoon. He wanted to explain what else he saw on Jamie's CT scan and X-ray. He said he'd gone through Jamie's CT scans since his DOI (Date of Injury) to investigate any imperfections or issues.

"Let me start with Jamie's esophagus," the doctor began. "He may have an abscess or infection in a small spot on his esophagus. But, I cannot go in and cut it out of that area. Jamie's spleen is also enlarged. His colon has a thick wall on part of it, and he has a large vein going from one side of his stomach to another."

"Regarding Jamie's TEF [Tracheoesophageal fistula]," I asked, "what are your plans?"

Before he was able to answer, I told him I had spoken with GI. It was almost as if I had to speak in riddles to get information. I told him how information was being withheld from us. I felt strongly that withholding information was the same as lying. I needed to know what was going on with Jamie so I could know how to make accurate medical decisions on his behalf. The GI service told us the stent was a barrier, and in three months there was hardly any possibility of it correcting the TEF.

"Yes," the doctor replied. "We know we'll be having major surgery, and that's something the thoracic surgeon and I have discussed."

"That's why the CT team follows Jamie..."

"That's correct."

"Knowing that would have helped us understand," I told him. "Tell me about the surgery."

"The surgery will consist of taking muscle or a foreign object and placing it in Jamie's esophagus to seal the hole. Of course he can't have surgery now. This will be down the road."

That was the route they were going to take. He was the type of doctor who fixes issues down range. I told him I appreciated his time and the information. It helped me connect the pieces of the puzzle.

I arrived at the hospital the next morning (Saturday, August 27, 2011) to see Daddy Jarboe out and about. I was able to meet with the night shift nurses who told me Jamie had a decrease in his blood pressure. They called the doctor and pushed fluids in him to help offset the blood pressure issue. Other than that, they said he had a good night.

I went in and spoke with daddy. He gave me the notes on when the RT was there and what had been done.

- 8:00 PM, chest PT.
- 8:15 PM, blood start for transfusion, two pints.
- 10:00 PM, chest PT.
- 11:00 PM, blood done.
- 11:08 PM, breathing treatment, BP meds, and chest PT.
- 12:33 PM, blood start, 2/2 pint.
- 1:55 PM, chest PT.
- 3:50 PM, chest PT.
- 5:20 AM, chest PT.

We met the first shift nurse. I greeted her, and I asked her to please keep us informed of what medications he was getting and when. That way we could keep up with the meds during the day and be aware of what was going on. She said, "No problem." Around 11:00 AM, the RT showed up with doctors to perform a bronchostomy. This would clean out Jamie's lungs. They would also collect a sample and then try to help him breathe on his own. They were successful.

Around 1:30 PM I noticed Jamie's gastric acid outtake was clamped. This was something new to me. Typically they wanted his gastric output recorded in order to monitor the amounts. We had had issues before where Jamie's gastric acid had caused distention and acid was leaking from his feeding tube hole into his stomach. I asked the doctor who was present about the gastric tube. She said she wasn't aware of it being clamped for any purpose. We asked the nurse who told us that was how she found him. She went on to explain that it was ordered by one of the teams of doctors, and that his gastric outtake should always be clamped. She said it was nothing new, and it was good for him in order to make sure his medications didn't back up into his gastric output and go out.

I explained to the nurse that in the five months we'd been there it wasn't usually clamped. I was concerned it was causing distention. Once again, she said it should always be clamped. I told her I was concerned because the previous night his gastric acid had backed up, and he had acid reflux causing acid to come out of his JP drain. I reminded her that my husband was already in extensive discomfort and I didn't want to contribute.

"It's all right ma'am," the nurse said. "This is what should normally happen. You should make sure its clamped from here on out."

"Thank you for helping me understand," I responded politely. "Can you suction Jamie? He's gurgling."

"He just had chest PT an hour ago."

"Yes, I know. But he's making serious noises. I'd like him to be as comfortable as he can be, and him gurgling without being suctioned concerns me."

She returned to do the suctioning forty-five minutes later!

At 2:30 PM they rolled Jamie. The nurse asked if I thought he looked distended. I told her yes. She put bacitracin on Jamie, but never answered the question. She took off his ortho boots and left to go do her charting. At 4:45 PM I submitted another request (for the forty-third time) to be transferred to Johns Hopkins Hospital. After doing my own research I found that they had done forty-four TEF corrective surgeries with a ninety-two percent success rate. That is where my husband needed to go.

ॐ

I showed up at 5:00 AM today because I wanted to be there to calm Jamie when they brought him out of sedation. When arrived in his room I noticed his ABP was high. The nurse said she had to restrain him during the night because he'd been moving all over, especially after an X-ray around 2:00 AM. I started cleaning his mouth and removing the gauze that was below his chin (which was saturated). I noticed he was very tight on his right side. I tried to massage out the muscles of his neck and shoulders, however nothing seemed to loosen him up.

"I'm giving him valium and methadone," the nurse told me.

"I hope that works," I said.

Just then she started removing the gastric tube to his feeding tube.

"What are you doing?"

"We feed him through gastric."

"I'm sorry," I said. "I wasn't told that. The instructions when Jamie first had his esophageal perforation was that he was not to have anything in his stomach due to acid reflux."

"I'm sorry ma'am, but this is in the order per the ICU doctor."

"No worries," I told her. "However, that was the order put in when the nurses weren't flushing with water after they gave him meds and clogged his feeding tube. Furthermore, we discussed the extent of the damage this was doing to my husband with the general surgeon. He had literally almost filled up his JP drain that drains out the back of his esophagus."

I asked her to please push his meds through the jejunum. She said she would go ahead and call the doctor. I asked her to make sure it was a doctor who was familiar with his chart. I didn't want anything to do with one who wasn't. That was the issue I'd brought up to the nurse the previous Saturday, and yet it was overlooked. No wonder my husband's lungs sounded terrible. He kept puking up the meds being put in his stomach. I told them to do what they needed to do, however, I would send an e-mail to the doctors, nurse case manager, federal recovery coordinator, and AW2.

℘

RT came in Jamie's room around 8:30 AM to do chest PT and breathing treatment. Now it was almost 3:00 PM and I hadn't seen anyone come in to help Jamie with the left lower lobe of his lung (which was being condensed with fluid). A nurse (a Major) came in and I asked him when they were supposed to do Jamie's mouth care. He said they were supposed to do it every four hours. However, he hadn't completed it yet today. I asked him if he needed assistance, or how he wanted to proceed. He told me he would send in a corpsman.

At 5:00 PM I questioned the nurse regarding Jamie's turn schedule that was hanging up in his room. He had not been turned every two hours. The nurse said, "I'll try to get to that. I have another patient I'm taking care of across the way."

It was now 6:00 AM Saturday morning, and figured I might as well bring my laptop to write down inconsistencies as they happened. This morning, the night nurse got his blood sugar and left the little T-thing with a needle inside of it in the bed near Jamie's toe. I found this an hour after his left ankle had been laying on it. Jamie's dad stayed overnight and he mentioned the issues with RT during the night were extreme. The RT came in and told Jamie to bend up and touch his toes. Jamie looked at her and asked for the acapella [a therapy system]. She said, "Well, you need to hold yourself up so I can do the percussor [for chest therapy]." Jamie said, "No. I can't. I'm paralyzed." The RT girl

250

said, "Oh, I'm sorry." Then she noticed Jamie was very congested, and his right lung was very coarse.

The RT asked the night time nurse to get a suction kit so she could suction down his nasal area. When the nurse came back, and the RT was getting ready to do the suctioning, Jamie's dad mentioned that he had a trachesophagial fistula. She said, "Oh, I didn't know. I won't be doing nasal suctioning. Thank you for telling me!"

The issue I pointed out to the nurse that morning was: What if Jamie was unconscious, or not in a good mental state, and you or the RT didn't read his chart accurately? Can you imagine the damage that would've occurred? The nurse said, "Yes ma'am." I told him we needed their help to stay consistent and to protect my husband. I asked them to please address those issues with the powers that be, because I would be sending an e-mail regarding my concerns.

The daytime nurse came on duty and introduced herself. I let her know that Jamie had one more stimulation to be done and he would be ready to clean up. She said as soon as she had the time (perhaps around 7:00 AM or 7:15 AM) she would come in and assist me. I told her it wasn't necessary since I'd cleaned him up three times that morning. I did it to assist the nighttime nurse because he was behind in charting, which also wasn't my problem. But, I didn't want my husband to be compromised due to the fact that they were short-staffed. Therefore, I did it. I was doing my husband's RT, PT, and KT each day.

Thirty minutes passed. At 7:30 AM Jamie called for the nurse to shut off his tube feed.

She opened the door and said, "What do you need?"

"Jamie would like to speak with you."

She said, "All right."

She suited up in her gown, mask, and gloves and then came in. Jamie asked her to shut off his tube feed because it was running at 30/hr. However, he had discomfort. She turned it off. He also asked to be cleaned up. She left the room and got a corpsman to assist. When they were both in the room, I excused myself to go down and get breakfast. As I was leaving I let her know his ortho boots were to be on every two hours, and then taken off for two hours. I also asked her if she saw the order in the computers from the doctors about Jamie's need to be turned every two hours, and how it was important for him not to be on his back. He needed to be elevated and up off his right side due to his lungs not getting better. She said, "All right," and I left to go down and get a drink.

I was gone for twenty minutes. When I got back (around 7:45 AM) I noticed Jamie's oxygen was at 88–89. I asked her how long his oxygen had been below ninety-four percent. She said, "Off and on for the last ten minutes."

"Has he been rolled or on his back?"

"I left him on his back," she replied. "He's due for his 8:00 AM medications."

"All right."

So when I came back, I put Jamie's ortho boots on, and at 8:15 AM I asked her to assist me in rolling him off his back. But, it was worthless. She took off his gown and said she needed to check his chart. The medical student came in with SICU and I mentioned to him that the order he wrote last night was not being followed by the nursing staff. If anything, within the last three hours I'd been there, Jamie had been laying on his back two hours. I was concerned about his stage 3 pressure sores. The only time he was turned was when his dad and I did it for his bowel stimulation. I asked the medical student if a bronchostomy was an option. It seemed as if it was an option Monday (before we requested to transfer and then it put on the backburner). Then Tuesday, it was mentioned and they declined it because they thought we were transferring. If anything, my husband's lungs were not getting better.

"How does the X-ray look?" I asked.

"The same as yesterday."

"Well, how about his white blood cell count, which was 15,000 yesterday?"

"Today it's 12,000."

"All right," I said. "We have an improvement. What you guys going to do to deal with my husband's right lung that isn't getting better? We're having issues RT not following through with therapy, which is supposed to be every four hours—*correct?*"

"Yes," he replied.

I said, "Well, she was here last night at 9:00 AM, 11:00 AM, and at 5:00 AM. Where is the consistency?"

"Let me address these issues with the team."

"As you can see," I told him, "he's on his back and his oxygen levels are down to eighty-nine percent. Last night he was on the nasal oxygen, and his oxygen levels went down to eighty-two percent and below. Jamie's dad took the initiative, putting on a mask to help assist with that issue. Please, give us direction or assist us in getting him better. Because at this point, I see regression not *progression.*"

He said, "Well, I heard you're suppose to transfer today."

"Supposedly," I said wearily, "we've been transferring every day for the past five days, and it's not working. Right now I'm concerned because Jamie is still laying on his back and I'm responsible for moving him off his right side."

I took care of rolling Jamie by myself to get him off of that side. We also did his breathing assistance, which was his acapella. I have to remind him to blow long breaths and not ten short ones. I told him to take his time with it. Sometimes he got so frustrated and just wanted to hurry.

I listened to the SICU doctors as they came in for their rounds. They wondered why his X-ray or lungs weren't getting any better. I told them know the PT wasn't coming consistently as their orders directed. Additionally, I let them know that the nursing staff wasn't rolling him up off the right side as requested. I explained how I had taken time forty minutes earlier to elevate him off his right side, and that his saturation level went up from ninety-one to ninety-seven percent. I told them Jamie had issues the night before with the nasal canual that wasn't producing enough oxygen. So, they switched it back to the mask.

The physician in charge told the team to schedule a meeting with the nursing staff and RT to go over their orders. Then he told the team they needed to ramp-up his tube feed.

"Excuse me," I interjected, " but, Dr. Jamie requested the tube feeds be shut off forty minutes ago due to discomfort."

"What kind of discomfort?" asked the doctor.

"His stomach and lower abdomen."

"Well, as long as there isn't any tube feed coming out of his gastric."

"But doctor, tube feed was coming out of his gastric outtake, and Jamie was hiccupping. So he had tube feed in his stomach even though it was being fed through his jejunam."

The doctor said, "All right, let's get a KUB X-ray to see what's going on."

I also asked about Jamie's opiates and breathing issues at night. It seemed that most days he did well, however, I wondered if what he was getting at night would lower his oxygen level. I asked if the Percocet's would've had bearing on that (as if I didn't know the answer). The doctor said, "That very well could be. Let's switch that to PRN instead of scheduled, and switch his Ambien to PRN so he has to request instead of schedule. Let's also try to eliminate this slowly. He'll still get Valium, but we'll lower the intake of everything else."

I said, "Sounds great doctor."

Then the doctor said, "Melissa, please make sure he's off that right side, and turned q2."

I said, "Yes doctor. I'll do my best. However, please speak with nursing if you have time. The chart is in the room, but it's being overlooked."

"All right," he replied. "Make sure he's up at 45%-60% most the day, and go back and forth."

I asked him if we could get Jamie sitting up in the chair. He said that would be fine to help the lungs.

ತಿ

X-ray came in to do the KEG. Instead of the nurse coming in to assist, she sat in the hallway speaking to a coworker about having to work Labor Day weekend. The X-ray guys came in and began to lower the head of Jamie's bed below twenty degrees. I told them it needed to stay higher due to aspirations. Then they started to slide the plate under his shoulders, and I had to let them know he had a JP drain in his left shoulder. I asked them to please be careful. They thanked me for assisting them, and for getting Jamie ready and comfortable as they were leaving.

After the X-ray was taken, the tech said he would call the

doctor immediately. I was glad because we would know the results soon. I thanked them, and said, "Have a great weekend." Then Jamie and I put in *Elf* to watch so we could relax.

Within ten minutes Jamie was snoring and sleeping like a baby. I laid there watching him sleep. Unfortunately, the nurse came in and let the door slam behind her. It startled Jamie so that his entire body shook. I asked her to be more courteous when my husband was sleeping. She said she was sorry, and that she would open the secondary door.

The GI doctor was next door seeing a patient, and afterward he stopped at our door and said hello. I was glad because I wanted to thank him again for using the metallic stent. He said they'd put the plastic one in first and figured it wouldn't be as reliable as the metallic. Then he told me that if he ever got injured, he would want his wife to be like me—*knowledgeable*. I thanked him for his kindness, and asked him his opinion on Jamie's injury. He said it was probably the biggest hole he had ever seen in someone's trachea and esophagus. He said it wasn't going to be an easy fix. But, with time, perhaps things could be corrected.

I asked him why it was such a rare injury. He said you just don't see it in adults. Newborns and infants, yes. But in adults…very seldom. And, the difference when you see it in newborns and infants is their trachea and esophagus aren't actually developed. The two areas are separated. Therefore, it's an easier corrective surgery. In Jamie's case, he's an adult and has an adult's esophagus and trachea. Having them grown together does not facilitate an easy correction. Yet, with time and perhaps rehabilitation, a lot could happen. I asked him if he were Jamie, what would he want his wife to do. He said, "Everything you're doing." I thanked him again, and told him I didn't want to take too much of his time.

Today I'm sending my fifty-second request for transfer from Walter Reed Bethesda to Johns Hopkins. I was being told that Tricare had not approved the transfer. I told them I would pay the medical bills, so please just transfer us. Earlier in the week I submitted my letter of resignation and forfeited my partnership with the company where I thought I would spend the rest of my life. A company I had started in the Midwest territory with two offices (doing $800,000 per year) to a company with eight offices (doing $8,000,000 a year). It was a company I'd dedicated my life to, working seventy to eighty hours a week. A company who had a West Point graduate as a CEO who told me to let go of my husband and let him die, because trying to save him wasn't working. However, I preferred trying to save my husband and exhaust my entire life saving, and sell everything I had, rather than give up. And, that is what I did.

I went in the room, and Jamie was still sleeping. I sat and watched him again. His feeding tube was still off. So at 11:00 AM he wasn't receiving any nourishment. Jamie couldn't feel hunger because of his injury. It was hard to make good judgment calls from my standpoint. Another doctor came in and we discussed Jamie's lungs. He said that when Jamie was being taken off the ventilation that he might of aspirated. That may have been why his white blood cell count went up, and could've been the reason the X-ray of Jamie's lungs hadn't gotten any better.

At 1:30 PM I asked to see the SICU doctor regarding concerns about the CT scan, KEG X-ray, and the tube feed being stopped. The nurse told us she put bacitracin on Jamie's wound at 9:00 AM and that it was charted. I asked her *when* she did it she said, "Earlier." I asked her what specific time, and she said, "Oh, I haven't. It's in the room on the counter." I told her I didn't see it. She said, "Let me get it for you." So she was entering into the computers as being done when it wasn't. Neither was his mouth care that she'd marked down as being completed. Jamie should've had mouth care every four hours. It is 1:30 PM (six and a half hours after her shift started) and she hadn't done his mouth care *once*! As usual, I went ahead and did it.

At 2:45 PM I told the doctor and nurse that Jamie had had a mental change within the past six hours. He'd been going in and out. He could be talking to you and then suddenly fall asleep, or he would go into the similar zone-out like he was doing weeks ago. The nurse would simply ask him if he was asleep. Then Jamie would fall asleep and never answer the question. I told her again he had an altered mental state.

"Well, he's on a lot of medications," came her answer.

"He's been on these medications for nearly five months," I said rather frustrated. "I'm concerned there's a new infection or something else going on in his body."

The doctor came in and said the X-ray looked great. He said his feeding tube was in the right area. He told the nurse they were going to order a CT scan, and around dinner time he would go down and have it completed.

"Doctor, what do you want to do about nutrition?" I asked.

"Does he have a port for TPN?"

"Yes. He was receiving TPN until yesterday at 3:00 PM when they stopped it after I informed them it had expired."

"He has a port?"

"Yes," I told the doctor.

He pressed on Jamie's stomach and said, "Does this hurt?"

"I can't feel pain," Jamie said. "I can only feel pressure, and right now I don't feel any. I feel all right."

The doctor explained his orders to the nurse. Then, she rolled Jamie and put new bedding on his bed because I noticed that there was fecal matter on it since that morning at 6:00 AM. When she changed him the previous night I had asked her, "Is the poop on his sheet a concern. She said, "Well, we could probably change it."

❧

The next day I went in early to do Jamie's bowel regiment. I noticed his gastric acid was clear in color. I didn't feel it was necessary to complete stimulation right then due to the fact that his stomach was empty. They discussed starting the tube feed and revisit the TPN later. I requested TPN immediately pending the trickle on the tube feed starting at 20. Jamie's jejunam had been backing up his tube feed at least three times a month. The question before we left Bethesda was is his gallbladder, which was enlarged, the culprit of the tube feed backing up? They ordered an ultrasound of the liver and gallbladder. His CRP (C-reactive protein) level was elevated to .7. His white blood cell count spiked from six thousand the day before to twenty-four thousand that morning.

The team was waiting for infectious disease from Bethesda for a consult regarding regiments of antibiotics, surgeon op notes from past surgeries, and blood cultures from May when the infection in his hardware started. All in all, Jamie was stable—critical but stable. I would wake him up every so often to do his "E" exercises. He would say the letter E for a couple of seconds to build up the muscles inside his throat. With the stent being 15cm long, the team was concerned that the stent was not allowing him to swallow adequately. Additionally, with his Amylase levels at 66,000, his saliva was eating away his esophagus. All we knew was tomorrow would be a great day. The doctors were going to take him into surgery to remove the stent, check for leaks and issues, and then make their movements accordingly.

-20-

Johns Hopkins

We finally made it to Johns Hopkins. For so long I felt like I was "the hard to impress wife." I was impressed by the consistency of the nursing team (doing their evaluations and assessments), their ability to read charting and follow orders, and the doctor's quick proactive approach to even the greatest nature of concerns. My stress level had decreased. Finally I could be a wife. I could sit next to my husband's bed with no worries or concerns. Just having faith, hope, and love, and knowing that today was another blessing that I was forever thankful for.

As I watched Jamie rest peacefully, I tried not to think of how hard it was to get him to a civilian hospital, or the difficulty in finding a doctor who had done over forty trachesophageal surgeries. It was comforting knowing we were in good hands.

I sat in a chair next to Jamie's bed each day as he rested. I understood his body's needs. But, the days grew longer he seemed to sleep more and more. The doctors came and went. They asked questions as they tried to compile data in order to understand Jamie's medical history. The night we transferred from Bethesda, only six pieces of medical history were sent to the staff at Johns Hopkins. Connecting the rest of the dots of his complex medical history was left to me. I referred often to my journal, photos, and videos as I tried to explain what happened to Jamie and why.

It had only been three days since we arrived at Johns Hopkins, and his doctor had a sense of urgency to get Jamie into surgery to correct the hole in between his esophagus and trachea. Jamie and I were both nervous and excited. As Jamie laid there, and only woke up a few moments every couple hours, I was reminded of the man I married. I saw the man he would be once again. All we needed was each other.

Jamie was taken away to surgery, and once more I was left alone in a waiting room. I was hopeful. I was also very aware of the pros and cons of him having surgery. The surgery would be longer than most. Jamie would be behind closed doors for twelve to fourteen hours. I never took the time to question the doctor as to why, how long, or what if... Once again, I took my place as a strong wife, full of faith, on a path we were chosen for. I remembered the prayer we prayed before Jamie was taken to surgery. As the staff surrounded Jamie's bed, we prayed, "Heavenly Father, we come before you today to ask Your forgiveness, and to seek your direction and guidance. We are Your forever indebted and humble servants, and we give thanks for You allowing us to hurt and to heal. Forever in your name, amen."

As I said these words over and over in my head, I

remembered that no matter how much life hurts there was always a lesson to be learned. There was a point. There was a life that had been chosen for me and I could not control the outcome. All I could do was control my reaction to each new situation that arose.

As I began pacing the floor during the thirteenth hour of his surgery. The phone rang. It was the doctor. He said the surgery was a success. However, Jamie had to be intubated again for a short amount of time. The doctor told me to get some sleep and return in the morning. I thanked him for his concern, but I was not leaving the hospital that night. I knew my place. I knew where I belonged, and it was next to my husband when he awakened. It was *my face* he would see, and my love he would feel.

A few hours later, Jamie's bed was wheeled into the ICU room where he would be staying. I assisted the nursing staff with his history, and rolled a recliner next to his bed where he could see me if he woke up. As the nurses finished up around 2:00 AM, I snuggled into my plastic chair with my hospital blanket wrapped around my yellow polyester nurses gown. My feet were snug in my pink fuzzy slippers as I drifted off to sleep.

⃝

The next morning I awoke to find no change in Jamie's medical condition. He was still very sedated, and his oxygen levels were hard to maintain. I could see my husband was tired and weak. I had the feeling that what he wanted to happen wasn't happening. The doctor came in and said the chance of Jamie being able to eat by mouth were slim. He might have to eat by feeding tube the rest of his life. His esophagus had narrowed due to all the surgeries, spasms, and scar tissue. During the next week nothing changed. Jamie's lifeless body lay in his hospital bed as he clung on to the life we'd always dreamed of.

The doctor asked if I had access to any more of Jamie's

medical reports or operation notes from previous surgeries. I gave him numerous email addresses to make contact with the military hospitals so he could obtain the necessary information and paperwork to help care for Jamie.

෨

It had now been nearly a month since Jamie was admitted to Johns Hopkins Hospital. He'd been vitamin K deficient, endured one fourteen hour surgery, and numerous other minor surgical procedures. His medical files had been requested by the me and Johns Hopkins. Yet, we still had not received any of the information requested which would help ensure Jamie's adequate care in a hospital that had the ability to do so. They just didn't have his medical history from the military hospital.

Jamie's doctor at Johns Hopkins asked if we had thought of specific spinal cord rehabilitation facilities. I told him there were a few we had discussed where Jamie could learn how to live his life as a quadriplegic. He wanted to go to a rehabilitation center in Denver, Colorado. That would also take us closer to Kansas, which would make it easier on his soldiers who desired to come and see him. There was a facility I'd been in contact with, but it was in Georgia. That would take us further away from Jamie's soldiers and our family. After days of discussing it, it was confirmed that Jamie would like to transfer to Denver, Colorado. I supported his decision and understand why it was so important to him to be close to home. I also missed everyone.

We let a social worker and Jamie's doctor know about our decision. After telling him about our decision, the doctor informed us that the Military hospital was requesting that Jamie to be transferred back to Washington D.C. for observation. They informed John's Hopkins that he might be able to transfer from there to the civilian rehabilitation facility in Denver. After hearing this, Jamie and I looked at each other with tears in our eyes. We felt overwhelmed! After the doctor and social worker left, we both begin to cry.

Being told we had to return to the military hospital put us both in a state of shock. A feeling of defeat overwhelmed us. As I looked at Jamie, I saw tears rolling down his face.

"We've come too far to go backwards," Jamie said. "I won't return to the military hospital."

I agreed with my husband, but we just received medical insurance approval for Johns Hopkins. I knew that I wouldn't be able to afford to pay for his rehabilitation facility, his private medical needs, the equipment he needed, or a private nursing staff. I started making phone calls to find out who was requesting Jamie's return to the military hospital and why.

A few days passed, and I found out the neurosurgeon wanted to remove the hardware in Jamie's back at some point. I asked if a neurosurgeon at Johns Hopkins could look at his medical records to provide a second opinion. I reminded Jamie's medical insurance company that he was requesting a transfer to a civilian rehabilitation center. I asked them to confirm that they would cover the cost of rehabilitation and equipment.

After taking those preliminary steps, we spoke to his doctor and social worker at Johns Hopkins, and we let them know we were denying the transfer back to the military hospital. We reiterated our decision to transfer to the civilian facility for which we had received approval from the medical provider and Veterans Affairs. Later that afternoon, I received a call on my cell phone from an unknown number. It was a sergeant at the military hospital requesting information on Jamie's whereabouts, the hospital name, and the room number. He told me he was at Johns Hopkins with a medical team to transfer Jamie back to the military hospital.

Earlier in the month we'd chosen to make Jamie's room number confidential because people had shown up at the hospital while Jamie was sleeping to take photographs of him. In life, we believed everything happens for a reason. We didn't try to understand it, we just accepted the life we were given. Interestingly, having that particular issue arise earlier in the month worked in our favor in this new matter. The military could not come in to a civilian hospital and remove Jamie unless they had the necessary information. I wasn't willing to give them the information.

"I appreciate your service, time, and commitment," I told the sergeant. "However, my husband will be transferring to a civilian rehabilitation facility, and will not be returning to the military hospital in D.C."

"Do you understand your husband is on active duty orders?" he asked.

"Yes, I understand that. Do you understand, sergeant, that my husband has been fighting for his life since the day he took a bullet for his country? Do you understand that my husband wants to live and come home to his family? Do you understand I have been by his side vigilantly since he was shot, and if he says he does not want to return to the military hospital that he will not return to the military hospital? Take away his paycheck; take away his medical; take away everything the military has threatened us with because at this point we don't give a damn anymore! The one thing that matters is my husband! Thank you for your time and consideration and good bye."

As I ended the call, Jamie looked up at me smiling and said, "I love you. And, when I think I couldn't love you more than I already do, you prove me wrong. Thank you for taking care of me."

As Jamie and I began doing his stretching and exercises, in my mind I wondered if we would ever have to quit fighting. I wondered if we would be able to live our life like we had always dreamed. Either way, I knew one thing…I was never going to give up on my husband.

On top of dealing with medical, military, and everyday life issues, I was dealing with the fact that fourteen years of my life in the corporate business world was going to have to come to a close. I chose to resign from my management position, and I declined further partnership in the company I'd built since 2006. When Jamie was first injured, I thought we would be home in a month. I envisioned us modifying our home to be handicap accessible. I saw us operating my company together as a husband and wife duo. Each day after Jamie was shot, I knew more and more that I had an unrealistic idea of the life we would have to live.

Caring for Jamie was a full time job. I realized that once we got home it would consume most of our lives. I was all right with that. For so long I believed that to live life and be happy a person had to be wealthy and have all the amenities to make their life valuable. The last few months of our lives the only things I needed were in front of me—my faith, my husband, and my children. Nothing else mattered anymore.

Being in the fast paced business world, I had learned a lot about marketing, sales, operations, and management. Those tools helped me tremendously in Jamie's recovery. Looking back, I felt blessed within the career path I had chosen. Making 200,000 dollars a year proved to be beneficial, but not just from a financial standpoint. I was also able to save money, now using it as a backup in the event Jamie wasn't able to have the medical care, equipment, or anything else that would help him overcome the obstacles of being a quadriplegic.

Prior to our transfer to Johns Hopkins, we had numerous people tell us that if we left the military hospital, the VA (i.e. the government) wouldn't pay for Jamie's treatments, equipment, or prescriptions. That's when I began contemplating resigning from my career knowing that each day might be a battle. I needed to give Jamie a fighting chance by staying by his side and being his legs when he couldn't walk. I needed to be his voice when he couldn't speak and his strength when he was tired. As soon I was done stretching Jamie's legs, I asked him if we could talk about our life? He said, "Yes. Always babe."

I went on to tell Jamie that I submitted my letter of resignation because I wanted to be by his side. Jamie's eyes got big. He nodded his head no and said, "I can't let you do that. Melissa, you love your career so much, and I don't want to be the reason you leave it."

"You're not the reason I'm leaving my career," I told him. "I am. I know where I belong and that's next to you. I want to wake up with you in the morning, make the girls breakfast, and spend the day with my husband loving the life we have together."

I would never tell Jamie about the comment made by the CEO of my company. It was history now.

Using what little strength he had left, Jamie raised his arms and motioned me to come closer to him. He held on to me and began to cry. Once more he said, "I cannot believe you would give up your life for me…for us."

"If you can take a bullet for our country, I can make muffins for breakfast for the rest of our lives, caring for you my amazing husband."

I laid my head on the side of Jamie's hospital bed and watched him drift off to sleep. The doctors kept telling me his energy level and strength was weak. So I stayed next to his bed as he slept. I went over his medical records. I searched the Internet for different options he may have as a quadriplegic. I wanted to determine what would be the best quality care for my husband, and if what he wanted was for the best.

It had been six months since Jamie was shot by the sniper in Afghanistan. It had been six months since he fought to come home to American soil—home to Celeste, Alexa, and me. It had been six long months of ongoing medical issues. I tried not to share my frustrations or show my sorrow with Jamie. I tried to focus only on the positive. It was hard to see other soldiers, marines, or other wounded warriors injured just a month ago already reunited with their families. I watched many be released from intensive care, leave the hospital, and begin living with their loved ones in their own private apartments as one big happy family.

As Jamie slept, I paced around his hospital room cleaning, organizing, researching, and documenting anything that would make the time go faster. There were days I tried to remember what it was like before Jamie was deployed. I remembered the man he was—a spontaneous, rambunctious, crazy man. That was the man I fell in love with. I could still see a glimpse of that man inside of my husband. I knew he would stay strong for me just as I was doing for him. I tried to stay focused on the life he had. I knew that four or five of his fellow soldiers from the 4th Calvary would not be coming home or even have the option to come home to their families. How could I be so ungrateful? My husband was laying in front of me. He might not be able to walk, talk, eat, or drink fluids, but he could open his eyes and show me he loved me. For now we focused on the simple things in life—the things we thought mattered the most.

I also thought about how for a woman to be successful in business ten or twenty years ago she would have to be a strong cutthroat type who worked fourteen to sixteen hours a day. You'd have to be able to network, sell, and be on call twenty-four hours a day. After fifteen years in the corporate world, I was alone in the hospital laying next to my husband waiting for him to wake up. Now the only thing that mattered to me was that when he woke up he sees I'm right next to him. I wanted him to know I would protect him.

⅚

Several days passed and we received acknowledgment that Jamie would be flown to Denver by a private civilian medevac. It was a small plane with medical equipment on it. We were both eager to leave the hospital and start rehabilitation. We couldn't wait to start moving forward again. The doctors, counselors, and social workers provided us with the proper medical paperwork we needed for transfer. They sent electronic copies to the rehabilitation center and gave us paper copies to take with us just in case.

Since Jamie was still active duty we had to correspond with the Department of Defense, a Wounded Warrior advocate, a Warrior Transition Unit, the Warrior Transition Brigade, the Federal Recovery Coordinator, and a nurse case manager. To make things easier, I started sending everything via e-mail. I didn't communicate by phone to any of the individuals caring for Jamie or keeping track of his care. I would send group e-mails updating them on Jamie's status, his requests, or anything else that would benefit him during his relocation. Some days I would courtesy copy his doctors, nurses, rehabilitation therapists, speech pathologists, urology, neurosurgeon, general surgery ENT, and any other medical physician following Jamie's care. That way we ensured that everyone was on the same page and was following the same directions. The intended outcome was that Jamie would no longer fall through the cracks.

It was now the morning of October 20th, and was our final day at Johns Hopkins Hospital in Baltimore, Maryland. We were eager and excited to leave. We would finally be going back to the Midwest. It had been a *very long* six months on the East Coast. We missed everything beautiful about the Midwest. We missed our friends and our family in Kansas who would only eight hours away. We couldn't wait!

-21-

Finally on Our Way

A representative from the hospital informed us Jamie's transportation had been placed on hold pending approval. I pulled up my e-mail and forwarded it to the representative. The e-mail showed we had confirmation from our a W-2 advocate and our nurse case manager saying the recovery coordinator, our doctor at Johns Hopkins, and Tri-care approved the transport. Everybody was on board. How could we possibly be held up at this point? The representative didn't have an answer. All she gave me was the information on the card, which was a telephone number for the name of the company managing the medevac. I asked her if they had all of Jamie's medical records and files. She said they did.

The doctor came in and asked if there was anything else we needed pertaining to Jamie's transport. The doctor told us he was good to go. I picked up the phone and dialed the telephone number on the card. A woman answered on the other end.

"I'm Melissa Jarboe," I told her. "I am Jamie Jarboe's wife, and he is scheduled for transport today at 10:00 AM. I want to confirm that payment and approval has been accepted."

"It's pending approval," she said.

"Are we still cleared to transfer today from Baltimore to Denver?"

"No," she replied.

"What's the main holdup regarding transfer? Is it the medical records?"

"No."

"Is there a question about Jamie's medical stability— whether he's stable enough to be transferred?"

"No."

"Is it a financial issue? Are you worried about receiving payment?" I asked.

"We have not yet received approval for payment of $30,000 for transport."

"Can I give you my credit card number? Then you can authorize the amount needed for the transport and then we could still leave this morning at 10:00 AM."

"Yes," came the reply.

I looked at Jamie who had tears in his eyes as I read her my credit card number. I hung up the phone and asked him, "Do you want to leave Baltimore right now?" He nodded his head yes. I went over and gave him a hug. A moment later they picked up our suitcases.

He was transferred down to an ambulance that took us to the airport where they loaded him on a private plane. I looked behind us and felt freedom. An enormous weight had lifted off my shoulders as the plane took off. I looked down and saw everything getting smaller. Jamie slept during most of the three-and-a-half hour flight to Denver. As the elevation increased, so did the oxygen that was needed to help Jamie breathe.

Tears fell from my eyes once again as we landed. Army members greeted us and saluted Jamie as he was taken off the plane. I could feel the emotion in the air. I could also feel the love my husband had for his fellow soldiers. I felt that everything in life was good.

 &

As we rode in the ambulance to the rehabilitation facility, Jamie had complications breathing. His oxygen levels decreased. They administered oxygen by inserting a nose tube in the facemask. He often had flashbacks of the morning he was shot. He remembered when he was on the "bird" on the way to the Kandahar hospital. They put the plastic facemask over his nose making him feel as though he would suffocate. Now, anytime they try to put a facemask over his nose he has an anxiety attack and freaks out.

I asked them to get the nasal cannula as I tried to calm Jamie down. I said, "You've got to let the paramedics take care of you until we get to the hospital." Jamie nodded his head yes and calmed down. They inserted the nasal cannula and Jamie's oxygen started going up. I asked Jamie to relax as I rubbed my hand on his chest and belly to soothe and calm him with my touch. We were greeted by admissions at the new facility. We were given a brief tour of the hospital as Jamie was being taken up to his room. His doctor was on vacation. He was treated and seen by another physician the first day. They did their best to understand the complexity of Jamie's injuries. I walked them through our entire journey.

As the days went by, Jamie and I adjusted to a different schedule for his body per the rehabilitation hospital's request. They moved his bowel stimulation from 6:00 AM to 4:00 PM every day. His physical and occupational therapy were decreased from three times a day to fifteen minutes once a day. The staff at the rehabilitation center told us they wanted to build from where Jamie was. They encouraged me to enjoy being a wife. So, for the moment I was no longer needed as his physical therapist, his occupational therapist, his speech pathologist, or his nurse case manager. They would take care of everything.

Instead of going to Jamie's room at 5:00 AM, I would go in at 7:00 AM to find him still asleep in his bed. They changed some of his medications and introduced Klonopin to his nightly meds to help him sleep. Jamie was still on Methadone, Gabapentin, Neurontin, and Lovenox. They also introduced Lyrica. It was discovered through X-rays and testing that he had had heterotopic ossification (HO) of his hips. It's commonly found in paraplegics or quadriplegic as well as amputees. It's a condition causing extra bone growth or calcium deposits to form in certain areas. They started Jamie on medication to help diminish the HO.

One night when they were doing his bowel stimulation I saw the nurse immediately leave the room and return moments later with the doctor. Jamie was asleep in his bed. I asked the doctor and nurse what was concerning them. Jamie had blood in his stool and they weren't sure why. Within the next hour they transported him to an ICU at a hospital a block away. Unfortunately, Jamie didn't have a picc line, and they said they could no longer feed or give medications through his stomach. His veins were so small and frail they couldn't get an IV in his arms. The ICU team asked me to leave the room. They said since they couldn't administer medications or narcotics any other way, they would have to insert a picc line through his neck while he was awake.

I didn't understand why they could no longer use Jamie's jejunum to give him medications. I asked the doctor what happened. He said Jamie had a gastrointestinal bleed, but they weren't sure why. He said they were doing everything in their power to correct it. As the nurse walked with me to the waiting room, I could hear Jamie scream. I stopped and turned to walk toward his room. The nurse held my arm and told me that they would take care of him. He said it would be best for me if I waited in the waiting room. I told him my husband needed me. He needed to see me and know it was going to be all right. And, I needed to know he was going to be all right.

Ⅎ

A few hours passed until I was finally allowed to see Jamie. He was resting peacefully on his hospital bed. The nurse said they had given him the allotted dose of synthetic morphine to numb his pain. I pulled a chair up to his bed and laid my head next to his arm. We both rested as I held him. The doctor came in and said they would have to scope Jamie's small and large intestine. He asked what kind of medications he was on, and if there was anything new. I told him the only changes I was aware of was the Klonopin at night and the medication for the HO.

The nurse asked if there was anything and she needed to be aware of regarding Jamie's care. I asked her if she ever cared for quadriplegic before, and she said no. I told her that Jamie completes PT and OT three times a day and has bowel stimulation. I explained that if he doesn't have bowel stimulation at a certain point in the day, then his autonomic dysreflexia can be quite severe. (Autonomic dysreflexia is a potentially dangerous clinical syndrome that develops in individuals with spinal cord injury, resulting in acute, uncontrolled hypertension.)

There were often times I wondered if this would ever get easier. Would we find a doctor that could treat Jamie for his quadriplegia, his tracheal esophageal fistula, and a medical staff equipped to answer my questions about his prognosis? Until then, I understood that I was the only continuity in his medical care. I was his advocate, his wife, his biggest supporter. You would never hear me say, "I'm tired," "it's too much for me to handle," "I quit," or "life wasn't fair." Those words were not in my vocabulary, nor will they ever be.

As I sat in the ICU watching Jamie sleep, I waited quietly hoping that soon he'd open his eyes. I hoped that soon we could talk again. I knew his body was weak. I knew he was tired. But, I also knew we could fight this. I kept focusing on our goal. We both desired to get home to Celesteal and Alexa. We wanted to begin the process of reintegration into civilian life. We wanted to grow our family and live happily ever after. These were the things Jamie and I dreamed about since we were children.

We had both come from broken homes. I didn't know much about Jamie's childhood because he told me it was part of his past, and he wanted to focus on the future. The only person I ever heard him talk to about it was his father. He looked up to him so much. Before he was wounded, I think he actually called his father every single day (if not twice a day). When he got a new iPhone, he learned how to conference call. A few times a week he would conference me and his father. I always laughed at the silliness.

Jamie was born at Fort Bragg, North Carolina. His father

was active duty, and was deployed to Korea when Jamie was just a baby. His mother and father got divorced shortly after his father returned from Korea. It had only been in recent days that he started talking about his childhood. He slept twenty to twenty-two hours a day. He cried out sometimes while he slept. I ignored it the first few times it happened. I thought it was part of his PTSD from what he saw in combat after serving two tours in Iraq and one in Afghanistan. Over the course of a few weeks I started noticing a pattern. He would relive certain moments of his childhood over and over. It would start very slowly, with the movement of his head from left to right. Then he would mouth the words, "I'm sorry," or say, "I promise it won't happen again."

After speaking with some of the doctors, psychologist, psychiatrists, and others from mental health, I decided to try to wake Jamie in the middle of his dreams. I wanted to see if he could remember them. I was trying desperately to understand what was going on with my husband, and what I could do to help.

One day when I woke Jamie up from a dream, he asked me if I had cleaned up the Kool-Aid that he had spilled in the kitchen. I asked him where it was spilled in the kitchen. He said it was on the counter and on the floor. He told me to hurry before the man sleeping on the couch wakes up. Before I knew it, Jamie was sleeping again. A few moments later Jamie's upper body started shaking. Instead of his head going from side to side, it was going back and forth. I wasn't sure what to do. I placed my hand on his shoulder and whispered in his ear, "Jamie wake up. I'm here. You're all right."

Jamie opened his eyes. He had a fearful look on his face. I'd never seen him like that before. I asked him if he was going to be okay. He asked me if I remembered the old Tupperware pitchers? I said, "The plastic ones? Yes, why?" Jamie went on to tell me that one of his first memories was a painful one of when

279

he was a little boy in the kitchen. His mother was at work and he was thirsty. He went into the kitchen to get himself a glass of Kool-Aid from the refrigerator. He did his best to make sure he was quiet because he didn't want to wake up the man sleeping on the couch. I asked him who the man was sleeping on the couch. He said he didn't remember his name, but he remembered his face. It was a man who would watch Jamie when his mom was gone. Jamie asked me if I remembered the sound a pitcher makes when you pour liquid out of it. He said, "Gurgle gurgle"—making the sound he distinctly remembered. It was the sound that woke up the man on the couch, and it was the man's face Jamie remembered as he banged his childhood body on the floor. Jamie's head moving back and forth was from the memory of the man's hands on his shoulders banging him up and down on the floor.

Speechless, and not knowing what to say, I asked him who in this world does he trust? Without hesitation he said, "I trust you, I trust my dad, and I trust God." I asked him to name the five men in his life that he would trust no matter what. He said, "I trust my dad, Dennis Shirer, Carl, and that's about it." I asked him to name five women in his life that he trusted no matter what. He said, "I trust you, and that's about it besides the girls, Celesteal and Alexa."

I paused and asked him again, "There's no other females in the world that you would trust?" Jamie became frustrated with my questions. I then named off people that have been in contact with me asking about Jamie's prognosis. As I went through the names, there were many people he didn't remember, or that he hadn't seen and five, ten, or fifteen years. I asked him about his aunt Mary Jane and his cousin Abby. Jamie smiled at the thought of the names. He said he wished he'd seen them more, and that he used to stay at Mary Jane and uncle Jim's as a child. He said he loved every second of it. The only part he didn't like was when he had to leave.

I spent as much time as I could with Jamie at the hospital. All we had was each other. We focused on our life; we embraced our past; and we looked forward to our future. I'd learned more about my husband in the past few months than I had in the last three years. There were times I felt guilty for working so much and not focusing on what really mattered. Time was the most valuable thing we had as a family.

While in the ICU, the doctor start running various tests on Jamie. They were trying to trend his vitals, his inflammation markers, his white blood cell count, and his nutrition level. They needed to understand what a strong baseline would be, especially with him being a quadriplegic. Due to the issue with the GI bleed, Jamie was being fed through an IV in his chest. I was told it was called intravenous feeding and it was the only way he could receive nourishment.

The doctors were doing rounds each morning. Before they would come, Jamie and I discussed questions or concerns he had. One day he asked a question I'd never had thought of. He asked if he be able to have children? I told him that no matter what we had to do, we would have a son to carry on the family name. He said he wanted to know if he could do his part to have a son; a child of our own to carry on the family name. In the back of my mind I was afraid to ask. Normally, Jamie would go back to sleep before the doctors would come around. But, that day he was alert and awake.

As the doctors visited and went over Jamie's care plan, they asked if we had any questions. Before I could say anything, I heard Jamie's weak voice. He simply asked, "Doc, I want to know, with all your tests and with my medical history, what is your

281

professional opinion on me being able to have children with my wife when we get home?"

Five doctors stood outside Jamie's room. They were all speechless as they starred at a soldier who only weighed ninety-two pounds. One spoke up and said they would send in a referral and request to find out the information he desired. Jamie wouldn't accept that answer. Once again he asked, "In your professional opinion, what are the chances? Give me percentages of what you think is the possibility of me being able to give my wife a son."

The only doctor who had the courage to address the question put on a gown and came in the room. He sat down next to Jamie and me as a nurse followed him in and closed the glass door. He said, "I'm not a specialist in that area, and I don't want you wondering about my professional opinion. Given the nature of your injury, excessive surgeries, and the long term prognosis, I would say that in your physical condition as of right now, the likeliness of you being able to give your wife a son is very slim. I'm not saying in the future that it will be impossible. What I'm saying is, right now your body, with all the antibiotics and all the treatments, will not be able to perform the way it used to."

Jamie looked at me and squeezed my hand. Tears welled up in his eyes as he whispered the words, "I'm sorry." I laid my head next to Jamie on his bed as we both cried. The doctor and nurse left while Jamie and I mourned over the devastating news. It was news that in the back of our minds we already knew, but we wanted to hear. Amidst the bad news, there was some good news. Jamie would be able to be transfer out of ICU and back to rehab before Thanksgiving. I invited his father to join us and give thanks during the holiday season for bringing Jamie home.

ಬ

I noticed a changed in Jamie as we returned to the

rehabilitation hospital. I asked him what was on his mind. He told me he was worried about the day he would be able to come home. He wondered if he would be able to protect his family. I asked him what he thought we needed protection from. He replied, "Everything!" He went on to say his biggest fear was one of us being injured or hurt and he wouldn't be able to help us. He was worried about the day Celesteeal started to date and brings a boy home for the first time. Who would he intimidate sitting in a wheelchair and not being able to move?

I told him he was being silly. It had been over seven months since he was paralyzed from the chest down, and I could name a few dozen people who were very intimidated by Jamie Jarboe. In response he did his little sideways smirk and nodded his head yes. Then he said, "I know...*I'm such a badass.*" I told him not to worry about giving me a child, we have other options. As far as having a boy, I reminded him about adoption and how I remembered my childhood in a foster home. All I wanted was two loving parents. I told Jamie that's what we were—two loving parents. We may not be able to have a child on our own, to carry on his family name, but we can choose to adopt a son to carry on his family name. Either way, we'll still be two loving parents.

As we sat back and discussed options, values, and goals, we reminded one another of how much love we have for life. If we focused on putting God first, spouse second, and children third, we would overcome. We had to relinquish our worries to a higher power and focus on the day we can change for the better.

It was nice to have our family reunited for Thanksgiving! I saw a spark of energy in Jamie when the girls were around. Celesteal and Lexi were growing up so fast! I could just sit and stare at them all day. As the months went by I could tell it was getting harder for both the girls to have me gone. I knew because each day I didn't see them, or him not with them, I felt a void.

Over the holiday, Jamie's doctor came to speak with us about removing the stent that had been in his tracheal airway since the middle of October. He told us they had a thoracic surgeon there that was willing to remove the stent.

I asked the doctor if we would be able to discuss the procedure with the thoracic surgeon. I'd been told he was very busy, but he may swing by a few days before the surgery. I also asked him all the basic questions I normally did with any doctor or surgeon performing surgery on my husband. I asked questions like, how many times have they performed a tracheal airway stent removal? He didn't have an answer. I asked him what the date was that the doctor from Johns Hopkins recommended the tracheal airway stents be removed? He said that with all of Jamie's medical issues, the surgery would have been hard to perform. With Jamie in the ICU, he was not medically stable for surgery.

I told the doctor that I understood my husband was not medically stable for the procedure. Yet, my understanding and the directions I received (both written and verbal) from the doctor at Johns Hopkins was that the tracheal airway stent was to be removed no later than two weeks after the initial surgery date of October 18, 2011. My concern was further complications from leaving the stent inside Jamie's airway. And, if there were complications during the surgery, I wanted to know his care plan as Jamie's attending physician. Furthermore, what was the surgeon's plan if issues should arise during surgery? He told me he would look into it and get back with me.

As the doctor turned to leave, I told him I appreciated him coming. Especially during the holiday season since he had to be away from his family. We were thankful for the time he had taken to care for Jamie, and we knew Jamie's medical condition was very complex. We just wanted to understand and make sure that all the bases are covered and Jamie is protected.

A few days later it was confirmed that Jamie would be going into surgery the early part of December. The thoracic surgeon stopped by to talk with us. When I asked him how many times he had removed the tracheal airway stent, he paused for a long time. He told us it was not a procedure or surgery he had completed in the last few years due to the nature of injury. With Jamie's condition the surgery itself could be complicated. However, he had spent countless hours reading through the file, speaking with the surgeon from Johns Hopkins, and trying to create an adequate care plan and alternate care plan in the event anything happens. I continued to do my best to understand the nature and extent of this upcoming surgery. Jamie had made it clear in the past six months that he was fearful of dying. He just wanted to go home with his family. He wanted to see his friends. He just wanted to be normal like the day he left for deployment to Afghanistan.

The morning of surgery arrived. Jamie's hospital bed was wheeled over to the surgery pre-op area. I was able to sit with him once more. We said a prayer. It wasn't to prayer for well-being, riches, or help. We said a prayer and gave thanks to God for allowing us to hurt and to heal. We prayed that He would lead us on the path chosen, and we pledged our dedication and loyalty to serving others on our journey.

Jamie and I gathered our strength in knowing that we all have a purpose in this life. We knew we were not a failure or mistake. We were chosen and created for struggle and hardships. It was our faith that would see us through. Our unconditional love for one another, our ability to relinquish and release our fears, and our strength to never give up on our lives and to live each day as if it's our last.

A few hours passed and I was called inside the operation prep area to speak with the surgeon. He told me Jamie was still very sedated and the surgery was completed. However, he was afraid that there was another hole in between Jamie's esophagus and trachea. I asked the surgeon if the hole from the previous surgery in October had opened out. He said no. The tracheal stent created a new one.

As the doctor went on to tell me about the surgery, my mind went blank. It was nearly eight months after Jamie's initial injury and five months after the military hospital found the tracheal esophageal hole caused from the esophageal stent and the tracheostomy, and now we were trying to figure out what we were going to do. The surgeon gave me a photo of what Jamie's trachea looked like on the inside after they removed the stent. The next photo showed the stent in place. The thoracic surgeon said it was important to replace the area with a larger stent due to the soft tissue and damage sustained by the smaller tracheal stent.

I took the photos back the rehabilitation hospital. I found Jamie's attending physician and showed him the photos. I asked him if this injury was within his scope of practice. The rehab doctor told me he was familiar with esophageal perforations. Without looking at the medical records, but seeing the photos, he believed in time that the hole may heal with proper nutrition. I reminded the doctor of Jamie's weight loss since we'd arrived nearly two months ago. He had lost nearly ten pounds and he was on intravenous feeding only. I said, "With all due respect, you find it in Jamie's best interest to stay at the rehab hospital knowing that he cannot get into rehab due to bed sores? Or, do you believe it would be beneficial if we transferred to Johns Hopkins to evaluate the hole and get a second opinion from a qualified surgeon?"

The attending physician told me he believed everything would be all right with time. He said we needed to be patient and let them do their jobs. I assured him that I had the utmost faith and confidence in his ability as a rehab doctor. At the same time, I believed the nature of my husband's injury was out of his scope of practice. I told him that in the morning I would be contacting our nurse case manager, Tri-care, our Wounded Warrior advocate, the recovery coordinator, and the counselor for the hospital to discuss options that would ensure my husband's tracheal esophageal injury was handled by experienced medical staff.

As I rushed back to the operation room waiting area, the receptionist told me my husband would be in the ICU within ten minutes. As I waited in Jamie's room, I went over what I would say to him. How would I explain to him that after eight months he has another hole, and that we may have to make a trip back to Johns Hopkins? How could I keep telling him to hold on and to keep his faith? It had been nearly eight months! Eight months of his life he had laid inside a hospital room without eating, drinking, or breathing on his own. He hadn't been able to walk, but I was walking every day. I ate whatever I wanted. I drank my Diet Coke. I breathed the mountain air in beautiful Colorado. I would be trying to tell him everything would be okay. How big of a hypocrite was I?

As I was sorting out my thoughts, the operating team brought Jamie to his room. The anesthesiologist said he was very surprised they had to increase the sedative after giving him four different doses and Jamie didn't fall asleep. I smiled as I told him my husband's looks are deceiving. He might only weigh ninety pounds, but his body is accustomed to the narcotics, sleep medications, and sedatives. He replied, "Obviously, we found out the hard way. We ended up giving him Ketamine during the procedure. He'll most likely sleep well tonight. I thanked the operation team for their diligence, and for caring for my husband. They waved as they walked out the door.

The ICU nurse came in and confirmed Jamie's medical history. She asked if there was any way she could be of assistance.

I told her the same thing I told all the nurses. If they had any questions or concerns about Jamie's medical history to please let me know. I respected the job they had to do, and I just wanted to ensure that nothing in my husband's complex medical history and condition was overlooked. The nurse smiled and said, "If it was my husband, I would do the exact same thing Mrs. Jarboe." A few moments later she brought me in a chair so I could sit next to Jamie. As I sat down next to his bed, I held his hand and fell asleep for the night.

❧

In the morning I sent e-mails to everyone in charge of Jamie's medical care plan. I requested their professional opinion on what the next move should be. Half the team said to transfer Jamie back to Johns Hopkins for observation. The other half said keep him in rehabilitation. But, at the rehabilitation hospital Jamie had developed a stage two sacrum wound and was unable to participate actively in physical therapy. He wasn't allowed in his wheelchair any longer than an hour, and sometimes he had to be put back in bed within a half hour. There were many decisions to be made. The final decision would have to come from Jamie's understanding his new injury.

A few days before Christmas, there was a care meeting with all the various teams. A few out-of-state individuals voiced their opinions, concerns, and suggested options by phone. Among others, the meeting involved the Fort Carson WTB unit, a Fort Carson surgeon, the Department of Defense, and the Army and civilian doctors who had been treating Jamie for the past two months. Everyone had a different opinion about the best options for Jamie's medical care plan. At the end of the conference Jamie spoke up and said he felt his best option was to return to Johns Hopkins to evaluate the new fistula [hole]. He had the utmost faith and confidence in the ability of the surgeon at Johns Hopkins.

As we got back to Jamie's hospital room, Celeste and Alexa were waiting for us. The girls were there for the holiday. Instead of focusing on the new problem, the transfer, or the upcoming surgery for Jamie, we decided to focus on our family. On Christmas Eve the girls and I dressed in our pajamas and decided we would make Christmas Eve cookies. We asked the nurse if it was all right to use the kitchen in the cafeteria. She said it would be fine.

Ian, a retired Army Staff Sergeant of the First Infantry (the Big Red 1) showed up with a young boy named Cole. After introductions, it was time to make Christmas Eve cookies! I asked Ian if he would give us a hand, and we loaded the girls up with different kinds of cookies dough and gingerbread houses. We went to Jamie's hospital bed and I said, "You didn't think you were going to get out of making cookies did you Sgt. Jarboe?" Jamie laughed and said, "You know I'm restricted to my hospital bed. I can't get up in my wheelchair, so how do you expect me to come to the cafeteria and help make cookies?"

To Jamie's surprise, the doctor and nurse came in with a travel oxygen tank. They started disconnecting and reconnecting Jamie's monitors to portable monitors on his bed. Jamie looked at me and said, "You're really taking me to the cafeteria in my hospital bed aren't you?" I smiled as I saw the excitement in his eyes. For a moment—*just a small moment*—he thought we would leave him alone in his hospital room on Christmas Eve while we made cookies. He thought he was going to get out of making Christmas Eve cookies. Not a chance in this family! "It's a team effort," I told him as I helped the nurse get Jamie prepped for transfer.

As we walked down the hallway next to Jamie's bed, I could hear the excitement from the children in the cafeteria. Lexi, Cole, and Celeste were being silly and the sound was music to our ears. Jamie and Ian watched as the children and I made brownies, cookies, and did our best to build a ginger bread house. Hours passed, and finally it was time snuggle up and get ready for Santa Claus. I think we were all excited about being together on Christmas morning!

&

Christmas morning was amazing! We watched as the girls opened their gifts with smiles on their faces. We were so happy to have our family together. As the doctors did their rounds that day, we were told that Jamie's white blood cell count jumped up to 44,000. Jamie looked at the doctor and told them he felt fine. He didn't have a fever or the chills. So what would be causing the increase? The doctor said she wasn't sure, however, they would look at a few other blood test results to find out.

Jamie fell asleep a few hours later. He had tried so hard to stay up and be awake with the girls and me that he'd worn himself out. I took the girls down to the family room to watch television without waking Jamie. I went back to the room to sit next to his bed as I did every day. I would stretch his legs, massage his body, and give him all the love he can take. Two days passed, and Jamie was exhausted. I packed up his hospital room to get ready for his transfer to Baltimore. I tried to be quiet, but *nothing* was waking him up. He was sound asleep.

We had two car loads of boxes to take home to Kansas! I asked Ian to come sit with Jamie while I drove to Kansas to drop off the first load and then I would drive back the next day. It was nice to have people you could trust. People you knew would do their best to care for your loved one. I felt blessed that Jamie had Ian as a part of his life. He helped give Jamie the support from the military side that I wasn't able to give, and he kept pushing him to do better and keep going.

Since I hadn't heard anything regarding Jamie's transfer to Johns Hopkins, I sent out a group e-mail to the necessary people. I received a phone call from the commander who told me that it may take up two months to have Jamie transferred. He said there was a lot of paperwork needing to be completed. I told him I appreciated his time, but I was already in contact with Johns Hopkins. They were expecting Jamie. The rehabilitation hospital has transferred his medical history to Johns Hopkins. All we are waiting on was transportation. It was an urgent matter that Jamie get there in a timely fashion due to the severity of the hole and new stent in his airway.

I was told that since the transfer was a request, and not a lifesaving measure, it could take up to two months. I told the commander how much I appreciated his time, but I would send a follow-up e-mail regarding our discussion. I told him I would pay for the medevac again if I had to. My husband made the request to go to Johns Hopkins, and that was where he was going sooner than later.

After a few e-mails, I contacted the medevac company regarding the transfer. Then, I spoke to the social worker at the rehabilitation hospital and a few others who needed to be on board with the pending transfer. Within a week, Jamie was confirmed for transfer to Johns Hopkins. He would transfer the second week of January 2012 for a pending surgery.

-22-

Back in Baltimore

The surgeon came to speak with us after we arrived at Johns Hopkins. He talked to us about what we could expect. He requested a few tests before Jamie was taken to surgery. Within a few days, Jamie was back in the operating room. Within a few hours of the start of the surgery, the surgeon requested to speak to Jamie's dad and me in the OR consultation area. Our hearts dropped. Why were we being called back there? What had happened?

As the two surgeons came in, we were told that the stent that was placed in Colorado was too large, and it had torn about four inches through Jamie's trachea and esophagus. It was now compromising the original surgery planned by the team. The doctor asked me what my preference was: did I want Jamie to be able to talk or eat? I told him that whatever decision he makes, we were behind him one hundred percent. The doctor started to draw a picture of the damage sustained from the larger stent. I told the surgeon that if Jamie could eat, it would be beneficial to his rehabilitation. The two surgeons left as quickly as they showed up. Jamie's father and I went back into the waiting room to do what we did best…wait.

It had been six hours since we'd heard from the surgeons. The waiting room lights were shutting down and it was quiet. I must've fallen asleep because I woke up to the surgeon telling us that Jamie made it through the surgery. He would be transferred to the ICU shortly. Jamie's dad and I were so thankful. We packed up our belongings at midnight and started walking to the ICU. I was so thankful for Jamie's dad being there and showing support. Without him, I don't know what I would've done. They brought Jamie into his ICU room. He was on a ventilator again. He was still heavily sedated and the surgeons went over the surgery with me.

After everyone left, Jamie's dad and I found chairs to rest in and get some much needed sleep. I would be flying out in a few hours to start moving our belongings into a handicapped accessible rental property in Topeka. It was so hard for me to leave Jamie, but I knew Daddy Jarboe would take good care of him. He would call me every few hours.

As my plane touched down in Kansas City, I was happy to see my beautiful daughters and eager to get all of our belongings moved into a place Jamie could come home to. A home where he would feel free until we could build a better home to help give him his independence. After being home for less than two days, packing, moving, and unpacking, I was on a plane back to Johns Hopkins. As I touched down I received a call from Daddy Jarboe.

He said Jamie was having a hard time breathing after he was taken off the ventilator the day before. I told him I would be there as soon as I could. I hurried off the airplane to a car waiting, and I went straight to the hospital.

When I arrived, Jamie was groggy, but somewhat alert. I asked Daddy Jarboe a lot of questions. What he couldn't answer, the nurse did. Jamie's CO_2 was elevated, so he wasn't able to breathe or push out the air in his lungs. That can make people lethargic or non responsive. The nurse went on to say they had alerted the surgeon. After being there an hour, I told his father to go to the hotel and get some sleep. I was going to stay with Jamie that night.

I snuggled up in my chair next to Jamie's bed as he stretched his arm toward me. I stood up, smiled, and asked, "Did you miss me lovey?" He nodded his head yes. Well, I have our new home all ready for you. And, the girls are ready for us to come home. Only a little bit longer and we'll be there Jamie. We got this…*right?*

I kissed his lips, his cheek, his shoulder, and all the way down his arms. And then I kissed his hand as tears ran down my face seeing the discomfort he was in. I tried to control my emotions. I asked him if he was ready for me to shut off the lights after he got his night medicine so he could go to sleep. He nodded his head yes. The nurse came in and gave him his night medications (methadone, neurotin, and klonopin). She shut off the lights as she left.

Within a few moments Jamie jerked his arm to get my attention. I turned on the light to find he was white and choking. I told him to stay calm and keep breathing. I pressed the call light and went out to the nurse's station to get assistance. As the nurse came in I told her get ready to call a code blue because he would

295

code any second! As soon as she questioned me, Jamie's heart stopped and he flat-lined on the monitors. The code blue team came in and started placing a plastic bag over his mouth to push air into his lungs. I stood at the foot of the bed as the team scrambled. They brought in the ventilator. I told them to contact the surgeon because they placed it due to the narrow airway Jamie had after surgery. It needed to be done with a special tool or fiber optic. I stayed at the foot of Jamie's bed and watched the team working ensure the continuity of care remained.

Once Jamie was alert, the surgeon and his team arrived and made the decision to put him back on the ventilator. Jamie gasped for each breath as he asked the doctor if he could talk it over with his wife. As I walked up to Jamie's bed with tears in my eyes, he said, "Baby, I don't want to go on the ventilator." I told him, "I know Jamie, but if you don't, the next time you die you may not get to wake up. Please do it for the girls and me. We need you!" He nodded his head yes, and within seconds the team began working on inserting the ventilator through Jamie's mouth and down his airway while doing their best not to puncture or create any more holes.

The doctor complimented me on my quick wits and the fact that through the entire scenario I remained calm. I told him how after seeing him code a dozen times, the unfortunate reality is that you get used to seeing your husband die. Through all that, you learn what works and what doesn't.

ॐ

Days passed by and Jamie wasn't able to be taken off the ventilator. He had increased CO_2 levels again, and he wasn't able to follow commands any longer. My concern was prolonged brain damage from the lack of oxygen and carbon dioxide levels. The doctors reevaluated the ventilator. Within hours Jamie's CO_2 levels lowered and the next day he woke up.

Each day, the doctors would make rounds and go over Jamie's medications. We noticed how Jamie coded three straight nights after he received his nighttime medicines. I realized they were giving him too many benzodiazepines. He was receiving klonopin and medazol which are strong medicines. I asked the doctors to discontinue the klonopin because whenever they gave it to him it was causing his respiratory failure which made him code. The attending doctor told me they didn't want to make any immediate changes to his medications due to the severity of his condition. I told the doctor that I understood his approach. Nevertheless, I'd been by his side for nine months and I had managed to taper off his medications when he didn't need them. I asked very respectfully that he discontinue the use of the klonopin, or as Jamie's medical power of attorney I would refuse it for him.

A few hours later the doctor came back to discuss his his concerns with me. I listened, and I thanked him for his time. I fully understood that Jamie wasn't an easy medical case to walk into. I understood he had a job to do. I told him that I also had a job to do. My job was to keep my husband alive. As the doctor left the room, he saw Jamie open his eyes. He walked over to Jamie, shook his hand, thanked him for his service, and told him to take good care of his wife. He said, "She's a keeper." Jamie nodded his head yes.

That evening they determined it was time to take Jamie off of the ventilator and to see how he did breathing on his own. We were all excited. But I think Jamie was more excited than any of us. Within seconds the ventilator was out of Jamie's airway and he was breathing with the assistance of the nasal cannula. Success! Finally, we were moving forward again!

We received a visit from the social worker to discuss where we wanted to be transferred once Jamie was medically stable. We looked at a few places for rehabilitation in Georgia and Nebraska, however, Jamie wanted to go home to Kansas. He knew it was time for his unit to come home, and even though he couldn't be there for the homecoming, he wanted to be close so they could visit him. The surgeon discussed Jamie's decision, and told us that Kansas may not have the kind of medical attention he needed. It might in his best interested to stay close to Johns Hopkins.

With the assistance of the military and Tricare, we looked for a facility that would take Jamie as a quadriplegic inpatient. The only place we could find was a nursing home six miles away. Jamie immediately refused. He said being a twenty-seven-year-old man in a nursing home wasn't something that was going to happen—*no matter what!* He wanted to go to Kansas to be close to his soldiers.

-23-

Going Home

We found a hospital in Topeka that would accept Jamie. The Johns Hopkins team did their best to verbally communicate Jamie's medical history, and they sent a detailed medical history to the team at the Topeka Hospital. Within a few weeks Jamie was scheduled to fly home to Topeka, Kansas!

What a glorious sight we saw at the airport as Jamie was carried off the private medevac airplane to a stretcher. He made a snide comment about how no one was there to welcome him home. Just like his first two deployments, no one there to say thank you to the soldiers for putting their lives on hold. Just when the paramedic wheeled Jamie's stretcher around the plane, we saw a hundred people holding American flags and saluting Jamie for his service and sacrifice. Jamie smiled from ear to ear as he used every last bit of his strength to wave to the on looking crowd. I leaned down to give him a kiss, and I told him to quit talking crap. America does support our military and we just proved him wrong. He laughed and said, "Babe, you always seem to surprise me."

As we loaded up in the ambulance, bikers followed and led us to the hospital. As we entered the hospital bay, there were dozens of people waiting to see Jamie to shake his hand and say thank you for his service. It was a truly blessed event to see all of these people take time out of their schedule to support this one soldier.

An ongoing discussion Jamie and I had (even months before he was deployed or wounded) was how forgotten soldiers feel. How do Americans live their lives day in and day out while not even considering the sacrifices made by our military? He would often say there's little to no support for our military. I would always counter his argument saying people *don't know how* to support our military. Well, that day, Sgt. Jamie Jarboe felt the support from America, and his mind was changed. He saw how much America cares for their military and he gave them a way to show their support.

It was time to get acquainted with yet another hospital room in another hospital. But this time we knew we were just that much closer to being home for good. Within a few days we had an entire staff assisting Jamie with his medical care needs. I'd made arrangements with Tricare to get Jamie a private care nurse who would stay by his bed at night or during the day in the event that I was gone. I was able to wake up with the girls in the morning, make them breakfast, and then get them off to school. Then, I spent the day with Jamie doing his therapies or just talking about how wonderful it was to be home. At night I would pick up the girls from school and we would go back to the hospital to have our family time. The girls would do their homework while Jamie and I watched in amazement at how much they had grown.

Within a few weeks of being in Topeka, a few of Jamie's closest friends were able to come and visit. This was a huge morale boost for Jamie since he hadn't seen some of the guys since the day he was shot. Life was smoothing out. We had a new schedule, new doctors, a new plan, and we were ready to put the past behind us. But then, Jamie's body started growing weak. His oxygen levels started decreasing and his carbon dioxide levels increased. Within a few weeks after his homecoming, Jamie was being transferred to ICU.

Early one morning he was scheduled for a bronchostomy to evaluate his lungs and air flow. As the procedure was being performed, Jamie's heart stopped and he coded again. As I sat there watching his lifeless body being resuscitated, I asked the Lord for the strength, understanding, and to have mercy on us for all we had been through. The doctor spoke to me after Jamie was alert. He told me the tracheal airway was narrow, and that the corrective skin graph was detaching. He said once it completely detaches, it would only be a matter of time before Jamie suffocates. Finally, the severity of Jamie's injury was becoming a truly harsh reality and punishment desiring our acceptance. Jamie and I refused.

When I got back to our room I made a call and sent out three hundred e-mails to every doctor, surgeon, and military official I knew. I asked that Jamie to be transferred into a stem cell research program up north. It was Wednesday, March 14, 2012. We were going to beat this! Within the first ten minutes I received close to fifty emails from surgeons, military officials, and doctors directing us to the stem cell research facility. I forwarded our e-mails to the facility, and requested they accept my husband. I contacted Jamie's doctor asking if he was stable enough for transfer because we were trying to get him into a stem cell research

301

program for a new airway and esophagus. She told us she would look into it, and then said we would be visited by palliative care physicians later in the day.

We were happy. Another specialist to help us. Someone who could look at all of Jamie's records and help him get better so he could come home to his family. We were going to beat this! With all of our energy and excitement to move forward, with our "happily ever after life" always in view, we both forgot something the surgeon told us at Johns Hopkins. As I started reading medical history, e-mails, and files, I came across one section that was written explaining the nature of Jamie's injury from the larger stent put in place at Denver. It explained how it would be Jamie's last and final surgery to be completed on this area due to the deterioration of his body. This was a result of being malnourished; it was due to infections; and the fact his body was shutting down little by little.

Once I read that and looked back at video and photos, I began to cry. Was it true? Was Jamie terminal? Did this mean the end for my husband who had fought for the last eleven months of his life to stay alive? Were there no other alternatives for Jamie who had endured over one hundred surgeries and surgical procedures, and who fought for his life on the battlefield to come home to the girls and me? Was this is the end?

Jamie woke up from his nap and asked me why I was crying. I showed him the notes. He said, "Yeah, that figures." For once I let down all my emotion. I sat next to his bed and cried for hours as he comforted me. I knew these would be some of the last days I would be able to feel my husband's touch. As we laid there in his hospital bed holding one another, we only exchanged the words "I love you" a hundred times over. He asked me if I was done crying yet. I laughed and said with a stuffed up nose, "Be nice to me." He said, "We have more to talk about."

He asked me to get a piece of paper and a pen. As I got up to get them, I looked back at him staring at our family picture (which we hung up in his room). I sat next to his bed as I always did, and told him I was ready when he was.

The first thing he told me to write was:

I love you and don't you ever forget that.

Immediately I began to sob uncontrollably. The second thing was:

Don't ever forget how much I love you and the girls. Tell them every day.

Third:

Keep helping my soldiers and their families. Take care of my soldiers and don't ever let them forget they have our support.

Jamie said, "Don't you ever go back to work. Focus on our family and caring for my soldiers. That should keep you busy the rest of your life. And, you're not allowed to be the old cat lady. Promise me this, Melissa."

When I looked up at Jamie, I could see tears in his eyes as he said, "Promise me you will love again. Promise me you will not be bitter or heartbroken, because you are the best thing that has ever happened to me in my life and I wouldn't change this for anything. God gave me you and I have no regrets in my life because it all lead me to our life together."

As I cried uncontrollably, I told Jamie that I would keep fighting, and we would beat this. He would come home to the girls and me where he belonged. It's our life, and that's what's supposed to happen. He looked at me, smiled, and said, "No, this is our life. This is how it's supposed to be. You remember when I told you people didn't support our military? Remember how you proved me wrong? I'd been on two deployments and there was never a homecoming like the one I had here. No one knew me before I was wounded. After I was wounded, you made sure everyone knew about me, about us, and about our new life. And now I know after I die, everyone will care because you will show them a way to care."

As we talked into the night about his funeral, his soldiers, and his family, we fell asleep just like old times. I was sitting in my chair with my head resting on his bed holding his hand. When I woke up, Jamie's breathing was shallow. I pushed the call button for the nurse. She said she was just coming in to wake us up to transfer Jamie to another room in ICU. As I gathered our things and walked next to Jamie's bed to ICU, my body was weaker than it had ever been. Each step felt like a hundred pounds was being dragged behind me. Once we got into the new ICU room, I began bathing Jamie and caressing his body as the nurse took his vitals and asked questions.

Jamie looked up at me and smiled as his heart stopped. The nurse said, "Did he really just do that?" She pressed the code blue button and the team came in to resuscitate by using the bag to fill up his lungs once more. The doctor came in and told me that Jamie's airway is breaking down, and it was only a matter of time before they would no longer be able to resuscitate him. I ask the doctor to keep my husband here as long as he could.

The doctor introduced the bipap machine which pushes constant air into Jamie's lungs. It looked like the most uncomfortable thing to wear, and after eighteen hours of it Jamie demanded it come off. I begged him to keep it on and stay with me. He told me, "You need to let me go. I'm ready to die, and it's going to be all right." The doctor began to remove the mask from Jamie's face as I held on to his hand. A few hours passed and they increased Jamie medication for comfort purposes. As I met with the palliative care doctor once more, I asked him what "palliative care" meant. He said, "It's comfort care—similar to hospice."

Not knowing what to say, I went back to my chair and held Jamie's hand. My great aunt came in to sit with me as I laid next to Jamie rubbing his head and touching his cheek with my cold nose. She captured a photo of us in our own little world. The doctor came in the room and said they would like to transfer us to a private room without all the sound. One more time, I walked next to Jamie's bed to a private corner room.

The girls had gone with a family member to pick up Cole from the airport. Celesteal, Lexi, and Cole were on their way to the hospital. As the children walked in, I could see Jamie moving his head a little bit. I asked him if he knew who was here. He nodded his head yes. Then Celesteal, Lexi, and Cole came up to Jamie's bed and they each greeted him. Celesteal and Cole opted to stay with me for a few hours. We sent Lexi home with family.

The children and I shared stories around Jamie's bed about how crazy, wonderful, and amazing he was. We would look up and see the smile on Jamie's face as we laughed. He was heavily sedated, not able to open his eyes, but his smile was priceless. It got late and I told Jamie I needed to get the children home for dinner and bed. Daddy Jarboe was there to be with him. I kissed Jamie's lips, and the children said goodbye. The car was silent as we drove home. All of us were immersed in our own thoughts. We got to home, relaxed, and went to bed.

Within a few hours my phone rang. Daddy was calling to tell me Jamie was losing his color and his breathing was extremely shallow. I drove to the hospital as fast as I could. When I got to Jamie's room, he was taking four breaths per minute and his color was a light blue. I said Jamie's name and kissed his cheek. Within a few minutes his breathing had increased. I laid next to him on his hospital bed resting my head on his chest. I could hear his faint heartbeat. Daddy and the nurse both said his color and breaths had been shallow for hours before they called me. I told them not to worry about it right now, let's get some sleep.

I fell asleep for one last time in the chair next to my husband's bed. When I woke up, his breathing once again had turned shallow. I said Jamie's name again, and said, "Hey lovey, I'm right here." He started breathing again. A few hours later I got up to call and check in on the children. When I went back to the room, the nurse asked to speak with me. She said the entire time I was gone Jamie's breathing got slower. She went on to say that he's waiting for me to tell him it's all right to die. I told her with tears in my eyes, "It's *not* all right! I need my husband!"

I walked back into the room, greeted Jamie with a kiss, and rubbed his legs a little bit. I asked him if he was awake. He nodded his head yes. I asked him if my name was Betty. He nodded his head no. Then I asked him if he was in any pain. He nodded his head no. As I laid next to him on his hospital bed, I asked him if he wanted to let me go? He nodded his head yes.

I started to cry once more at the thought of losing my Jamie, and then he nodded his head no. I told him I loved him so much, and he nodded his head yes. I asked him if he knows how much everyone is going to miss him, and he nodded his head yes. I told him I remembered everything he told me to do, and I will promise to do it. He nodded his head yes. After I kissed his lips, I told him I knew he had struggled more than humanly possible, and I was sorry for being so greedy and keeping him there because I didn't want to let him go. He nodded his head no, and I gave him one last kiss before he took his last breath. The private care nurse said she'd already made the call to the doctor.

At 9:25 AM, on March 21, 2012, my husband took his last and final breath.

Epilogue

After watching the last shovels of earth cover Jamie's casket, I gazed up into the sky. The beautiful idea of Jamie's forever-life now looking over me comforted my heartbreak. While knowing I would never again physically be able to kiss the lips or feel the touch of the love of my life, I walked away from his gravesite with an overwhelming strength. I was overcome with the feeling of his love all around me. As long as the sun shines, the wind blows, the rain falls, and the birds sing—I feel Jamie all around me.

Months after Jamie's passing, I started receiving phone calls, e-mails, and social media requests from people all over the world for themselves or their loved ones. The first case was an active duty soldier who had been thrown from a guard shack to the ground. It occurred as their forward operating base was under attack. Fortunately, he didn't appear to be physical wounded. But, whenever he walked he would experience a jolting pain up his back as well as seeing black dots. The soldier followed protocol and requested medical assistance. He was able to get an appointment with the unit doctor who prescribed Percocet and Ibuprofen and told him to drink water. This soldier took the Percocet when he felt pain, but it would make him drowsy to the point where he was unable to perform his duties.

He contacted me for assistance after nearly passing out one morning as he was walking to the chow hall. I stopped what I was doing and drove to the base. Once I arrived, I picked up the soldier and took him to a civilian doctor for treatment. Neither one of us could believe what the doctor saw in the X-rays. This soldier's spine had twisted due to the impact from the fall. His L2-4 was fractured! He needed immediate corrective surgery. The doctor gave us the X-rays, a medical referral, and a direct line for the military doctors to contact him.

While checking out at the front desk, the clerk asked the soldier how he would like to pay his bill. He told her he didn't have any money, or a referral for insurance. He asked if he could make payments. To me, it felt right giving the clerk my credit card to pay the soldier's bill. "After all," I thought to myself, "look at everything he has given for me. It was the least I could do."

We discussed his options as I drove back to the base. I asked him who he had assigned as his medical power of attorney. Since he was a single soldier, he needed to make sure he had someone who could advocate for him. The following day, he went to the legal department and created a medical power of attorney for his mother. I educated his mother concerning what to do if something were to happen to her son. I helped her understand who to contact, how to navigate the MEDCOMM (the military medical system), and how to best assist her son. That was just the beginning. Soon after I was inside Walter Reed National Hospital educating a wounded warrior and his wife on programs and Tricare benefits that were available to them. Then I assisted with the transfer of a blind quadriplegic veteran who had been at the Veterans Administration Hospital for over a year with minimal quality of life. I was able to assist in having him transferred to a civilian facility while paying for any expenses incurred that were not covered, or that may have delayed the transfer.

Each person who reached out to me for medical assistance had a unique case. None of them were the same. But, each person needed help and I was fortunate enough to use the experience of what I went through with Jamie to assist them. Before I knew it, I had a team of a dozen volunteers assisting with intake, medical records, medication lists, referrals, case management, and ensuring that each veteran or service member received the adequate medical care they deserved.

In August of 2012 I reached out to a local attorney to find out if I could create a non-profit organization to perpetuate what I was doing. Within days the Jamie Jarboe Foundation was created. We filed the necessary legal work with the Kansas Attorney General, and we requested an IRS EIN (employee identification number). With the help of Jamie's life insurance and my savings, I was finally able to operate and carry on Jamie's dying wish: "To care for his fellow service members."

Finally, everything in life was making sense. I remember leaving a hospital at Fort Bragg where I had met with a young military couple. The soldier had gone in to have his wisdom teeth pulled. Afterward, he was diagnosed with a traumatic brain injury from lack of oxygen. As I drove to meet the nurse case manager, I remembered Jamie and I sitting in his hospital room in October of 2011. As we talked about life, I remember him asking me if I believed he was made for human sacrifice. After all, everything in his life had been a struggle. Nothing had ever come easy for him. I remember looking at his tear-filled eyes and thinking of everything he'd been through in his childhood and adult life. I answered, "Yes, *we were* made for human sacrifice—together my love. Each of us were created for a purpose. Perhaps our purpose is to suffer and overcome." As we talked, we began to cry. We weren't crying out of self-pity due to the life we were created for, but rather knowing that we were chosen for this path and that we accepted it. Never would we falter or lose our faith.

It's been nearly two years since Jamie took his last breath. In that time the Jamie Jarboe Foundation's name was changed to the Military Veteran Project which provides a broader description of our mission. Our project is military veterans. We assist with rehabilitation, reintegration, and rebuilding soldier's lives during or after their service. We've assisted over 2,000 active duty, reserve, wounded, and retired service members. Each day we're moving forward to assist thousands more.

Today, I think back to the weekend before Jamie left for Afghanistan. I was making breakfast for my family. Celesteal was by my side setting the table, and Lexi was running up the stairs to wake up Jamie. I remember hearing Lexi giggle after Jamie pretended to be asleep and then grabbed her to play tickle monster on the bed. I wasn't thinking about the effects of the budget cuts our military was facing, or the downsizing of our troops and the short staffing in the military medical facilities. At the time, those things weren't having an impact on me or my family. After all, my soldier was home safe and sound with his family. How could we be directly impacted by those changes? Little did I know at the time that I would receive a phone call on April 10, 2011 that would forever change my life.

ABOUT THE AUTHOR

Melissa Jarboe is the widow of SSG Jamie Jarboe. SSG Jarboe was shot by a sniper in the Zhari District of Afghanistan while on patrol in April of 2011, and he passed away in 2012. To carry on her husband's dying wish to care for his fellow service members, Melissa founded the Military Veteran Project (a military nonprofit) as well as Topeka's Veterans Parade.

Melissa is a former corporate executive who resigned after her husband was wounded, choosing instead to dedicate her life to philanthropy. Now she donates her time to her extended military family by assisting veterans in receiving adequate medical care and educating military families on PTSD, TBI, and creating peer-to-peer mentorships. She serves on the Military Relations Committee and is a Christopher Reeve advisor. She also volunteers countless hours assisting active duty and reserve service members, as well as wounded and retired service members and their families. She has received the following awards and accolades:

Topeka's *Top 20 Under 40*

Named Politico's *Women Who Rule 2013*

American Red Cross *Military Hero*

5-Hour Energy's *Amazing Person Award*

City of Character

Distinguished Kansan of the Year

VFW's *Keeping America's Veterans and Families Strong Award*

To contact Melissa Jarboe, or for more information about the Military Veteran Project, visit www.melissajarboe.com.

ABOUT THE MILITARY VETERAN PROJECT

At MVP we recognize the service, honor and selfless contributions made by ALL our Military Veterans! We provide financial assistance for desperately needed therapies and services for injuries like Traumatic Brain Injury (TBI) and Post Traumatic Stress Disorder (PTSD), that are not currently provided or covered by the U.S. Department of Veterans Affairs. We feel that in return it is important for MVP and our nation to help each of our veterans be reintegrated into the civilian community.

In order to accomplish this, MVP helps raise awareness in our communities by giving support and aid to our military veterans and their families. MVP will act as a liaison for military veterans and their families with the Veterans Administration while assisting with navigation through the military medical system. We do this through education, reintegration, and service programs.

The Military Veteran Project also provides financial assistance for medical services and treatments to veterans who have served our country. ALL veterans are welcomed at the Military Veteran Project! Pre 9/11 and post 9/11 service members and veterans are eligible to request medical assistance. Military Veteran Project has a network of medical professionals to provide quality care for service members and veterans who have been put on waiting lists or denied treatments by the Department of Defense and Veterans Administration.

Since August of 2012, Military Veteran Project has assisted thousands of military veterans and families with medical assistance from MRI, CT Scans, X-rays, medical transportation, transfer to civilian hospitals, counseling, family temporary housing, airfare and prescription reimbursement. Most needed therapies are ongoing rather than a one-time fix. Military Veteran Project has one goal—advocating, educating, and honoring our military veterans. *We need your help!*

To find our more, visit: *www.militaryveteranproject.org*

All of the proceeds from this book go to the Military Veteran Project.

Additional copies can be ordered on Amazon and other online outlets, or you can visit www.militaryveteranproject.org.